WHY AMERICA?
500 years of a name

Germán Arciniegas

WHY AMERICA?

500 years of a name

The Life and Times of Amerigo Vespucci

Translated from the Spanish by
Harriet de Onís

Villegas
editores

This book has been published
in Colombia by
VILLEGAS EDITORES S.A.
Avenida 82 No. 11-50, Interior 3
Bogotá, D.C., Colombia
Telephone (57-1) 616 1788
Fax (57-1) 616 0020 / 616 0073
e-mail: informacion@VillegasEditores.com

Publisher
BENJAMÍN VILLEGAS

Art Departament
ENRIQUE CORONADO

First edition, October 1952
Second edition, October 2002

ISBN

958-8160-18-9

Pre-press
ZETTA COMUNICADORES

Printed in Colombia by
QUEBECOR WORLD BOGOTÁ S. A.

Page 8:
Johann Ludwig Gottfriedt,
New World and American Stories,
1631. Frontispiece.
Maps and illustrations by
Mattheum Merian.

VillegasEditores.com

HISTORIA
ANTIPODUM
oder
Newe Welt
Das ist:
Natur vnd Eigenschafft deß halben theils der
Erden, so Westindien genennt wird der Ele mē
ten, Geschopffen Nationen vnd Inwohner, vnd
wie diß alles durch mancherley Schiffahrten
entdecket worden, mit fleiß zusam getrag durch
Johann Ludwig Gottfrid.
Mit Landtafeln vnd Kupfferstucken ge
Zieret vnd verlegt
durch
Matthæum Merian.
1631.

CONTENTS

To Aurora Angueyra, my mother
To Gabriela Vieira, my wife
To my daughters, Aurora and Gabriela.

Preface

Benjamín Villegas

As Germán Arciniegas shows in this fascinating portrait, the Florentine navigator Amerigo Vespucci had such a profound knowledge of the world that, only ten years after the voyage of Columbus, he was able to affirm that the new lands discovered by the immortal admiral were not part of Asia but a completely New World– America.

Vespucci was never present at the baptism of the new lands. It occurred in the old monastery of Saint Dié, in the heart of Lorraine. "The name *America*," writes the author, "was the expression of delight that filled a group of disinterested, lyrical scholars when they learned of an explorer who found the recompense of his labors, not in power or conquest, but in the discovery of the constellations of the austral firmament queened over by the Southern Cross."

Previous historians, mostly relying on his letters, had invented a kind of dark legend about his life. Intrigued by their discrepancies, Germán Arciniegas decided to uncover the real story. As we approach the 500th anniversary of the naming of America, Arciniegas's masterly study–originally published in 1952–is more timely than ever.

Much remains to be said about the navigator who lived in a privileged time of discovery. Nevertheless, we expect that this book will fascinate anyone who wants to know more about a man who changed the course of our world.

Sandro Botticelli, Portrait of Amerigo Vespucci,
(Present location unknown; courtesy of Frick Art Reference Library)

FOREWORD

GERMÁN ARCINIEGAS

The case of Amerigo Vespucci is one of history's oddest ironies. The names of famous heroes, writers, and artists have been commemorated in rivers, cities, squares, or streets; whole countries have been named for a small few—Bolivia for Simón Bolívar, Colombia for Christopher Columbus, Rhodesia for Cecil Rhodes. For Amerigo Vespucci alone the honor of a hemisphere was reserved. And yet in this whole hemisphere, from Alaska to Tierra del Fuego, not one statue has been erected to him.

Two of Vespucci's letters—The *Mundus Novus* addressed to Pier Francesco de' Medici and the one to Piero Soderini containing the account of his four voyages—were the greatest literary successes of the sixteenth century. Within a few years they had been translated into nearly evey tongue and published in the leading countries in Europe, and had wrought a profound change in the geographical sciences. Whereas Columbus's letter telling of his discovery, which was published in Rome in 1493, caused hardly a ripple in scientific circles, those letters of Amerigo had a decisive influence on the earliest maps, and so aroused the enthusiasm of a group of geographers and poets of Lorraine that they launched the idea, which immediately caught on, of giving the name *America* to the New World. There is no comparable example in the history of European literature.

But at the time that this was taking place, Amerigo Vespucci was being made the target of the heaviest barrage of vilification to blacken the name of any mortal. Father Bartolomé de las Casas—one of the great historians of the era of the discoveries—launched this campaign of character assassination, alleging that Vespucci, out of envy, had artfully contrived to rob Columbus of his rightful glory. This was the line followed by nearly all the Spanish historians, and later by those of the rest of the world, Portuguese as well as English. The words of Ralph Waldo Emerson, written in 1856, have become famous: "Strange... that broad America must wear the name of a thief. Amerigo Vespucci, the pickle dealer at Seville... whose highest naval rank was boatswain's mate in an expedition that never sailed, managed in this lying world to supplant Columbus and baptize half of the earth with his own dishonest name."

Biographies, some of them famous, have been written of all the great figures of the discovery and the conquest, and even of explorers of second and third rank. But the life of Amerigo Vespucci is as yet unwritten. School texts go on repeating that Vespucci was a scoundrel, thus closing the door on the students' curiosity. Nobody has made an effort to dispel the shadows to which he was relegated by those who maligned his fame. Hundred of books and studies have been devoted to his letters. Few other documents in the history of América have been subjected to such minute and implacable scrutiny as the letters of Vespucci. But nobody has taken the trouble to step outside this vicious circle and seek the man himself, reconstruct him in his human likeness, round out his character. In 1779 Angelo Maria Bandini wrote a biographical sketch of Amerigo which subsequent investigators have copied without further amplification. The paucity of information concerning the man is all the more perplexing in the light of the controversy over his letters, which has been a favorite topic in the polemics on the New World.

The reasons for such diametrically opposed attitudes are not too far to seek if one bears in mind the circumstances surrounding the process of the discoveries in Spain and Portugal. By inverting the terms in which the case of the two great Italians of the epoch has been presented, it could be maintained that instead of Amerigo's robbing Columbus of his glory, it was the impassioned controversy over Columbus that ricocheted against Vespucci. Columbus and Vespucci were close friends in Seville from 1492 until the former's death in 1506. There is no evidence of a hint of rivalry between them, nor did Columbus's sons ever voice the slightest complaint against the Florentine. As lasting testimony of the warm understanding that existed between the two men, we have the letter of Columbus to his

son Diego written shortly before his death: "The
bearer of this, Amerigo Vespuchy, is going there to
the court where he has been summoned in connection with matters of navigation. It has always
been his desire to give me pleasure; he is a man of
good will; fortune has proved contrary to him as to
the others; he has not profited from his labors as
justice would demand. He is acting on my behalf,
moved by a great desire to do something which
shall be to my benefit if it lies within his power.
From here I do not know what I can enjoin upon
him that will be to my benefit, because I do not
know what they want of him there. He is determined to do everything possible for me. See there
what would be advantageous, and work toward
that end and he will do everything and talk and
put it into effect; and let all this be done secretly so
no one gets wind of it…" This document, written
two years after the publication of the *Mundus Novus*
letter, and a year after the letter to Soderini describing the four voyages, is tacitly confirmed in
the life of the Admiral written by his son Ferdinand,
in which there is not the slightest trace of a griev-
ance against Amerigo. But a spate of impassioned
literature was flowing out of Spain; historians, poets, dramatists were presenting Columbus as the
victim of the Crown. Castile had not fittingly rewarded his merits, had thrown him into irons, had
tried him like common criminal, had allowed him
to die in poverty. And Amerigo was caught un-
awares in the acrimonious crossfire of charges and

counter-charges. Father Las Casas never knew how the naming of America by the canons of Saint Dié had come about, but in the heat of the controversy he threw the first stone against the good name of the Florentine. This book grew out the simple desire to approach Vespucci as a human being. It is not a work of vindication, nor is it my intention to enter the lists of academic quarrels. The end result of this study will, I believe, reveal an Amerigo Vespucci different from both the figure presented by his revilers and that drawn by his panegyrists. But all these conclusions should be considered as purely accidental. I did not set out to find documental support for any preconceived idea of my own regarding Amerigo. In a sense, I stumbled upon the theme. For years now I have been studying the lives of the Vespucci during a century of Florentine history. As is obvious, I came to Amerigo in the course of this investigation. Some day I hope to present others of the Vespucci. But from the present work it can be seen that the navigator was a good man and a cultivated man, trained in the best school of humanism, who went to Spain by chance, one might say, and found himself plunged into the epoch of voyages and discovery. He was not impelled by the spirit of adventure or by the vocation of a hero. His whole career was conditioned by two fundamental qualities: the spirit of scientific inquiry guided by his natural genius, and the reputation, which he never betrayed, of being a man of trust. It has been alleged that he was a "publicity hound," that he invented his voyages, that he always sought to further his own glory. The study of his life reveals that he was a man of great discretion, so much so that once he had officially entered the service of Spain and become a Spanish national he never again wrote to his people in Florence, nor by a single word revealed any of the secrets confided to him by King Ferdinand the Catholic. Amerigo Vespucci is a singular example of a man who, in those hazardous times, enjoyed the complete confidence of the Medici of Florence, of the Florentine bankers in Seville, of Columbus and his family, of King Ferdinand, of Philip the Handsome, of King Manuel of Portugal, of the great navigators of his day–men like Juan de la Cosa, Díaz Solís, and Hojeda–and of the man who sailed before the mast, the common sailors.

It is evident that Amerigo Vespucci had at his command knowledge nobody before him had possessed–knowledge that enabled him to make his great affirmation that the new lands, whose location Columbus had discovered by his genius, were not Asia, as the Genoese believed, but a new world. This was his joyful news, the basis of his glory. But if we stop to consider how he came by this knowledge, how he informed Florence of his findings, we will see that that road he traveled in no way resembles that of the great heroes whose reckless bravery captures the imagination. Everything in him followed the peaceful paths of a bourgeois spirit that leaned toward ideas rather than trade. There is more in his life of a musical and poetic substratum than of the stuff heroes are made of. He had a closer affinity with the star-set sky of Dante, with the Renaissance poetry of Politian and the paintings of Boticelli, than with the intricate problems that tormented Columbus.

The fact that the disinterested enthusiasm of the group of canons and poets of Saint-Dié should have moved them to give the new continents the name *America* is perfectly explicable, and the angry reaction provoked in persons to whom it had never occurred that the New World should be called Colombia or Columbia in honor of Columbus is somewhat irrational. Before the Saint-Dié group had thought of the name *America*, and after they had put it in circulation, Spain's idea was that the new hemisphere should bear an Asiatic name–that to Gangetic India, Indochina, and the other various Indias of the Far East, there should be added the Western Indies. Amerigo suggested a name that seemed to him more suitable–the New World. His admirers replied with *America*. But there was more than enough glory for Columbus. The Atlantic Ocean should have been called the Columbian Sea. That it was not is an injustice! Columbus opened up this sea by his daring, his determination, his perseverance, his blind faith and piercing vision. Columbus and Vespucci are in no way mutually exclusive, but brothers joined in a common enterprise. It was their destinies that differed, and their natures, which were antithetical.

Since the end of the eighteenth century, eminent scholars have taken up the cudgels in Amerigo's defense, men like Angelo Maria Bandini, Stanislao Canovi, Francesco Bartolozzi, Alexander von Humboldt, Francisco Adolfo de Varnhagen, Armand Pascal d'Avezac, Jules Marcou, Henri Harrisse, Gustavo Uzielli, Charles Edward Lester, John Fiske, Lucien Gallois, Ida Mansetti-Bencini, Henri Vinguad, Stefan Zweig... But decisive as have been their findings, the explanations they have put forward, they have been unable to erase the widespread, conventional impression. Recently Alberto Magnaghi has tried to work out a compromise formula that would settle the Vespucci controversy by considering the letters published during his life time as complete falsifications denying two of his voyages, and on this basis granting him a measure of recognition. Frederick Julius Pohl and Thomas Oscar Marcondes de Souza have been influenced by Magnaghi. In my contribution to the volume commemorating the fifth centennial of Amerigo Vespucci, which will be published by the city of Florence, I have given in some detail my reasons for not accepting Magnaghi's thesis. The most recent works refuting his position are those of Roberto Levillier of Argentina and Edmundo O'Gorman of Mexico. Levillier bases his conclusions on a monumental study of the cartography of America, O'Gorman his on considerations that fall within the province of the philosophy of history.

If my simple human presentation of Amerigo in this book has any moral purpose, it is to show the common reader of the Western Hemisphere that he need feel no embarrassment at hearing the name *American*, which brought a blush to Emerson's check. On the contrary, it becomes clear as one studies the life of that man of Florence that the name *America* was the expression of delight that filled a group of disinterested, lyrical scholars when they learned of an explorer who found the recompense of his labors not in power or conquest, but in the discovery of the constellations of the austral firmament queened over by the Southern Cross.

In the preparation of this book, and of the research I am carrying out on the Vespucci family, I have had the generous cooperation of many institutions and friends. I wish first to express my gratitude to the Bollingen Foundation of New York City, which made me a grant for this work, and to Columbia University, where for several years, as Visiting Professor, I have been allowed opportunity to carry on my investigations; to the directors of the European archives and libraries in which I have worked–Rome, the Vatican, Florence, Paris, Brussels Ghent, Bruges, Saint Dié; to the sometime ambassadors of Colombia to Rome and the Vatican, Jorge Zalamea and Carlos Arango Vélez; to Count Carlo Sforza; to my friends in Florence, Piero Bargellini, Giovanni Papini, Primo Conti, Romualdo Cardarelli, and Mayor Giorgio La Pira. I am especially indebted to Dr. Marcelo del Pizarro, of the State Archives of Florence, who for five years has been invariably helpful in securing for me copies of hundreds of letters of the Vespucci family preserved there. At Columbia University, Professor Emeritus Dino Bigongiari has given me the benefit of distinguished scholarship in the translation and study of the letters that will serve as the basis of the general study of the Vespucci family; and Giuseppe Prezzolini and Enrico de Negri, of the Italian Department, have always honored me with their friendship. In my workshop, which is the Spanish Department of Columbia University, and in the Renaissance Seminar there I have always found the academic stimulus indispensable to an undertaking of this sort. My publishers, Alfred and Blanche Knopf; Herbert Weinstock, my editor who read the original manuscript or manuscripts with infinite patience; and my able and discerning translator, Harriet de Onís, are responsible for this book's publication in English.

It is evident that my constant companions in this work have been men who have long since departed this world, but who will live forever in the heart of those interested in Amerigo Vespucci and his achievements: Angelo Maria Bandini, Alexander von Humboldt, Gustavo Uzielli... To their names must be added that of a man like Roberto Levillier, who continues with unabated interest his endeavor to clarify the Vespucci problem.

And among these personal references, which I make with all modesty, it is superfluous to say that the names of the four women to whom this book is dedicated are self-explanatory: my wife and my daughters, who have welcomed the invasion of Vespucci which has been going on in our home for years, and my mother who in my far-off native land, in the saintliness of her threescore and five years, awaits these pages with the love with which mothers always wait, and, in this case, with the marvelous lucidity of her incomparable spirit.

Rome
November 1954

AMERICUS VESPUTIUS

I

AMERIGO'S CHRISTENING
(1454)

March 18, 1454 was March 18, 1453 in Florence by what was termed the "Florentine style." There was no uniform method of reckoning time in Europe. In some places the new year began with Christmas Day. The Florentines, like the English, preferred Lady Day, March 25, when the Archangel Gabriel announced to the Virgin Mary that the Word had been made Flesh in Her womb. The new year began for Florence in memory of this celestial Annunciation, a popular motif with its painters.

It was a Monday. From one of the Vespucci homes there emerged a small group carrying a nine-day-old infant to the baptismal font. Although the child had been born in Ognissanti (All Saints') parish, he was about to receive a name that is not to be found in the saints' calendar: Amerigo. For reasons we need not explore here, no Amerigo ever achieved sainthood. Amalaric, Aymerillot, Amaury—old forms of the same name—all smack of *chansons de geste*, not of sanctity. Amalaric was the first Gothic King to occupy the throne of Seville. In Tuscan, Amalaric becomes Amerigo, and as the infant's grandfather was called Amerigo, he was to receive the same name. But it is always advisable to give a newcomer the

John Ogilby, Amerigo Vespucci, *London, 1671.*

protection of a saint, and so the priest called the babe Amerigo Mateo. The Mateo was promptly forgotten; he was never called anything but Amerigo.[1]

The four or six gentlemen attending the christening set out along the street leading to the Baptistery. Every self-respecting Florentine family made this journey annually. It was a routine affair. The years a couple had been married could be calculated by the number of children–at least the early years. Six generation earlier, the Vespucci of Peretola had moved to Florence. By the grace of God and their love they had multiplied and been fruitful. Each new family always managed to house itself alongside another Vespucci in the same quarter, Ognissanti. They grew after the fashion of coral reefs. Ognissanti was inhabited exclusively by Vespucci and friars. The friars, of the Lombard Order of Humiliati, had installed themselves in the same place and at about the same time. This religious family and this lay family had been living side by side for over a century. And, like brothers, at times amicably, at times quarreling. Disputes arose as to which should have more authority in the neighborhood. It was hard to say which were richer, the Vespucci or the friars. They all worked, the friars carding wool and weaving it into cloth that was exported all over Europe; the Vespucci selling

---

1.   G. Uzielli, in his notes to the *Vita di Amerigo Vespucci* of Angelo Maria Bandini pp. 68 ff.) definitely established the year of birth, 1454, from the baptismal record of the Cathedral. Bandini had given the date as 1452, taken from the State Archives, and this has been followed by subsequent writers.

first wine, then silk, sometimes wool, and engaging in banking and commercial operations. The friars built the church, the Vespucci the hospital. Those Tuscans who felt that God had called them entered the convent and lived out their years in its cloisters, weaving their wool, ringing the bells, and praying in Latin. The daily devotions of the Vespucci were performed in the same church, and there their bones came to rest. The friars were buried in the courtyard of the convent, the Vespucci in the chapels of the church. The friars said Mass and wore the vestments; the Vespucci listened to the Mass and adorned the altars. When, in 1388, Simone Vespucci founded the hospital, he wanted a chapel of his own in it. The jealous friars raised a great hue and cry, whose echoes reached Rome. The cardinals intrigued, and the Pope intervened, authorizing Simone to carry out his wish. In his will Simone left instructions that the hospital was never to be managed by the friars.[2] Of such kidney were the Vespucci and the friars of the Order Humiliati.

Close beside the Vespucci lived, or had their yard, the Filipepi, a family of tanners.[3] The smell of the hides was anything but pleasant, but everyone accepted it. Florence was a republic of workers, and Florentine leather was famous all over the world. The hides were tanned, polished, and stamped with

2. L Passerini: *Storia degli stabilimenti di Beneficenza della città di Firenze*, pp.396 ff.
3. H.P. Horne: *Alessandro Filipepi, commonly called Sandro Boticelli, painter of Florence*, p.360.

gold designs. It was a beautiful sight to see a gentle-man on a horse-back with all his saddle gear look-ing like a jewel box. Mariano Filipepi had his full complement of children, eight of them.

The youngest was Alessandro, but they called him Sandro. By the time he grew to manhood the family name had dissapeared, too, and he was known as Boticcelli, in reference to Juan Filippi, who was called *Il Botticello* because he was a great winebibber and shaped like a barrel. Filippi had taken Sandro from his father's yard and put him to work in another section of the city. People began to call him Botticello's Sandro; that is to say, Sandro Botticelli. The Vespucci and the Filipepi were good friends. The tanners had set themselves up in Ognissanti because it had water in abundance. It was the confluence of the Mugnone and the Arno, an ideal location for a tanner, as well as for those working in flax, straw, or wool. Ognissanti was the industrial quarter of Florence. The Vespucci, too, took advantage of the water sup-ply: they had a mill.

The Baptistery was a leisurely ten-minute walk from the home of the Vespucci. But the group moved slowly and with dignity and probably employed some twenty minutes in the trip. Friends wanted to have a look at this latest addition to the family, congratu-late the father, and reflect on the baby's future. What would fate hold in store for this third son of Staggio Vespucci? Rather than ambition, the infant's father had wit and humor. He was close to twenty-eight, and he did not yet have a home of his own. If short of money, he was long on friends. Beside the father walked the grandfather, Amerigo the Elder, beaming with pride at the fact that his granchild was to bear his name.

The streets leading from Ognissanti to the Duomo were, and still are, narrow and winding, like all the streets that came into being during the Middle Ages. They were bounded by stone and sky–more stone than sky. The air was impregnated with the odor of wine, which clung to the damp cellar walls and permeated the wood of the casks. A babble of noise poured from the workshops, half of it coming from the artisans' hammers, half from their throats. Sleek cats moved lazily aside as the party passed, and pages gaily attired in colored hose. It passed the wall of a square tower in which the citizenry could defend itself with machines of war, and yawning stone mouths through which to pour boiling oil on attackers. In a corner niche stood a terra-cotta image of the Madonna garlanded with fresh flowers. All these things were an everyday sight, and yet at times it was as though one were seeing them for the first time.

The party had reached the Piazza del Duomo. Across from the Duomo stood the Baptistery. Everything looked new: Giotto's campanile, pink as a stalk of lilies; Brunelleschi's red and white cupola, completed so recently that the lantern had not yet been put in place. The doors of the Baptistery–the Gates of Paradise, Michelangelo called them–had been completed by Ghiberti barely one year before, and glittered with their recent covering of gold.

The priest came to the door of the temple and asked the infant: "What do you ask of the Church of God?"

The goodfather, who may have been Amerigo the Elder, answered for the child: "Faith."

"And what does faith give you?"

"Life everlasting."

"If you would enter upon life everlasting, keep the Commandments. You shall love the Lord God with all your heart, with all your soul, with all your will. And your neighbor as yourself."

These words are always employed when an infant is about to be christened. In this case they were to have special significance. The child was going to be named Amerigo, and as a result the New World was to be called America. In a sense, it was not the son of Stagio Vespucci being christened, but the New World. When the priest said Amerigo, he named America. It was a sort of geographical annunciation, an anticipated greeting given to the lands set along the western rim of the Atlantic. In this light the ceremony takes on a deeper and more exact significance.

The priest blew his breath upon the child, made the sign of the cross three times, and ordered the Devil to emerge from the body of Amerigo: "Foul spirit, come forth from him (or her, the ritual provides), and yield place to the Holy Spirit."

The priest prayed, Amerigo the Elder and his son Stagio prayed, and all blessed one another.

"Per Christum Dominum nostrum."

"Amen."

The priest laid his hands on Amerigo's head and said: "God all-powerful and eternal, Father of Our Lord Jesus Christ, turn Thy glance on this Thy slave, whom Thou hast deigned to initiate into the rudiments of the faith; remove all the blindness from his heart; break all the chains of Satan that enslaved him; open to him, Lord, the gates of Thy mercy so that, signed with the seal of Thy wisdom, he may be free from evil desires and drawn by the gentle perfume of Thy precepts, he may joyfully serve Thy Church and grow in virtue from day to day."

The priest gave the infant the salt of wisdom to savor, which elicited a whimper of resentment, followed by a smack of satisfaction and the new taste.

"Amerigo: *abrenuntias Satanas?*"

"*Abrenuntio.*"

The priest dipped his thumb in oil and anointed the child on breast and back.

"Amerigo: do you desire baptism?"

"I do."

"Amerigo: I baptize thee in the name of the Father and of the Son and of the Holy Ghost. Amerigo, go in peace, and may the Lord be with you."

Those present answered with one voice: "Amen."

There is an entry of a single line in the baptismal record of the Duomo under date March 18: *"Amerigho et Matteo di ser Amerigho Vespucci, po S. Lu Dognisci."*

The use of the form Amerigho for Amerigo is an instance of the orthographic anarchy that existed in the spelling of proper names. Nastagio was the father's name: Stagio was the familiar form. And where the priest wrote: *"Po S. Lu Doggnisci,"* what he meant was the parish of Santa Lucia d'Ognissanti.[4]

Amerigo Vespucci was born on the frontier between two epochs: the autumn of the Middle Ages and the spring of Sandro Boticelli. As a matter of fact, the calendar still fluctuated to the rhythm of the movable feasts; the science of the astronomers had not yet affected this vital aspect of the Magic Age. But Florence was modern and rational. It had developed as a burghers' city in the struggle against the Teuton barons who ruled the neighboring countryside. Every family that had come in from the "counties" to settle within the city walls had turned its back upon feudalism and joined together in a republic of workers. The barons would have wished to reduce the city to a factory of servile hands to weave them cloth, forge them arms, and tan them leather. This was not the destiny of Florence. The workers developed a growing pride in their achievements and waxed bold on the fire of their own speeches. Their ambition was to be free, independent. They were willing to suffer internal tyrannies in exchange for a halt to the inroads of the barons. They were bent on developing their foreign trade, bringing wool from Flanders and selling their cloth wherever they could find a market. The barons attempted to shut the city within its walls. The Floren-

---

4. G. Uzielli, op. cit., on p. 68 publishes the note of the church record.

tines responded by enlarging the walls, seizing castles and bringing them under their dominion, subduing cities, making theirs the valley and the hills. The guilds or corporations were not organized for the single purpose of displaying their banners in holiday procession; they were animated by a spirit of combat, conquest, and victory.

And this was not the history of the city alone; it was that of each family. The atmosphere was one of bourgeois pride resting on generations of forebears who had amassed fortunes by industrial or commercial activities. The Vespucci belonged to this bourgeoisie. Simone, who founded the hospital in 1388, had made his money in silk. He was one of those who took part in the assembly that in 1382 settled the differences between the populace, which had revolted at the instigation of the Ghibellines and the oligarchy. In 1400 Piero, his son, was in Bruges, Antwerp, Ghent, working with the Florentine bankers, selling grain, signing letters of exchange. There were many Vespucci like Simone and Piero. This far-flung commercial network was giving Europe the air of a huge bourgeois community. The preoccupations of the gloomy Gothic forest held little sway over the minds of the new scions of work. Hitherto Holy Writ had been all. Now there were Holy Writ and letters of exchange. And the center of this ambitious economic awakening was Florence. It might be said that since 1400 there had been in Europe a New World whose capital was Florence. Between this new Florentine world and the medieval world

yawned abysses far wider than the oceans that separated the continents. The rich formed a united front
that displaced the privileged classes of the theocratic
epochs. Self-sufficing feudalism was succeeded by
commercial interchange, and Europe, which had
been an archipelago, became a continent, It was
held firm in a web woven by thousands of such
workers as these friars and the Vespucci, or the
Medici, whose role in the history of bourgeois
economy rivals that of the Fuggers.

The Medici had banks in Rome, Milan, Pisa, Genoa,
and Venice; in Lyon, Antwerp, Bruges, Avignon,
Lübeck, Geneva, and London; in Valencia and
Barcelona. Their agents traveled to Constantinople
and Alexandria, to all the known world and a little
beyond. The Vespucci were often employed by the
Medici, at times in Florence, at times in other cities of
Tuscany or other regions of Italy, or outside Italy.

Florence was also a frontier in still another sense,
as was the greater part of Italy; the west ended there
and the East began. The Vespucci like all other
Florentines, knew this, for they were dealers in silks,
which were shipped by galley to Constantinople,
and they had listened to the Greek philosophers who
had come from the Near East. Nowhere else in Europe so strongly as in Italy was the attraction of Asia
felt, the need to establish contact with Arabia, with
Persia, with India, with China. The voyage of Marco
Polo, the Venetian, had made a deep impression,
and for a long time his *Book* had been a work of the
greatest appeal. One of the Corporations of Florence

was that of the spice-dealers; painters, doctors, and pharmacists were members of this guild. From the most distant countries came pigments for the painters, dyes for textiles, and cloves, cinnamon, pepper, and nutmeg for culinary purposes. Apothecaries employed exotic ingredients in their pharmaceutical products. From Beirut came the ash of certain plants which was utilized in the manufacture of glass and soap; from Damascus, attar of roses. According to Marco Polo, Sumatra produced the best cinnamon, and there was a time when that of Borneo commanded a price one hundred times that of China. Ambergris, frankincense, balms, and myrrh were brought from far off for perfumes.

The greatest stumbling-block the Pope always encountered in his war against the Turk was the determination of Venice to maintain at all costs its friendship and trade with the Porte. The humanistic revival in Florence was a consequence of the arrival of the Greek philosophers from Constantinople, with their Eastern beards and damask capes, like the Three Kings of Orient. It was thus that Benozzo Gozzoli painted on the walls of the Medici chapel in what is now the Palazzo Medici Ricardi the entry of the Emperor Manuel II Palæologus into Florence. There in the same painting, the birth of Jesus and that of the Renaissance in Italy are fused with Oriental pomp.

A breath of Oriental magic was quickening the life of Italy, suspending the Gothic soul, the civilization of the West. Romanesque and Gothic art lived on only as the skeleton sustaining the body of the churches. But the colored marbles, the Byzantine mosaics, the damask hangings, all had an Oriental flavor. Such great ports as Pisa and Venice were like orient pearls. In Florence, leather was worked in the Persian fashion, silk in the manner of Damascus, and pearls of Ophir adorned the throats and the hair of the women.

How to reach the Orient was for a Florentine, as for any Italian, the guiding thought of the fifteenth century.

Florence was concentrated within a limited compass. So small was it that the circuit of its wall could be made in an hour. It was all spirit. It is stated that it had some forty thousand inhabitants, which does not seem possible. The correct figure would be closer to twenty thousand, and not inhabitants, but souls. And what souls! When Amerigo Vespucci was nine days old, Lorenzo de' Medici was six years old, Domenico Ghirlandaio three, Leonardo da Vinci and Savonarola, two. Neither Leonardo nor Savonarola were born in Florence, but they established themselves within its walls. The list of Amerigo Vespucci's contemporaries contains names that fill the pages of the history of art and of statecraft. If these names were expunged, the Renaissance would become a void.

Leonardo da Vinci, Self-Portrait, *Red chalk drawing, 33,3 x 21,3 cm, Turin, Royal Library.*

II

THE FAMILY

Amerigo's father was Stagio Vespucci. He was a notary, as his father had been before him and as his eldest son was to be. The corporation of notaries and judges headed all the other guilds of Florence. Such distinguished men as Francesco Guicciardini the historian belonged to it. But in 1457 Stagio Vespucci was only the notary of some tanners, and he had five mouths to feed, according to the tax register. These did not include his mouth and his wife's, but only the mouths of his five living children: Agnoletta, who was one year old; Bernardo, three; Amerigo, four; Girolamo, five; and Antonio, six. Stagio lived in a rented house. The tax-assessors put down his income or "substance" at four florins, "perhaps so his name could be included among those of the taxpayers of the Republic."[1]

By 1470 Stagio's affairs had improved, but he still lived in a rented house belonging to the brothers Lorenzo and Luca Bartolegli, which was situated between the one owned by his father, Amerigo Vespucci, the Elder, and the hospital founded by the Vespucci. He paid no rent. Stagio had lent the Bartolegli two hundred florins, and "they utilize my money, and I

1. G. Uzielli, op. Cit., p. 74.

Ghirlandaio, La Pietà e La Misericordia, *Fresco in the Church of Ognissanti, Florence. In the upper part, portraits of the Vespucci family.*

their house," said Vespucci in a statement to the tax-collectors, with a touch of irony. Stagio needed to be very clever to outwit these officials. In a poem Bernardo Cambini, recounting incidents of the Florentine love of a joke, alluded to the hunter's wiles the tax-collectors had to employ to draw a bead on Stagio, a master in the art of defending himself "with documents and papers."[2]

To Stagio money seems to have been only a means of finding those places where life took on a pleasant warmth. When he came to a man's estate, his father, Amerigo the Elder, made over to him a house in Peretola, a little village near Florence.

"I have let my uncle live in it with his family," said Stagio, "because they are very poor." In Peretola, too, he bought from his brother Giorgio Antonio a piece of land that their father had given the latter. To be sure, this land was not going to bring Stagio any income, but it was a piece of Peretola, to which the Vespucci family was linked by tradition. Stagio spent his money on manuscripts worth their weight in gold to the humanists. The two brothers, Stagio and Giorgio Antonio, pooled their resources for such purposes. In a manuscript copy of Martial there is this inscription on the first page: *"Liber fo. Anastagii Vespucii & Giorgii Antonii eius fratris."*[3]

In Stagio's opinion, life was to be enjoyed. He liked an occasional spree, a night with the boys, and see-

2. Verses of Bernardo Cambini, in the Ginori-Venturi Codex. Quoted by Uzielli, op., cit., p. 74.
3. A. M. Bandini: *Vita di Amerigo Vespucci*, p. 12.

ing the sunrise on the hills after a convivial night. On one occasion, in the company of Zuta the tailor, who must have been a bird of the same feather, he knocked at the door of the priest Arlotto in the early hours, of the morning. The priest was a great wit, whose sallies are still recalled in Florence, where they have been collected in a delightful volume entitled *Facezie.* Stagio and the tailor watched as Father Arlotto Mainardi opened the door and, lamp in hand, peered out like a ghost, attired in nightshirt and nightcap.

"Father," they asked, looking at him with eyes aglitter with mischief, "can you suggest a medicine to rid us of this fog that obfuscates our senses?"

Ceremoniously the priest asked them to hand him the wineskin. He, emptied it into a pitcher, drank it off without stopping for breath, and, without blinking, replied: "To dissipate that fog all you have to do is imitate me and say: 'Fog, fog, morning fog, May the dawn, with the help of this overflowing pitcher, cure and carry you off.'" It was not in limping prose that he said it, but in improvised verses:

Nebbia nebbia mattutina,
Che ti levi la mattina,
Questa tazza rasa e piena
Contro ti sia medicina![4]

It required no great effort on the part of Stagio to improve his position; his native wit and the standing

4. Quoted by Uzielli, op. Cit., p. 74.

of the Vespucci sufficed. But he was not ambitious, not because he was lazy, but because his philosophy provided a bulwark against fallacious hopes. Shortly after he had served as the tanners' notary, he became the notary of the Signoria. In 1470 he bought himself a house in Florence, land in San Felice and in Signa, about seven miles from Florence. But instead of living in his own house, he preferred to live in that of Guido Antonio Vespucci at an annual rental of eighteen florins. There was one thing that Stagio did desire: that his children should receive a good education and know Latin as well as he did.

Amerigo's mother, Elisabetta, Mona Lisa as she was called in the Florentine manner, was much younger than her husband. It is impossible, however, to know the difference in their ages. In the tax declaration of 1457 she stated that she was twenty-two, and Stagio thirty-two. In that of 1470 she was thirty-six and he forty-two. In that of 1480 she was forty-six and he fifty-three. Perhaps it was in the first declaration that she did not tell the truth; she had wanted to seem younger than she was, but she soon got over it. Stagio was amiable; Mona Lisa was stern and harsh. She had concentrated all her love on her eldest son, Antonio, and had no tenderness left for the others. As Stagio died long before her, Amerigo and the younger children suffered from her lack of affection. Girolamo, who became a Hierosolymite friar, wrote complaining letters to Amerigo from Rhodes. In one of them he said:

You tell me that Bernardo has gone to Hungary to better his fortunes. May God assist him, for we are in dire need of money. You add that Mona Lisa is in good health, but that she lives for Antonio, without giving thought to us. We have given her no reason to be ashamed of us. On the contrary. We honor her, and more than she deserves, taking into account the attitude she displays toward us. I asked her, by someone, to send me shirts and sheets, but she has paid no heed to my request. She has reached such an advanced age that any day may be her last, and for this reason I ask God in my prayers to give her whatever her heart desires. She will have to give an accounting of her acts to God. I beg you to read her all this. I write with some heat, for I feel that my complaints are just. During the nine years that I have been far from home, she has never thought to mention my name, as though I did not exist. May God forgive her... Bad luck has pursued me. Some days ago I was robbed. I lost all my clothing except what I have on. I am ashamed to appear before respectable people. And I have no hope of being able to come by a new suit through my own efforts. You can imagine how I feel... There is little more that I can say. Remember me to our father Messer Giorgio Antonio (their uncle) and return his greetings a thousandfold. The same to Messer Niccolò Canigiani, even though he has not answered my letters. And to Messer Guido Antonio Vespucci, and tell him not to forget me. And to all the rest of our family...[5]

5. A.S.F. (State Archives of Florence), M.A.P. (Mediceo Avanti il Principato), F. LXVIII, c. 203 (published by Ida Masetti-Bencini and Mary Howard-Smith in *Rivista delle biblioteche e degli archivi*, Vol. XIII, No. 10-12, Florence).

These were not the complaints of children. Girolamo was thirty-seven when he wrote this letter,
Amerigo thirty-four. In his monastic life in Rhodes,
what Girolamo suffered from was Mona Lisa's indifference. But Amerigo in Florence felt the direct effects
of her partiality for the first-born. Not to judge Mona
Lisa too harshly, it should be pointed out that she was
no different from the other women of her times in this
marked preference. In keeping with law and tradition,
so many considerations were reserved for the eldest
son, who carried on the family name, that to favor him
and enhance his position all other affections were relegated to the background. Even Stagio, who was eager to see that all his sons received an education, and
did what he could to see them well established, wanted,
above everything else, to see the eldest become a notary like himself and carry on not only his name but
also his profession. Antonio was the only one sent to
Pisa to receive a university education.

Agnoletta, Amerigo's only sister, must have died
very young. She is mentioned in the tax register of
1457 as being one year old, but no reference is made
to her in that of 1470. Stagio had hoped to set up
Girolamo, whom we have seen as a friar in Rhodes,
in industry and trade. In his tax declaration of 1480
Stagio said: "Girolamo is a member of the Wool Guild,
but at the moment he is unemployed." It was about
this time that Girolamo left for Rhodes. Eight years
later he wrote to Amerigo:

*Dear brother Amerigo: I cannot but complain of all
of you at home. I wonder that you hold me in so little*

esteem. It has been over two years since I have had a letter from you, and I cannot understand why. I can only attribute it to the scant love you feel for me. I do not believe this is caused by my conduct. Up to now, by the grace of God, I have done nothing to cause you to blush for me, and I trust this will continue to be so, God willing.

The object of this letter is just to ask you to commend me to Messer Guido Antonio and Messer Giorgio Antonio so they shall not forget me, and the same to my dear mother and all of you.

I have sent you word of my needs and sorrows, and I see that I just wasted time and paper. You do nothing for me. Why not give me what you lay out in alms every year? As I am poor, I will accept it for the love of God. It would be better for this money to go to me, who am one of the family, than to strangers. I do not want to say any more, except to ask you to write me from time to time. It is two years since I have heard from any of you, and this amazes me. I repeat this twice, so you will remember me. I am not in some inaccessible spot of the world. Every day people come here on their way to Venice or Naples, and everybody gets letters except me. I want to add one thing. I have heard that the benefice of San Jacobo has been taken from Messer Luigi Tornabuoni and given to Giovan' Battista Martegli. For that reason, I feel that it would be only fair for them to give me that of San Alucio. I should like to make every effort to secure it, in view of my rights as a monk, and I implore you to talk with Guido Antonio and Giorgio Antonio and

*ask them to tell me what I should do. Commend me to
my dear mother...*[6]

It is evident that Girolamo was somewhat embit-
tered, but basically he must have been a good man.
Years later, attracted by the doctrines of Savonarola,
he returned to Florence, entered the Convent of San
Marco, and died almost in the odor of sanctity. On
the scroll of the good sons of the convent– *"Albero di
Religiosi Morti in Concetto di Santita nel convento di
San Marco"*–there is the inscription: "Father Fray Girolamo Vespucci was a perfect son of Santo Domenico.
All came to him, and he heard them as a man of the
Church and a man of learning, because he was a man
of both high intelligence and devout life. He possessed all the virtues. Thus, reputed saintly by both
his order and the world, he departed this life the tenth
of April of 1525."

Amerigo's younger brother was Bernardo. Stagio had
said of him in his tax declaration of 1480: "He is ap-
prenticed to the Wool Guild, without salary." At this
time he was twenty-six years old. After Stagio's death
Bernardo went to Buda, the capital of Hungary, somewhat in the role of an adventurer. From there he wrote
to Amerigo. Like Girolamo, it was to Amerigo, and not
to Antonio, that he addressed himself, because Amerigo
was the brother they trusted, the one who listened to
them, the one who had the best connections in Florence; he was closer to their influential uncles, Giorgio
Antonio and Guido Antonio.

6. A.S.F., F. LXVIII, c. 197 (Masetti-Bencini, op. cit.).

Bernardo's letters to Amerigo convey a vivid picture of that poor vagabond's life. He begins by saying that he has found work keeping one Chimeti Camici's books for the sum of forty florins a year, and then adds:

I have engaged to do this for a year. Then I will try to return to Italy. This is how things stand with me here. Others will tell you that I am not doing too badly and that I am not easily discouraged; that my plans are promising. There is only one danger, and that is that the reigning King may die. If he should, all the Italians here will have their throats cut. It seems that he is the custom here. I am sure that if I perish here, many other Italians–a hundred, perhaps–will suffer the same fate. For that reason I pray every morning that God will preserve the King's health. He is our best friend, and our safety rests upon his health.

Bernardo added news about the life of the daughter of the Duke of Milan, who was married to a son of the King, and then gave a vivid picture of his adventures and those of others who, like him, had gone to seek their fortunes:

My dear Amerigo: When I return I shall enjoy life more. I have endured great sufferings here. Time and again I have had to sleep in the woods or in hay carts. Not a day goes by that I do not find a louse on me. And it is not my fault, because I never fail to bathe twice a week. I don't understand where they come from; I think it must be the air that breeds them. All these Hungarians, young and old, are covered with lice...

The King has Carlo Macinghi, a Florentine, a relative of ours, shut up in the tower. The reason is that the Florentines have been receiving certain privileges from the Venetians, with the result that they have more power than the King himself... Carlo is completely incommunicado. His cell is such that he cannot stand up and has to be lying down all the time. God preserve us from such misfortunes!...

Commend me to the love of our dear mother and remember me to all the others.[7]

Some time later Amerigo received another letter from Bernardo: "I have heard that you are well established. May God help you to earn money, because the poor are despised; I know this by experience." And he goes on to say that when he was without money, his friends grew tired of helping him out with loans and avoided him, and he took to gambling. Now he had found work again, had saved a little, and planned to return to Florence. Then came the news of the city:

Certain Venetians, accompanied by other Italians, were set upon in the street by several gentlemen. Two of the Italians were killed, and the others managed to take refuge in a villa. They are in the custody of a page of the King. The aggressors have been caught. Among them, as their leader, is Corvatti Paolo, well known to the Florentine people. In a few days he and his companions are to be garroted. This is the only kind of execution I have not seen. I have seen people burned alive, broken

7. A.S.F., M.A.P., F. LXVIII, c. 197 (Masetti-Bencini, op. cit.).

*on the wheel, hanged, and thrown into the waters of
the Danube. What cruel justice!...*

*I would ask a favor of you, and that is to call on our
dear mother and tell her I will soon be with her and
spend the whole month of October if nothing unforeseen happens. Try to cheer her up. Remember me to
Giorgio Antonio...*[8]

Amerigo's oldest brother was Antonio the notary.
During his student days in Pisa he made friends with
persons who later became outstanding figures in the
Republic. His uncle Giorgio Antonio had recommended him to men like Riccardo Becchi, who in
later years was Florence's envoy to Alexander VI when
the fate of Savonarola was being discussed. Antonio
Vespucci and Riccardo Becchi were two untrained
young men whom Giorgio Antonio guided with the
authority of his learning and of his reputation as a
great humanist.[9]

At the age of twenty-six Antonio married, and his
wife, Catarina, gave him child after child until her
death. Eight of them lived. When he was left a widower, Antonio remarried. His second wife was
Margheritta delle Galvane. Antonio was close to sixty
at the time, and there is no indication that he had
children by this marriage.

Antonio's career as a notary was a brilliant one. He
became notary of the Signoria and of persons of the

8. A.S.F., M.A.P., F. LXVIII, c. 219.
9. Bandini (op. cit., p. 11) publishes a letter in Latin and Greek
   containing moral advice to the two young men. In this letter
   Antonio is referred to as A., giving rise to its reading as Amerigo.

standing of Lorenzo di Pier Francesco de' Medici, in whose business establishment Amerigo was employed. In addition, he served as notary for Spanish merchants who had important dealings with Florence. Eleven volumes of documents notarized by Antonio Vespucci between the years 1472 and 1532 are preserved in Florence; they provide an economic history of the Republic. When Amerigo went to Spain, Antonio's connections with that country grew, and we find him notarizing documents of merchants from Burgos, Valencia, and Salamanca.[10]

In spite of the resentment that Mona Lisa's predilection for Antonio aroused in her other sons, as manifested in Girolamo's letter, the relations between Amerigo and Antonio were thoroughly cordial. After Amerigo had left his native land and settled in Spain, he included words of affection for Antonio in a letter to the Gonfalonier Soderini.

10. In the Archivio Notarile Antecosimiano, Florence, there are eleven volumes of notarial documents drawn up by Antonio Vespucci (1472-1532). Masetti-Bencini lists among the Spanish merchants whose names appear on them Juan and Pedro Sánchez, Juan Rana of Zaragoza, Diego and Sancho Miranda of Burgos, Martín Roys of Valencia, and Diego of Salamanca.

Leonardo da Vinci, The Sleeping Beauty, *Drawing of dead Simonetta. Florence.*

III

THE WASPS OF PERETOLA

To Amerigo and his brothers when they were children, home was not only the house where Stagio and his wife lived, but the houses of all the Vespucci, clustered together in the same quarter. There was the house of their grandfather, the house of the descendants of Giuliano Vespucci the banker, of Guido Antonio and Simone. Stagio and his family formed part of the tribe.

The quarter had a peculiarity of its own. The houses pressed one against another from Ognissanti to the Piazza del Duomo, a mass of turrets and stone balconies. From Ognissanti toward the wall, toward the Prato Gate, the street broadened, the houses had gardens, trees. The houses of the Vespucci were the last of the large city houses of wealthy burghers and the first owning a garden. To breathe pure air, however, one had to go outside the wall. Within, the streets were littered with filth and dust. The industrial pre-eminence of Florence rested upon a muck of leather trimmings, straw, wool. The streets of Ognissanti reeked of mule trains. The waters of the Arno and the Mugnone, which ran limpid into Florence, left the city dark with dyes. Between the street leading from the houses of the Vespucci to the Prato

Sandro Botticelli, Spring *(detail), tempera and oil on wood, 203 x 314 cm, ca. 1482-1483, Florence, Galleria degli Uffizi.*

Gate and the Arno, lay what was known as Sardigna Island, a foul-smelling refuse dump.

From the Prato Gate, which was only a few minutes from their houses, the Vespucci took the road to Peretola, a trip of about six miles. Peretola represented the rustic tradition of the Vespucci. There was the family seat, where they had always had lands, vineyards. Nothing delighted the boys so much as a trip to Peretola. Their uncles Niccolò and Giovanni lived there. Niccolò sold wines and kept an inn. Giovanni was a ne'er-do-well. He had never worked. Stagio said of him: "He does himself harm and is an embarrassment to all of us." But the fact that one of their uncles was a wine-seller and the other a good-for-nothing was a source of satisfaction rather than chagrin to the boys. They found these uncles most entertaining. Inasmuch as Stagio himself liked to sit down with Niccolò and Giovanni and have a drink with them and hear the gossip of Peretola, those eavesdropped conversations had the enticement of forbidden fruit for the boys. It was undoubtedly a pleasure for all of them to leave Mona Lisa in Florence and visit Peretola with Stagio.

A legend about Amerigo still exists in Peretola. It is told that on one occasion while Stagio and his brothers were discussing matters meant only for grown-ups, Amerigo ran away. It may not have been mischievousness, but only curiosity. The open air and adventure lured him on. He ran through the vineyards, across the field, and climbed a nearby hill, the way children chase a butterfly. He liked to scan the sky, to follow the course of a cloud, for clouds are rare in those limpid skies. When Amerigo's uncles realized that he was not to be found, there was consternation and excitement. They looked for him in the home of his poor uncle, in Giorgio Antonio's lands, in the fields. Finally they found him on the hilltop. He had just wanted to look at the sky. Stagio scolded him, but was inwardly amused. It was not a bad idea to leave the inn to climb a hill: when Stagio himself went to Peretola with his children, he was running away from home.

The name Vespucci is derived from vespa, wasp. The family coat of arms shows golden wasps on an azure bend in a field of gules. In 1428 Alfonso of Aragón, King of Sicily, a close friend of Giovanni Vespucci, authorized him to add a flower to the shield. There really was a wasplike quality about the Vespucci. They flew where there were flowers, sipped the nectar, and, if necessary, used their stings. There is a complete absence on their coat of arms of mailed fists, lions, castles, all the symbols of the warrior. Entomologists say there are ten thousand varieties of wasps, some social, some hermit. They belong to the order of Hymenoptera, "bearing love on their wings." And the Vespucci resembled them.

The Vespucci were descended from Count Soliciano, who had lived in Peretola in the thirteenth century.[1] The names that flowered on the family tree

1. A.S.F. A.S.F. for year 1226, Ancisa EE, Manoscritti 319, c. 344, contains a document of Vespucci, Dolcebene: *Dolcebene quondam Buonamichi del conte de Soliciano.*

had pleasant connotations. The early Vespucci were called Dolcebene, Bonamico (Sweet Good, Good Friend). From Peretola they moved to Florence. "Florence is like a tree in bloom," and wasps go where there is nectar. In 1309 Bruno and Bartolo, two remote forebears, signed a document with the sons of Vespino de Vespinello de Vespuccia. From that time on, no gathering, no intrigue, no convent, no government, no party, no guild, no gay group of night-wandering young sparks in Florence but included one of those wasps of Peretola.

In 1444 Giovanni Vespucci, who had been prior of the Signoria, commissioner in the war with Lucca, and a member of the Council of the Twelve, was named preserver of the laws. With other dissatisfied citizens he introduced a tax reform designed to increase the taxes of the Medici and curtail their power. The Medici moved quickly: Giovanni Vespucci was first imprisoned and then exiled. Pope Nicholas V had to appeal personally to Cosimo de' Medici to allow him to return to the City.[2]

In 1426 Piero Vespucci, who had been engaged in trade in Flanders, was appointed one of the three sea consuls. In this capacity he had a hand in drawing up the code by which the Florentine colony at Bruges was governed. This colony formed a separate nation, governed by its own laws. The statutes

2. G. Caponi, in *Storia della Repubblica di Firenze*, Vol. II, P. 34, states that Giovanni Vespucci twice paid with prison sentences for his disaffection to the Medici. The letter of Pope Nicholas V is to be found in A.S.F., Diplomatis Medicis, 1447.

drawn up by Piero Vespucci and his associates are a complete code covering all commercial, civil, and criminal cases. Piero was later named inspector of the port of Pisa. His son married the daughter of Luca Pitti, at one time the most powerful politician in the Republic.[3]

Bernardo Vespucci, the close friend of Pier Francesco de' Medici, who addressed him in his letters as "brother" or *"compare,"* after holding various posts in the government, was made captain of the Florentine galleys traveling to Sicily. Ten years later he was made captain of Leghorn and commissioner of Pisa, when those ports were vital to Florence's maritime trade.[4]

In 1447 Giuliano Vespucci, the banker, the first Vespucci to be chosen gonfalonier of the Republic–the gonfalonier was the visible head of the government–was made sea consul. And as consul he and two other citizens drew up the statutes establishing the routes and ports of call for the Orient and northern Europe.[5]

The name Vespucci appears repeatedly in the history of art. It was while Giuliano was in charge of the work on Santa Maria Novella that Giovanni

3. For Piero Vespucci's activities in Flanders, see Guilliodts-Van Severen: *Inventaire des Archives de la Ville de Bruges*, pp. 47-8. The statutes governing the Florentine colony in Bruges were published by A. Grunzweig *in Bulletin de l'Institut Historique Belge de Rome*, Vol. X (1930).

4. A.S.F. Manoscritti 52. *Onori delle famiglie fiorentini.*

5. A.S.F. Manoscritti 52. Idem. The navigational statutes were published by G. Uzielli: *Paolo dal Pozzo Toscanelli.*

Battista Alberti began the famous facade.[6] When
Vasari went to study with Michelangelo in Florence,
he lodged in the house of Niccolò Vespucci, and
Niccolò and Vasari became friends; Vasari wrote to
him about Pope Clement's rare ideas when he discussed with him two highly unreligious pictures:
The Toilet of Venus and The Battle of the Satyrs.[7]
Verrocchio lived in a house that belonged to Guido
Antonio Vespucci.[8] Andrea Sansovino was discovered and made known by Simone Vespucci.[9] The
relations of the Vespucci with Botticelli, Ghirlandaio,
and Piero di Cosimo play an important part in the
course of this history. Leonardo da Vinci was so
impressed by the virile beauty of Amerigo the Elder that he followed him about the streets until he
had fixed his features in his mind for the crayon
portrait he later drew. It must have been excellent,
for it is the only one Leonardo did in this manner,
as Vasari specifically mentions in his *Lives of the
Painters.*

Patrons of letters, the Vespucci were friends of the
poets and philosophers. Piero was a friend of Luigi
Pulci and Poliziano; Giorgio Antonio of all the humanists of Lorenzo the Magnificent's day. Agostino
was one of Machiavelli's most constant correspondents. Ludovico Ariosto stayed in Niccolò's house

6. Giuliano Vespucci was in charge of the work on Santa Maria
   Novella from 1462 (A.S.F. Manoscritti 52).
7. *Il cartegio di Giorgio Vasari,* pp. 3 ff.
8. A.S.F. *Diplo. Mediceo,* 1476, Nov. 7.
9. G. Vasari: *Vite dei Pittor,* Vol. IV, p. 510 (ed. Sansoni, 1878-85).

when he went to Florence, and it was there that the great romance of his life occurred.[10]

In Peretola, Amerigo and his brothers could see the soil from which their family tree had sprung, and breathe the atmosphere in which legends flourish. Some of the family annals were a source of pride; others, skeletons to be kept in closets. There had always been a sprinkling of ne'er-do-wells, and more than once the jail housed a Vespucci, as happens in all families. A man could easily fall into disgrace in those days of dictatorships, and the Vespucci were not always trimmers. Whether one was with the Medici or against them was a daily problem for over a century. Those who supported them could count on a post in the Palazzo della Signoria; those who opposed them ate the bitter bread of exile. In either case a moral was attached. To the children the accounts of those who knew which side their bread was buttered on were dull; those of the nonconformists were much more exciting. The Vespucci grew up on these stories, both in Peretola and in Florence.

As a matter of fact, the only distinguished family Peretola produced was the Vespucci. Today in the village square there stands a stone with this inscription: "In this village of Peretola the noble and powerful family of the Vespucci had its origin, one of whose sons was that great Amerigo from whom America derived its name."

10. G. Uzielli: *Ludovico Ariosto e i suoi amori* (Lapi, Firenze, 1905). Michele Catalano: *Vita di Ludovico Ariosto*, pp. 398 ff.

When Amerigo was a child, the people in Peretola amused themselves playing jokes on the Florentines who came there for a rest, or spinning yarns. Franco Sacchetti says that the Florentines, to get away from their wives, invented jousting matches in Peretola. They rented a field from a dyer, and armed themselves like knights to enter the lists. It was a shabby kind of tournament. The horses were bony nags, the arms whatever the jousters could get hold of, and the combatants anything but spirited. But the children enjoyed it immensely; sometimes they slipped a thistle under the horse's tail, with the result that it displayed a completely unexpected mettle, throwing its rider to the ground or returning him to Florence willy-nilly.

At the gatherings of the pages, slaves, and small fry, delightful stories were made up. Macchiavelli must have found in them the inspiration for his play *Belfagor*, which makes Peretola the abode of the Devil. This happened, so the story goes, because in hell the devils refused to believe any longer the Florentines' excuse that their wives were responsible for all their falls from grace. A devil was sent to Florence to investigate the situation. He set himself up in grand style in Ognissanti parish and married a daughter of Amerigo Donati. The wife turned out to be worse than the devil, and the poor imp, completely routed, fled to Peretola. There, in the house of a peasant, his peace of mind was restored and he made his way back to Hell, where he could enjoy the quiet and ease he had not found in Florence. He assured the other devils that the complaints of the Florentines were completely justified, and that in Peretola even a devil could enjoy a taste of paradise.

The citizens of Florence were born, grew up, and left this world amid the marvelous festivals that occasioned Savonarola's diatribes. When Amerigo was five years old, Pope Pius II visited Florence. He had come to preach the crusade against the Turk. The Florentines had little interest in wars of this type, and besides they cost money. They received His Holiness in splendid style, with a great cortege that accompanied him to Santa Maria Novella from the hills overlooking the city. There were processions, banquets, dances, and jousts. The Republic could imagine no other way to welcome a pope coming on such a mission. The Vespucci had a share in all these festivities, but especially in the jousts. Piero, a brother of Guido Antonio, is one of the seven champions mentioned in the chronicles. In gala attire, and followed by twenty squires into the Piazza di Santa Croce, young Piero Vespucci must have been a fine sight. In 1468 this childhood memory came back to Amerigo's mind when this same Piero took part in the jousts of Lorenzo the Magnificent, by which time Amerigo was fourteen. There was no official occasion for this tournament. It was in honor of the engagement of that gay blade, Braccio Martelli, one of the Magnificent's boon companions. Lorenzo appeared in the lists officially as the champion of his bride-to-be, Clarice Orsini, who was in Rome. But he really dedicated his victory to Lucrezia Donati, the wife of Niccolò Ardingheli, his inamorata, who occupied the most gaily decked balcony.[11]

Lorenzo entered the square wearing a surcoat of white and purple velvet embroidered with pearls; and the housing of his horse, which reached to its feet, was adorned in the same manner. Three hundred pearls trimmed his cap, and a gold buckle set with eleven diamonds. The contestants numbered thirteen. Piero Vespucci entered preceded by thirteen trumpeters with pennants displaying arrows and flames of gold. A page who might have stepped out of a painting by Benozzo Gozzoli carried his standard. The device it bore was a cupid shooting arrows of flame; a lady garbed in white gathered them up in a meadow through which ran a silver brook. The page was followed by ten youths carrying gold and silver lances, and another page bearing Piero's helmet on a velvet cushion. Behind him came Piero, wearing a robe of Alexandrian velvet over his armor. The trappings of his horse were trimmed with sable and a tree of pearls that weighed three or four pounds. Alongside him walked twenty-five pages wearing helmets and blue hoods. The accounts of the celebration do not record the names of the young lads who escorted the knights, but it seems logical to assume that Amerigo was one of them. Would he be carrying a silver lance or wearing a blue hood? Bearing a standard or carrying the helmet? Beyond

11. P. Gori: *Le Feste Fiorentine*; C. Carocci: *La Giostra di Lorenzo de' Medici.*

doubt he was present when Lucrezia Donati handed Lorenzo a garland of violets. Lucrezia was seventeen, and her beauty took the breath away. Lorenzo was eighteen, Amerigo fourteen.

Piero Vespucci was not merely one of those participating in the joust–he had helped with its organization. A few days before the event, he wrote to Lorenzo from San Gimignano: "As you requested, I have ready forty demijohns of Greek." This was the sweet wine with which the jousters refreshed themselves. And then his letter went on: "Please send the jugs to my house in Florence. If you don't do this, there will be no Greek… Don't worry, the wine will be there in any case… Incidentally, I would ask you to say a word on my behalf to Piero de' Medici at the time of the next tax assessment. And to the assessors at the right moment. Through you I hope to win grace and favor. All my trust is in you."

The tutelary divinity of all the Magnificent's spectacles was always the god of love. The game of love was so complicated that it is difficult for us to gauge just how far the liberties, the boldness, the respect for one's neighbor's wife or one's own, the virtue of married women, the generosity of the unmarried, went, the degree to which the poetry of the day reflected what actually took place. In so far as was possible to one of his years, Amerigo was fully aware of all that was happening at this nerve center of the Renaissance where the Vespucci played so important a part. Each group of friends was organized into a brigade. The brigades were the moving spirit in the

Pages 66-67: *Sandro Botticelli,* Birth of Venus, *tempera and oil on wood, 172 x 278 cm. Florence, Galleria degli Uffizi. Simonetta was the model.*

gay life of Florence, the carnivals, the balls, the jousts, the serenades. The older Vespucci had belonged to the brigades of the Medici. Giuliano concluded his letters with phrases of this sort: "Regards to Cosimo and Piero and the rest of the brigade." The Cosimo mentioned was to become the "Father of the Country." Some years before, the statutes of the brigades had been notarized, and there were the famous groups known as the Falcons, the Lions, the Knights of the Round Table. In the Academy, music was held in as high esteem as philosophy, and from music came the dance, and from the dance the gay, off-color carnival songs. One of the Vespuccis' best friends was the poet Luigi Pulci. He and Braccio Martelli have left us some of the most delightful pages about night life in Florence, with an account of the dance their brigade held on the outskirts of Florence, with the favor of the Donati girls. From a letter of Pulci's to the Magnificent, where the names are in cipher, it is possible to know all that took place, from the Morris dances that led off the festivities to the excesses of the morning hours. The merry dancers were already making their way home through the fields when the desire to keep the fun going made them turn back. They were soaked with dew, but the Donati girls warmed them up. "Now there are no flies in the honey": their husbands had left.[12]

The young lads took part in the nocturnal celebrations as pages, or footboys, or torchbearers. It

12. I. del Lungo: *Gli Amori del Magnifico Lorenzo*, pp. 32 ff.

must have been in some such capacity that Amerigo
participated in the serenade of 1468, famous in the
gallant annals of Florence. Piero Vespucci was one
of the moving spirits.

It was at carnival time. Bartolommeo Benci was
offering the serenade to Marietta Strozzi. His comrades were, in the order of the chronicle, Andrea
Carnesecchi, Iacopo Marsupini, Bartolommeo
Bertolini, Ludovico Pucci, Piero Vespucci, Francesco
Altoviti, Andrea Boni, and Ludovico Girolami. The
town-crier announced that if anything untoward
occurred that night–if, for example, someone was
trampled by a horse–no one would be held responsible. Bartolommeo and his brigade had the keys of
the city. This was the custom of the Republic.

At the first hour of the evening the group assembled at Bartolommeo's house, and the leader's
baton was handed to him. He had ordered a banquet prepared for them, and at the third hour they
set out for Marietta's house. The horses wore
saddlecloths of cramoisy and silver brocade. Each
of the nine gallants was followed by an escort of
thirty pages carrying lighted torches and displaying
their knight's emblem. Preceding the procession went
a float decked out with cupids and the coat of arms
of the Benci and the Strozzi, and atinkle with silver
bells. Next came musicians with flutes. Marietta appeared on her balcony, which was illuminated by
four flambeaux. The knights galloped past, laying
their arms at the foot of the balcony. The fireworks
began. The noise, the music, the shouting, the sparks

flew skyward. The young faces gleamed in the yellow light of the torches. Having done homage, the riders withdrew without turning their backs on Marietta. Of Marietta the chronicler writes: "In chastity and grace she was comparable only to Lucrezia." She must have been of exceptional beauty as the bust by Desiderio da Settignano bears witness, one of the perfect works of art of the Renaissance. She was spirited, proud, and charming, "half princess, half adventuress."

The members of the brigade, after honoring the lady of Bartolommeo's heart, left to go on with their serenading at other windows. Each of Benci's eight companions honored the lady of his choice in similar fashion. The streets were turning pink with the light of dawn, and the music and merriment still echoed in them.[13]

But there was one beauty who outshone all the others of Florence: Simonetta Vespucci. Or, to be exact, Simonetta Cattaneo, the wife of Marco Vespucci. She was exactly Amerigo's age. She was born in Genoa and spent her early years in Piombino with her sister, Battistina, the wife of the lord of the castle there, Jacopo III d'Appiano. When Simonetta was fifteen she married Marco Vespucci, a distant cousin of Amerigo's. She was about twenty when she first went to Florence. It was at that time, in 1473, that Simonetta was present at the ball given in honor of Eleanora de Aragón, daughter of the King

13. Gori, op. cit.

of Naples, who passed through Florence on her way to marry Ercole d'Este, Duke of Ferrara. Like all the other festivities arranged in Eleanora's honor, the ball must have been an extraordinary event. Rome had given her a truly royal welcome, cardinals and high church dignitaries going to meet her three miles outside the city, the Pope saying a Mass for her at St. Peter's, and after that the city becoming a theater of gallantry that gave the court of Pope Sixtus IV an air more of this world than of an eternal city. Florence's first act of public homage to Eleanora was a St. John, a traditional folk festival. It was followed by flag races, processions, fireworks, and a banquet, and reached its grand finale in the ball.

The ball was held in the open air, on the bank of the Arno, in the gardens of the Palazzo Lenzi, close by the houses of the Vespucci. It was in the late afternoon. The sun gleamed on the ladies' hair, held with strands of pearls and sprinkled with gold powder. Music was provided by lutes. The air held a warm sensuality. It was a preview of Botticelli's *Primavera.* The three graces of the ball were Eleanora de Aragón, Albiera degli Albizzi, and Simonetta Vespucci. Eleanora was to grace the learned court of Ferrara. Albiera was treading a dance of death, and every step she took, every move she made, was to take on a terrifying beauty in retrospect: before ten days had elapsed she was being carried to her grave. Simonetta's star was just rising. From then on she never left Florence except, perhaps, on the occasion of some festival in one of the neighboring towns.

The afternoon of the dance she was seen–and for Simonetta to be seen was to be loved–by all the young men of Florence. Above all, it was the ardent eyes of Giuliano de' Medici which followed her every incomparably graceful step as she moved through the dances. Giuliano, the brother of the Magnificent, from that time on worshipped her from a distance with manifest passion.[14]

Like all the Vespucci, Simonetta lived in the Ognissanti quarter. She was so close to Amerigo in that family atmosphere that the two of them are among the thirteen members of the family painted by Ghirlandaio. Probably Botticelli saw her frequently, as one sees neighbors, and her image went with him until the end of his days. Simonetta was the model of his masterpieces, *the Birth of Venus, Primavera, Venus and Mars.*

Two years after the ball, in 1475, Florence once more put on festive attire to celebrate a political triumph: its alliance with Venice and the pontiff. The Magnificent sent delegates to many cities bearing invitations to another tournament, at which Giuliano de' Medici was to be the central figure. His silver armor had been wrought by Verrocchio. According to the chronicle of the event, the jewels on his tabard and cap dazzled the eye. His horse had been sent as a gift from Apulia, and Sandro Botticelli had painted his standard. It represented Pallas Athena,

14. I. del Lungo: *La Donna Fiorentina del Buon Tempo Antico*, p. 184.

in a golden garment reaching to her knee, moving through a flowery meadow. It was in reality the portrait of Simonetta, for whom Giuliano had entered the lists. And Simonetta was queen of the tournament. On this occasion the Vespucci were not in the ring, but in the boxes. For reasons of a literary nature this tournament achieved a historic importance far beyond that in which Lorenzo contended. Giuliano was the champion. He was not so ugly as Lorenzo, and his brief life ended leaving no other memory than that of his ardent, ill-fated youth. The name of Simonetta, the queen of the tournament, naturally displaced that of Lucrezia Donati. But the thing that has immortalized this tournament is the poetic account that has come down to us. The description of Lorenzo's tournament by the poet Luigi Pulci is an uninspired effort. That of Giuliano, on the other hand, was described by Poliziano in one of his best poems, to be found in every anthology.

In allegorical form Poliziano presents Giuliano as a hunter who goes off to the forest, disdaining the call of Love. Cupid follows him and sets a springe for him. Giuliano sees a white doe run by and starts eagerly after her. He comes to an opening in the forest, and there in a flowering mead sees Simonetta as the living center, the axis of the enchanted forest. This is Poliziano's portrait of Simonetta:

White is the maid and white the robe around her,
With buds and roses and thin grasses pied;
Enwreathèd folds of golden tresses crowned her

Shadowing her forehead fair with modest pride:
The wild wood smiled; the thicket where he found
her,
To ease his anguish, bloomed on every side;
Serene she sits, with gesture queenly mild,
And with her brow tempers the tempests wild.[15]

In that proud brow which is modest, in that virtue which makes everything about her smile, in that cordial grace which melts bitterness away, in that serene regard which with its gaze calms the storm, Poliziano has fixed the traits of Simonetta, traits that reappear in all the writing and painting of which she is the subject. It is generally accepted that Botticelli found in this poem the inspiration for his Primavera. Even to the detail of her dress, which Poliziano probably took, not from that she wore the day of the tournament, but from the one she wore the afternoon of Eleanor's ball.

One year later, in the spring, Simonetta was dead. All Florence followed her to the grave. "The blessed soul of Simonetta is in paradise; it is Death's second triumph," a relative wrote to the Magnificent. When

---

15. *Candida è ella e candida la veste,*
   ma pur di rose e fior depinta e d'erba;
   lo inanellato crin dell'aurea testa
   scende in la frente umilmente superba.
   Ridegli attorno tutta la floresta,
   e quanto puo sue core disacerba.
   Nell' atto regalmente e mansueta;
   a pur col ciglio le tempeste acqueta...
   Translated by J. A. Symonds, in *The Renaissance in Italy.*

he received the news, Lorenzo had just seen a star that no one had observed before. "That is Simonetta," he said, and wrote the sonnet beginning:

Bright shining Star! Thy radiance in the sky
Dost rob the neighbouring stars of all their light.
Why art thou with unwonted splendour bright?
Why with great Phœbus does thou dare to vie? [16]

The lid of the coffin was left open as she was borne through the streets. Everybody wanted to have one last glimpse of her. She was still so beautiful that she seemed the Sleeping Beauty. Leonardo da Vinci, who formed part of the funeral cortege, sketched her head. The poets Giuliano de' Medici and Bernardo Pulci wrote elegies. Her slight body was laid to rest in the Church of Ognissanti. There, too, close beside the bodies of the Vespucci, the body of Sandro Botticelli was to lie.

16. *O chiara stella, cha co' raggi tupi*
     toglie alle tue vicine stelle il lume,
     perchè splende assai piu che'l tuo costume?
     Perchè con Febo ancor contender vuoi?
     Translation by E. L. S. Horsburgh, in *Lorenzo the Magnificent* (London: Methuen & Co.; 1908).

IV
AMERIGO'S STUDIES

Fortunately for Amerigo, he did not attend the university. To have done so would have meant going to Pisa. It had seemed to Lorenzo the Magnificent the part of prudence to get the turbulent youth of university age out of Florence, and to keep in the city only that literary club which was the Academy. There he could rub elbows with philosophers, poets, musicians, and learned men. Amerigo's education was entrusted to his uncle Giorgio Antonio, outstanding among all the Vespucci for love of learning. His wisdom was admired beyond the confines of Florence. For reasons undoubtedly related to Amerigo's own disposition, Uncle Giorgio Antonio showed a predilection for the boy among all his nephews.

Giorgio Antonio was eight years younger than Stagio. There had always been a close friendship between these two brothers, though they were very different in temperament. Their love of books and of Latin was a bond between them. But Stagio was made for the world and its vanities. He had a wife, his wife gave him sons, and, without being irresponsible, he loved a good time. He was the first-born of Amerigo the Elder. Giorgio Antonio, who was the

Ghirlandaio, Portrait of Giorgio Antonio Vespucci from La Pietà e La Misericordia, *Fresco in the Church of Ognissanti, Florence.*

youngest, remained single, completely given over to his studies, and said it was his intention to take orders.

So he did, and after having held the post of canon at the Duomo, became a Dominican friar.

We have a handsome portrait of Giorgio Antonio, the one painted by Ghirlandaio for the Ognissanti Church. The artist divided into two scenes the fresco behind the altar in the Chapel of St. Isabel of Portugal, a chapel belonging to Amerigo Vespucci and his descendants. The upper scene shows Our Lady of Mercy covering eleven members of the Vespucci family with her mantle, and the Archbishop Antonino, who was later canonized and by antonomasia is today considered the saint of Florence. The lower scene depicts the Descent from the Cross, and all the personages, with two exceptions, are Biblical. The two non-Scriptural figures are Giorgio Antonio and young Amerigo. Giorgio Antonio has an air of gravity and repose, and is fleshier than any of the Vespucci in the upper half of the painting. He has all the aspect of a scholar. His brow is furrowed by two deep wrinkles; his gaze is firm and alert, and his bearing is that of a man in complete control of himself. Whereas all but one of the sacred figures have their eyes turned toward Christ, and that one toward heaven, Giorgio Antonio's are on the spectators as though searching out the conduct of those contemplating the Passion of Christ. His lips are firmly set as though imposing silence. Amerigo is directly behind him, in the perfect attitude of the devoted pupil. His fair, curling hair is in contrast with the master's graying, close-cropped head, and his youthful attire with Giorgio Antonio's habit. There is a restrained quality in Amerigo's pose, as though the wise, experienced hand of the uncle were holding in check the tumultuous ardor of Amerigo's youth.

It may well have been that when Ghirlandaio painted this picture, about 1473, the Vespucci thought that Amerigo might follow the path of Giorgio Antonio and enter the Church, for he is shown with his uncle, and, like him, with the halo of sainthood, a device frequently employed in the paintings of the period. When Ghirlandaio painted this portrait, the most authentic that exists of Amerigo Vespucci, Amerigo was an unknown quantity, a stripling standing on the threshold of life. He might have become a friar and America have had a different name.

The history of this fresco of Ghirlandaio's is, like everything in Amerigo's life, a mixture of adverse and favorable fortune. Centuries were to elapse before the simplest details could be established. Years after the fresco was painted—well into the sixteenth century, when the friars of the Order of Humiliati, whose rules had become relaxed, abandoned the church and it was turned over to the Observantines—Alessandro Marzi-Medici, the son of Lisabetta Vespucci, was made Archbishop of Florence. The Vespucci and the Medici had intermarried. The Archbishop decided to redecorate the chapel, and he commissioned Matteo Rosselli to paint a picture of St. Isabel of Portugal to honor the name of his mother.

A new altar was installed, and Ghirlandaio's fresco disappeared for more than four centuries. Giorgio Vasari, however, had mentioned the fact that Ghirlandaio had painted in the Ognissanti Church a fresco containing a portrait of Amerigo Vespucci. In 1898 Father Roberto Razzoli published a monograph on the chapels that three of the Vespucci families had built in Ognissanti. This aroused speculation, and the commissioner of public monuments ordered the altar of St. Isabel moved, thus revealing the great fresco intact. As it was out of curiosity or devotion to the memory of Amerigo Vespucci that the investigation was begun, it then became necessary to establish which of the six male figures was Amerigo. Some of the experts chose one of the older men, others a youth with a bright, alert head. The latter won out, and even today this opinion is the most widely accepted. But it should be pointed out that whereas this is the portrait of a boy of about sixteen, Amerigo was twenty when Ghirlandaio's fresco was painted. Simonetta, who was Amerigo's age and is in this group, is patently not a child.

For decades the experts have argued about who is who in this picture. At least three claimants have been put forward as being Amerigo. Some have believed that he is the old bald man kneeling at the feet of the Virgin, with the result that an equally bald Amerigo has appeared in statues and on medals. Others have thought him the grave personage seen in profile in one corner, and we have engravings of Amerigo following this model. Others have used this same version, but have given him a long beard after the Greek manner. Others have found their inspiration in the sixteen-year-old youth. The figure they have least taken into consideration is that of the young man of twenty–Amerigo's age when the picture was painted–beside Giorgio Antonio. Yet this is the point at which the painting coincides with reality:[1] this is certainly Amerigo.

An interesting document of this period has come down to us: Amerigo's composition book.[2] It is written in a clear, careful, firm handwriting, in two columns, one the Italian original, the other the Latin translation. These are reflections of a moral nature, comments on the life about him. Giorgio Antonio directed the exercises; Amerigo set down either his own ideas or those of his uncle. In a sense, it was a resume of the dialogues that took place between them. The exercise might be a criticism of tyranny, of government based on injustice, with the sufferings to which this subjected the upright citizen. Sometimes the topic was scientific considerations, or family matters. The immediate object of these lessons was to prepare Amerigo in Latin, to familiarize him with all its moods and conjugations. But the secondary

1. R. Razzoli: *La Chiesa d'Ognissanti in Firenze*; E. Brockhaus: *Ricerche sopra alcuni capolavori d'arte italiana*; P. Bargellini: *Ghirlandaio*; R. Langton-Douglas: "The Contemporary Portraits of Amerigo Vespucci," *Burlington Magazine* (London), January-December 1944.
2. Preserved in the Riccardiana Library of Florence. Catalogue number 2649.

purpose was to inculcate in him teachings and examples of a moral nature. Through these exercises we catch a glimpse of the life of Florence and its customs. Amerigo writes:

I have always loved virtuous men and wished well to all who follow the paths of virtue... I should like to tell you about a group of wise and learned young men I saw a few days ago, who in their conversation revealed no other thought and no other goal than the study of letters... They were waiting for their master. When he appeared, they did him marvelous honor. After they had delighted themselves with his words, they accompanied him to his home... They have so aroused in me an ardor for such studies that I have put aside every other thought, to follow the path of virtue. From this I know that you, out of the love you bear me, will derive the greatest pleasure...

My father anxiously desires that I seek out and learn those things which may help me to win fame and honor. So far as I am concerned, I have endured and can endure all fatigue. I had taken no thought of such things, but I have now decided not to lose more time. I shall conquer myself, and I shall behave in such a manner as to put aside from me all lewd pleasures and give true signs of virtue... I have wished to tell you all this so that you may help and counsel me from time to time with your wise and kindly words...

A few days ago I bought a volume of Plato for the price asked by a bookseller I know. Some time later someone you know, learned in Greek and Latin, saw

*it and, after he had read it carefully, was of the opin-
ion that it was of scant value, and that I should not
have paid more than two or three florins for it. As I
paid more than ten, I am sending it to you to look
over and to tell me whether I should keep it or try to
sell it for what I paid for it, so that no one can accuse
me of being careless or extravagant...*

Uncle and nephew seem to have made a trip to
Rome together. In the long hours of travel, on foot or
muleback, during stops at monasteries or inns,
Amerigo would have made his first acquaintance with
the world of humanism. He knew the Renaissance in
the intimate aspect of serenades and tournaments.
He knew about the gay, licentious revels in the villas
outside Florence, and he had savored the sweet, faintly
melancholy side of life in his association with Simonetta. Now he walked in the company of a kindly,
upright man whose repugnance for tyranny was finally to align him on the side of Savonarola. On their
return from Rome, Giorgio Antonio dictated:

*Some days ago we left your home and set out for
Rome, passing by many cities and castles... We then
returned by the same route, and as soon as we arrived in Florence, we went to see your father.*

Then follows a moral portrait of Stagio. He was
just and good and will enjoy eternal bliss. He will be
known to posterity as an upright man, for he was
not one of those who live only for pleasure. Then
comes a description of a dinner said to have been
given in Stagio's home, but which may be rather of
a scene in the home of the sons of Giuliano Vespucci

the banker or in that of Guido Antonio and Simone Vespucci:

Yesterday we dined at your father's home. Many blackbirds, pigeons, capons, and other fowl had been dressed, which at this season of the year sit well upon the stomach, and we ate with pleasure to our fill. And the wines and desserts! We drank as though it was a wedding. After dinner he showed us handsome garments, woven of the finest wool and embroidered with great skill, which gave us an idea of the wealth of your house. With this motive we spoke of virtue, for you will not lack for the other things... Why, O mortals, build the walls of such a beautiful house, hung with paintings, and adorned with gold and silver, and displaying the handiwork of noble sculptors who cast and carved statues of metal and marble? Give thought to death, which, as the poets tell, comes when the Fate, Atropos, cuts the thread her sisters Clotho and Lachesis have drawn and spun on their distaff and shuttle. This shows the beginning, the middle, and the end of our uncertain, miserable lives...

The worst thing a man can do is to lead a sterile life:

In days past a man died who never awoke. He lived as though in a perpetual sleep. He contributed nothing to philosophy, he never engaged in a disputation or laid an argument before one who could answer him, or took part in battle, or occupied himself in trade. He spent all his time amusing himself, singing, strolling about the countryside with friends, fish-

*ing and hunting, given over to pleasure, and taking
pride only in some injury or villainy that he had done
his neighbor. Small wonder that he died poor and
full of regrets, bereft of the grace of God or man.*

The enduring influence of these lessons on
Amerigo can be appraised in his letters from the
New World. Thence he wrote to Piero Soderini:

*I recall how in the days of our youth... we used to
go to hear the principles of grammar under the good
example and teaching of that venerable ecclesiastic,
friar of San Marcos, Fray Giorgio Antonio Vespucci,
whose counsels and teaching would God that I had
followed, for, as Petrarch says, I would have been
another man than I am...*

Along with the moral precepts, Giorgio Antonio
planted in Amerigo's mind the love of travel, unroll-
ing before his eyes a colored map of the world. And
Amerigo became aware of those seas on which merchants voyaged, learned about unknown lands, and
acquired a broad vision of the universe. In the exercise book we read:

*Going back and forth to many distant lands, where
by talking and trading one can learn many things,
not a few merchants have become wise and learned,
something that cannot be explained in a few words.
Moving about and making inquiries concerning the
world, whose limits we have not yet completely ascertained, they can furnish valuable advice by word
and association to those who come to them in search
of counsel or clarification of some doubt concerning
matters of business and custom.*

Later on, during his life in Seville and Lisbon, the diligent nephew was to put this advice into practice. Above all, he was to apply it when, on the coast of Africa, at Cape Verde, he met Cabral's fleet returning from Asia, an encounter that provided him with a wealth of information, which he passed on to the Medici.

His exercise book continues:

I have been requested and begged to go to see you. But with these rains, and my poor health, the result of so much work and care... I have preferred to write rather than talk with you. Briefly, I wish to inform you that there has arrived in port a boat loaded with so many things that all who have heard of it find it incredible and are lost in amazement when they see it. Among the things I have heard that it is carrying is a great quantity of gold, and it is said that it has made very long voyages that are worth recounting...

Inasmuch as a companion of mine is leaving for the Orient, where he plans to buy and sell much merchandise that will bring him gold and fame, it has seemed to me well to inform you of this, in case you should desire anything from there, for he will serve you faithfully as he does me.

Giorgio Antonio was humanism made flesh and blood. He enjoined upon Amerigo the need of seeking a rational explanation of events and ceasing to lend an ear to theologians or astrologers who would explain meteorological phenomena as supernatural manifestations. He scoffed at those who believed that it rained blood or animals. If he was to be a friar, he was to be an enlightened one. Amerigo wrote in his composition book:

O priest, to whom people so often turn for advice, inquiring of you why lightning has struck, or hail, rain, or snow has fallen unseasonably, as though you were the god Apollo, who, poets pretend, can read the future as though it were the present, what would you reply to them if they were to ask you about the showers of stones, blood, or flesh so often mentioned in the old fables?

In another place he examines the problem of the emotions, seeking an explanation of physiological facts, following the type of question employed in academic circles, which was based on a different criterion from that of medieval fantasy.

What is the reason a man's blood heats or cools off? Why, at times, does a man pale, or turn red and again white, at times become bloated and then again gaunt? Why, at times, do his members refuse to obey him? Or he suddenly become gay when he should not? Or wax enthusiastic and laugh and show himself merry? Why does his countenance grow full because of certain things and waste away because of others? I should like to know all this, for I have heard it said that all the changes we undergo are caused by the action of the blood, which is the beginning and the origin, the reason of our life.

Another of his themes was political life. Florence was fickle, and every change in the Palazzo della Signoria meant an upheaval in the lives of many citizens. The wheel of fortune at times raises the

man tied to it to the upper regions where the air is
limpid and he beholds a firmament seeming to promise him everything. At others, it casts him down into
the mire. The symbol of the wheel was so often
invoked that it had become a commonplace, but
there is no doubt that it left a lasting impression on
Amerigo's mind. It made him canny, or at least prudent; and he often employed the metaphor in his
letters.

In the exercise book Amerigo set down the good
man's protest against tyranny which Giorgio Antonio had dictated to him:

*Who are those who have been so grievously oppressed,
despoiled of what was theirs–which was great wealth,
and which their oppressors prized and coveted? They
were our fellow citizens, the friends of your family. They
now depart to exile, and they have neither kin nor friend
who wish them well. Thus what was theirs has fallen to
their rivals or their very enemies.*

The moral counsels Amerigo received were not
mere words: Giorgio Antonio's life was his best teaching, and his authority was recognized not only in
Florence, but by all foreign scholars who visited the
city. He had begun his studies with an exiled humanist, Filippo di Ser Ugolino Pieruzzi, who lived in
the Monastery of Settimo (so called because it was
seven miles from Florence), where he collected one
of the largest libraries of his day. Women had no
part in his life; it was said that he died a virgin. The
injustices of Florence pained him deeply, but he
could do nothing against them. The humanists went

to see him, and his retreat became a university for
the most dedicated scholars. Giorgio Antonio was
then a boy. He visited the master continually, often
spending days and weeks in the monastery. Filippo
set him to copying Greek manuscripts, and in a short
time Giorgio Antonio had mastered the language.
Francesco Castiglione, who initiated Donato
Acciaiuoli in the study of Greek, affectionately referred to Vespucci as "our Giorgio Antonio."

Giorgio Antonio's great passion in his youth was
Cicero. He became impatient when Father Giovanni
of the abbey kept his copy of the great orator's *Rhetoric* beyond the time for which he had lent it to him.
When Giorgio Antonio went to Florence, he spent
long hours in the house of Donato Acciaiuoli, the
moving spirit of the Academy, taking part in dialogues on Latin or Greek themes. One day Donato
gave him a copy of the orations *Against Cataline* to
be returned to Filippo. Giorgio Antonio was to find
in the Ciceronian oratory a rod to scourge the corruption, treachery, and baseness that flourished in
Florence as they had in ancient Rome; a faint echo
of these readings is heard in Amerigo's book of dic-
tations. As Giorgio Antonio worked in the study of
an exile dedicated to learning, his thirst for justice
and his hatred for tyranny grew.[3]

At the Abbey of Settimo, Giorgio Antonio's horizons broadened in other directions. Filippo culti-

3. On Giorgio Antonio Vespucci and the Platonic Academy see A.
della Torre: *Storia dell'accademia Platonica di Firenze.*

vated mathematics and geography as well as literature. In the twilight of the cloister the lamp that lighted
the scholar's nights of study burned with a brighter
flame. Filippo had been a close friend of Paolo dal
Pozzo Toscanelli. The group which gathered around
him was the continuation of the one Toscanelli had
brought together in the Convent of the Angels, where
he and Filippo had often discussed astronomy, voyages, the form of the earth, and the limits of the
seas. Filippo transmitted to Giorgio Antonio his admiration for Toscanelli, familiarizing him with
Toscanelli's teachings. All these men–Toscanelli,
Filippo, Giorgio Antonio–had the scholar's vocation.
Filippo and Toscanelli were even more austere than
Vespucci, more harsh and intolerant in the defense
of their stern mistress, knowledge.

In 1473 Giorgio Antonio's study was a reproduction of the one in which he had received his own
initiation, Filippo's. His attitude was now that of his
master, his mission to carry on the work of Toscanelli.
Giorgio Antonio, his pupils, and his associates were
all followers of Toscanelli.

Young men of the best families of Florence, or foreigners drawn to the city by the irresistible lure of
humanism, gathered to listen to Giorgio Antonio's
teachings. There, alongside Amerigo, was Antonio di
Jacopo Lanfredini, who was to become one of the
directors of the Study or School of Florence, and Piero
Soderini, who was to achieve the unique honor of
being made lifetime gonfalonier, and who became
the recipient of Amerigo's letter concerning his dis-

coveries in the New World. Among the foreigners were Greeks or Byzantines bringing the message of the old learning, and Germans, to whom Florence was the Athens of the new world of Europe.

Here Amerigo could acquaint himself with the works of Dante and Petrarch and such classical authors as Plato, Heraclitus, and Democritus. He could take part in the discussions about Epicurean and Stoic philosophy, acquire knowledge of Ptolemy, smile at Martial's epigrams, read Livy, and come to know the contemporary poets of Florence: Franco, Pulci, Poliziano. The Latin taught by Giorgio Antonio was not the dead language of macaronic friars. It was a living key that opened the door to the science, philosophy, and literature of the past, which, grafted on the evergreen tree of knowledge, bore some of the finest fruits of thought which history records.

In 1476 one of those recurring plagues that decimated its population broke out in Florence. The activity of the workshops was paralyzed, and even the countryside received a mortal wound. In the city, within the confines of the wall, in houses crowded with old and young, the death toll was overwhelming. In many homes not one survivor was left. Over eleven thousand people had died in 1400 in a similar epidemic. Medicine could discover no effectual remedy. In Amerigo's composition book we find these lines, which sum up the advice of his uncle:

It would be well to remind friends and relatives that in times like these, when the plague is setting in, the only thing to do is to eat with moderation, avoid riotous living, and go to bed... I, praise be to God, am well, though at times the days are too prolonged with my many tasks...

Stagio did not think the danger could be withstood so easily. Like other prudent persons, he felt that the solution lay in getting as many of the family as he could out of Florence. He was not worried about Antonio, his eldest son, who was in Pisa. His greatest concern was for his brother Giorgio Antonio and for Amerigo. Both Giorgio Antonio and Stagio were good friends of Lorenzo di Pier Francesco de' Medici, who offered to make room for them in his villa at Mugello. There they continued the Latin lessons.

From Mugello, Giorgio Antonio wrote to Stagio, who had remained in Florence, reminding him of matters of urgency. A good priest by the name of Norotto acted as messenger. When Giorgio Antonio was unable to write, Amerigo did so in his name. But he had to write in Latin: Stagio was very strict on this score. Amerigo, fearful of making mistakes without his uncle at his side to correct him, nevertheless did his best:

"Honor. Pater & c. Quod ad vos non scripserim proximis diebus, nolite mirari..."

Translated, the letter, the first we know from Amerigo's hand, reads:

Venerated Father: Do not be surprised because I have not written to you these last days. I assumed that my uncle would do so in my name when he arrived. When he is away, I hardly venture to write to you in Latin, for I am ashamed of the mistakes I make even in my own tongue. I have been very busy writing out the rules of Latin grammar and the phrases I can use, so that when I get back I can show you that part of my exercise book in which I have set down your own examples. Of how I behave and what I am doing, you have been informed, I hope, by my uncle, whose return I ardently desire so that with your help and his I can devote myself more completely both to my studies and to your instructions. About three or four days ago Giorgio Antonio sent you several letters with Ser Norotto, a learned and obliging priest. He awaits your answer. Aside from this, I have no news to give you except to tell you how eager we all are to pack our belongings and return to the city. We don't know when this will be, though we think it won't be too long, unless the plague should get worse, a thing we trust God will forfend.

Giorgio Antonio hopes you will do something for a poor, unfortunate neighbor whose only hope and salvation are in us, a matter he has written to you about at length. For that reason I beg of you to take this matter upon yourself and take careful and diligent action in the matter so he will suffer as little as possible during his absence. I hope you are all well. Remember me to everyone, especially my mother and my elders...[4]

---

4. This letter was first published by Bandini, op. cit., p. 17. The original is in the Morgan Library of New York.

This letter and the exercises in his composition book give us an idea of Amerigo's development. His Latin was halting. But he was more than a lad beginning to see the world around him. Giorgio Antonio in his teaching used an extremely paternal tone toward his pupils. Amerigo was now adequately prepared to take his place in society, to be a merchant or a man of state, to have an amorous adventure or found a family. As a matter of fact, shortly after his return from Mugello the political situation of Florence brought about his engagement in diplomatic duties that marked the beginning of his life outside the city's walls.

Ghirlandaio, Portrait of Amerigo Vespucci detail from La Pietà e La Misericordia, *Fresco in the Church of Ognissanti, Florence.*

V

POLITICAL LIFE
(1478)

Cosimo de' Medici definitely established the power of his house in Florence and in the world. He was as shrewd a banker as politician. He never forced issues; he knew how to wait. On one occasion he was exiled; when he returned, he was received like a prince. Men of letters revered him; artists sought his patronage. When he died, in 1464, the Republic consecrated him "Father of the Country." Florence had never instituted personal titles. In other states the head was known as Dux, Marquis, Duke–or Pope. In the Republic of Florence a new gonfalonier was chosen every two months, and the Signoria was the visible supreme authority. Nevertheless, above the Signoria and the gonfalonier stood the Medici. They were dictators, though not of the breed of despots which sullied Rimini, Milan, and Naples–and even Rome–with their crimes. Their basic interest was in the wool trade, loans and letters of exchange, the Academy, and the artists' studios. Upon Cosimo's death the citizens of Florence turned their eyes to his son Piero, not yet fifty. Unfortunately, Piero was a sick man. He is known to history as Piero the Gouty. His control of the Republic lasted only five years. He left two sons, Lorenzo the Magnificent and

Sandro Botticelli, Giuliano de' Medici, detail from Spring, *tempera and oil on wood, 203 x 314 cm, ca. 1482-1483, Florence, Galleria degli Uffizi.*

Giuliano. Lorenzo, who was just twenty, was recognized as the head of the Republic by natural right; Giuliano was barely sixteen. He was a more dashing figure than the Magnificent, and his friends called him the "Prince of Youth." Poliziano called him "the delight of the youth of Florence." His love for Simonetta Vespucci, even if it remained on a purely Platonic plane, was none the less intense on that account. Not only did Botticelli delight in painting Giuliano and Simonetta together, as in the *Primavera* and *Venus and Mars*; Poliziano linked the two in his poem on the tournament. When Simonetta died, Piero Vespucci gave Giuliano her portrait and her personal belongings.

Not only for the honor of the family, but for his own interests, Lorenzo the Magnificent felt it fitting to give Giuliano an outstanding position. He thought at first of making him a prince of the Church and with this intention addressed himself to the Pope and to Cardinal Papiense. But the things of this world attracted Giuliano more than the Church. He carried on a clandestine love affair with a young woman of Gorini, who bore him a son, Giulio de' Medici. The existence of this child became known only after Giuliano's death, but as the boy had Medici blood in his veins, he became Clement VII. With regard to Giuliano's inclinations, Cardinal Papiense on one occasion wrote to Lorenzo suggesting that he be made, not a full-fledged cardinal, but a half-cardinal, "because as the layman that he is, to put him into a post of such eminence would be a thing that none of us could sanction wholeheartedly."[1] And the Cardinal was right. The better plan seemed to be an alliance with some powerful house, and the very year of Simonetta's death a marriage was arranged for Giuliano with her niece, Semiramide, daughter of Jacopo III d'Appiano of Piombino and Battistina, Simonetta's sister.

Through Giuliano's marriage to Semiramide, the Vespucci family would be closely linked to the Medici and the oligarchy. The proposed union gave much food for thought to the political world of Italy, especially in Siena.[2] Family ties between Florence and Piombino presupposed a political realignment. Piombino's importance had already been demonstrated at the time of Florence's war against Volterra. For Giuliano, in the flower of his twenty-three years, marriage to Semiramide was more than bringing Piombino within the sphere of influence of Florence; it was a blood tie with Simonetta. But destiny had decreed that this cadet of the house of Medici should die young, as had the beauty of the house of Vespucci. Giuliano lost his life in the Pazzi conspiracy of 1478. Semiramide entered Florence by a different route, Amerigo was thrust into diplomacy, Piero Vespucci was sent to prison, and a new phase of life began for Lorenzo the Magnificent.

All versions of the Pazzi conspiracy agree on the main facts. The Archbishop of Pisa, Francesco Salvati,

---

1. Fabroni: *Laurentii Medicis Vita*, Vol. II, p. 58.
2. Arch. Storico Siena, Concistoro, Copialettere, 1961, c. 230.

who lived in Rome, hated Lorenzo de' Medici with all his soul, because Lorenzo had blocked his ambition to be named archbishop of Florence and had secured the appointment of his own brother-in-law, Rinaldo Orsini. The banker Francesco Pazzi and Captain Giovan' Battista di Montesecco met with the Archbishop in his palace. The banker shared the Archbishop's hatred for Lorenzo from motives of business rivalry. Captain Montesecco was merely a soldier in the service of Count Girolamo Riario, nephew of Sixtus IV, and captain of the Papal Guard. The Count was consumed by hatred of Lorenzo de' Medici, who stood in the way of his unbounded thirst for power. The Count had hoped to convert his fief of Imola into a principality to outshine all rivals in Italy.

The three men discussed the manner of eliminating the Medici brothers, Lorenzo and Giuliano. The only one who had any scruples was Captain Montesecco; he would take part in the conspiracy only if the Pope gave his approval. The three went to call on the Pope. Sixtus said: "I want to see a change in the state of Florence, but without the death of anyone." They set forth that such a thing could never be. The Pope's nephew tried to convince him: "Everything possible will be done to avoid the shedding of blood, but if this should happen, Your Holiness will absolve the person responsible for it." The Pope replied: "You are a brute," and added: "In any case I want a change in the state of Florence, to get it out of the hands of Lorenzo, who is an evil man, a villain... but let there be no deaths." The Archbishop responded: "Holy Father, have no fear, for we are at the helm." And the conspirators left to work out plans for doing away with the Medici.[3]

Various methods were suggested and rejected. It was finally decided to do it in the Duomo while Raffaelo Riario, a twenty-year-old Cardinal, nephew of the Count, was officiating. Captain Montesecco, in the end, refused to take part in the crime, and his duties were taken over by one Antonio da Volterra and a priest by the name of Stefano. Giuliano was stabbed to death and left in a pool of blood on the Duomo floor. Lorenzo, though wounded, managed to take refuge in the sacristy. Florence was thrown into a frenzy by the news. The populace swarmed into the streets shouting the cry of the Medici: "Palle! Palle!" and Lorenzo's dominion over the city became stronger than ever. The Archbishop and his immediate accomplices were hanged from the balcony of the Palazzo della Signoria. Messengers set out post-haste to overtake those who had managed to escape.

Napoleone Franzeci and Bernardo Bandini were hotheaded, determined young men of the best families of Florence, friends of the Pazzi. The two had joined in the conspiracy, and they fled the city. Bandini was taken in Constantinople. Botticelli painted his portrait on the palace wall, below the balcony where the Archbishop was hanged, with

3. The phrases quoted are from *La Confessione de Giovan' Battista de Montesecco*, which, together with *La Coniuratio Pactiana* by Angelo Poliziano, was published by Adimari (Naples, 1769).

this inscription: "I am Bernardo Bandini, a new Judas, traitor to the Medici, who rebelled in the church only to receive a more shameful death." Napoleone Franzeci was aided in his flight by Piero Vespucci, Simonetta's father-in-law.

The Medici agents were never able to lay their hands on Napoleone. And his escape incensed the Florentines. In acting as he did, was Piero Vespucci aware of the risk he was running? Was he moved by humanitarian feelings, by his adventurer's lack of calculation, by his desire to help a fellow being in trouble? Did he have a foreknowledge of the conspiracy? Why did Napoleone turn to him? Did Piero Vespucci take satisfaction in the removal from this world of one who was reputed to be the lover of his daughter-in-law, and who had dared to write over-amorous poems about her? This is one of the explanations suggested.

Piero Vespucci connived at the escape of Napoleone while acting as commissioner of Florence in Pisa and enjoying the complete confidence of the Medici.[4] Possibly he thought his aid would never be known, for he took horse and calmly set out for Florence. He was arrested on the way and led into Florence beneath the balcony from which the populace had seen the body of the Archbishop hanging. Later his screams when he was tortured to make him confess could be beard for blocks. His torture lasted for twenty days. It was hoped that Franzeci

4. L. Landucci: *Diario Fiorentino*, November 14, 1478.

might have told Piero the names of those involved in the conspiracy. Whether Piero told anything, or had anything to tell, he was, nevertheless, sentenced to life imprisonment. Marco, his son, Simonetta's widower, was exiled.

All historians make mention of Piero's imprisonment. But none defends him–least of all his contemporaries. Poliziano, who had been his friend, exudes venom when mentioning him, calling him the black sheep of the family and stating that his father had disinherited him. In the homes of the Vespucci his name was never spoken. Nearly all of them fell over themselves to make public profession of their adherence to Lorenzo, as did all Florence. In part they were motivated by genuine friendship for the Magnificent, in part by the natural repugnance the brutality of the attempt had aroused. Only Piero's children kept up their efforts on behalf of their father. Ginevra, in a clear, neat handwriting recalling that of Amerigo, addressed a letter to the Magnificent. It has been held up as a model of the filial sentiments of a Florentine woman:

Best beloved, who holds the place of a good father: The motive of these sorrowful lines is not having been able to speak with you yesterday, as I had wished, to beseech you and remind you of the love and benevolence you have shown my house, the words and promises you have given me, and the charity you used with me when you called me sister... I implore you to think of the state in which my father finds himself... He has done penance enough for his sin... When I

*think of his years and his health, of the irons he wears
on his feet… my heart sinks…* [5]

For his part, Piero wrote from prison to Lucrezia
Tornabuoni, Lorenzo's mother:

*My dearly beloved Mona Lucrezia: If I have not
written you sooner, attribute it to the fact that I have
been so harried, attacked, and cast down by fortune,
and my ailments, dejection, and vicissitudes have
been such that for a long time now I have asked myself if I am really Piero Vespucci. Now I have had
good news from Lorenzo, saying that things are happening as he wished, and this encourages and in-
duces me to write to you. If I were to write you
everything it would be to my interest to tell you, I am
sure I would not only arouse your compassion, for
you have always been a woman whom I looked upon
as taking not only the place of my own mother, but
that of all those who had previously felt the slightest
affection for me.* [6]

Piero assures Mona Lucrezia that he is so completely
innocent that he would never have dared to write to
her if he had had the least evil intention in assisting
Napoleone to escape. If the charges against him were
true, it would be right that he should be in prison.
But he takes his oath, and calls upon God to punish
him in body and soul if he lies. Then he comes to the
subject of Giuliano and Simonetta, and writes:

5. This letter, signed "Ginevra Sventurata," was published by Lungo:
   La Donna Fiorentina del Buon Tempo Antico, p. 222.
6. A.S.F., M.A.P., LXXXVIII, c. 247.

When the blessed soul that was your Giuliano used to visit my house, he said to me many times in the presence of Niccolò Martelli that he was the unhappiest young man not only in Florence, but in all Italy. I had such pity for him, he aroused such sorrow, that to make him happy and give him pleasure both my son Marco and I did all we could to please him, as his kindness, correctness, and gentle breeding deserved. We gave him all of Simonetta's garments and her portrait. Marco and I did this with all affection. He aided us with money and in every way he could. How could I have plotted against him, taking part in the detestable conspiracy?...

Who has behaved more bravely and resolutely toward your house than I? Who has hunted down the traitors as I have done? How is it possible that I have been brought to this place–I, who revealed such important secrets to Lorenzo? I, who removed from the desk of the Lord of Piombino three letters from the King of Naples which made manifest the bitter hostility of that monarch toward Lorenzo? This was an affair involving great danger and expense. And I put them in the hands of your Niccolò, and Lorenzo did not even say: Well done! Through me Lorenzo received much secret information concerning the Duke (of Milan) and Roberto (di Sanseverino), but he attached no importance to it...

I decided to make my own way, and I went to Lorenzo and said to him: Brother, for certain reasons... I should like to be podesta of Milan. I did not get the post. Later I told him that I was thinking of going to Naples, and he said to me: Go, and follow

*the dictates of your heart; I am your friend. That is
what he said to me on the corner of the Giglio...*

Not long after writing this letter Piero was released
from prison. But that is another story.

The failure of the Pazzi conspiracy touched off a
conflagration in Rome. Count Riario, who saw his
plans wrecked, did everything in his power to move
war against Florence. The Pope at first had sent a
warm letter of condolence to Lorenzo, but later, at
the instigation of the Count, be made dire threats
against both Florence and Lorenzo. An Archbishop
had been hanged, and Cardinal Raffaello was still
being held a prisoner in Florence.

The Florentine Ambassador to Rome was Donato
Acciaiuoli, an eminent humanist, an old acquaintance of Giorgio Antonio Vespucci, a man more of
letters than of arms, like most of the Florentines.
Count Riario, at the head of the Papal Guard, entered the embassy, roughly seized Donato, and took
him to the Vatican with the intention of throwing
him into prison. As the Pope had said before, the
Count was a brute. An outrage of this sort was a
violation of all diplomatic conventions and proce-
dures. The Pope had to use all his authority to put
his nephew in his place and set Donato free. But
Donato saw that the threat of war against Florence
was imminent, and he dispatched couriers to advise
the immediate release of Cardinal Raffaello. The
Florentines realized that this was the proper course,
but acted with exasperating slowness. The Cardinal
was to spend many more days in prison, and when

he was finally released and reached Siena, he was the color of paper. It is said that, to the end of his life, he never lost this pallor, which fear had induced.[7]

The Pope fulminated the most hostile bull against Lorenzo. He called him corrupt, infamous, abominable, unfitted to hold any post, ecclesiastical or civil. The same document forbade anyone to associate with him or to have business dealings with him, and his houses were ordered razed or confiscated. The brief against Florence was no less minatory. Unless it yielded to the Pope's demands, if it did not set the Cardinal free and humbly ask forgiveness, he would put it under the ban. And it would be deprived of its episcopal dignity. In other words, this was war. Count Riario joined his forces—that is to say, the Papal troops—with the army of the King of Naples, under the Duke of Calabria as field commander. Lorenzo the Magnificent sought the help of the Duke of Milan and the King of France. Both the Church and Florence made a bid for the support of all the rulers of Italy, aligning them in a struggle in which the stakes were, on the one hand, the power of Florence and, on the other, the prestige of Rome.

Lorenzo recalled Donato Acciaiuoli from Rome to act as his ambassador to Milan and Paris. Guido Antonio Vespucci was sent to replace Donato in Rome. From then on, Guido Antonio was the leading diplomat in the negotiations between Florence and Rome, and his activities stand as one of the basic

7. L. Pastor: Storia dei Papi, Vol. II, p. 517

achievements in Florentine diplomacy. Guido Antonio's career was of paramount importance in the subsequent fortunes of the Vespucci family. He was about forty-two at the time, but his legal activities had been largely confined to Florence. His previous embassy had been to Imola at a decisive moment in the career of Count Riario. Florence had bought Imola without realizing or without wanting to realize that the Count regarded it as the key piece in his princely game. Under pressure from the Pope, Florence had had to renounce its purchase and allow the Count to take it over. But the Count was offended and rancorous. In his insatiable thirst for power be saw Florence as an obstacle in the way of his expansion. That had been his reason for participating in the Pazzi conspiracy.

Guido Antonio had so distinguished himself in Florence that he had been named Prior of the Signoria, and he had even sought to be made gonfalonier on the strength of his own merits and his friendship with Lorenzo the Magnificent. His fame as a jurist was such that he could make suggestions to Lorenzo as to professors for the University of Pisa. His economic position was good. With the other Vespucci, he had a share in the mill of Ognissanti. The house Stagio occupied was his, and two years before he had sold another to Lorenzo and Giuliano de' Medici, in which the sculptor Andrea del Verrocchio lived.

The relations between Guido Antonio and Stagio were especially close. They were third cousins, but treated each other like brothers. As for Amerigo,

Guido Antonio singled him out as though he were a favorite nephew. It may be that Guido Antonio took Amerigo to Rome with him to initiate him in the diplomatic career.

Guido Antonio's mission in Rome was of short duration. The troops of the King of Naples and the Church were already advancing on the Florentine border at Chianti, and the Pope was in no mood to make concessions. When the ambassadors of France, Venice, Ferrara, and Milan, and Guido Antonio for Florence, called upon him to attempt to work out a peaceful settlement, he answered them in even more aggressive terms than he had used when he had set about humbling Florence's pride.[8]

Florence's tactics aimed to win Venice to its side. At the same time that Guido Antonio was holding talks in Rome with the Ambassador of St. Mark's, Tomasso Soderini was on his way to talk to the Venetian Senate in the Magnificent's name. Guido Antonio's mission to Rome took the guise of a peace mission, but it was only a guise. The Pope was bent upon war. Guido Antonio returned to Florence.

There an unforeseen turn of events made necessary a change of plan. En route to France, Donato Acciaiuoli had died suddenly in Milan. A new ambassador had to be appointed immediately to replace him, and the Magnificent named Guido Antonio.

8. Part of the correspondence of the embassy in Rome has been reproduced in A. Desjardins: *Negotiations diplomatiques de la France avec la Toscane*. The rest remains unpublished in the State Archives of Florence.

In Rome the latter had become as conversant as Donato with the causes and the preparations for war; nobody knew better than he the ambitions, recklessness, and weaknesses of Count Riario. Lorenzo trusted him completely. It was not even necessary to draw up new instructions for Guido Antonio; a few slight changes in those Donato Acciaiuoli had been carrying sufficed.

Guido Antonio needed in his retinue a young man in whom he could place complete confidence, who knew how to keep a secret and write letters to the Magnificent and the Signoria. He chose Amerigo.[9]

9. In the tax register of 1480 there is this insertion: "Amerigo, son of Ser Nastagio, aged 29, is in France with Messer Guido Antonio Vespucci, ambassador."

Sandro Botticelli, Portrait of Cardinal Riario, detail from a fresco in the Sistine Chapel of the Vatican.

VI

AMERIGO IN PARIS
(1479-1480)

Perhaps Amerigo's biography should begin with
the time-honored formula of fairy tales: once upon
a time there was a boy–who had two uncles. The
next best thing for an Italian not fortunate enough
to be the first-born of the family was to have an
uncle. So important was the role of uncle in Italy
that a pope of the fifteenth or sixteenth centuries
might be defined as a great figure of the Church
surrounded by nephews. What Sixtus IV was in
reality was an uncle, and that was his undoing.
Possibly the psychological explanation is that in
their early years these uncles had suffered from
the preference and attentions shown eldest sons;
this left them with a gnawing resentment which, as
they grew older, shows itself in an exaggerated love
for those nephews who, like themselves, were second sons. At other times the uncle was a bachelor
who found an outlet for his paternal affection in
the nephew most in need of it. In the case of
Amerigo, his two uncles, Guido Antonio and Giorgio
Antonio, paid almost no attention to Antonio,
Stagio's eldest son: his father and mother would
look after him. But they showed a deep affection
for Amerigo.

Ghirlandaio, Portrait of Guido Antonio Vespucci from the fresco Cristo
chiama all'apostolato S. Pietro e S. Andrea, *in the Sistine Chapel*

In what capacity did Amerigo, at the age of twenty-four, become a member of Guido Antonio's staff on his mission to Paris? Nearly every embassy was made up essentially of an *oratore*, who was the ambassador; a canciller, who performed the duties of notary and secretary; and a *giovane*, who acted as attaché. There might also be minor personnel, if circumstances warranted. The main function of the servants was to look after the horses and mules, saddle them, be responsible for the luggage, and attend to their masters' needs at the inns. On embassies of brief duration, as when presenting greetings to a new ruler or dealing with some immediate problem, several ambassadors were dispatched. Missions of some permanence were entrusted to one or two. On Guido Antonio's mission of 1478, Amerigo went along as *giovane*, but be probably acted as his uncle's private secretary. As Gustavo Uzielli, an Italian scholar who has investigated such matters, says: "It will not surprise those familiar with the customs of the Florentine chancellery that the letters signed by Guido Antonio may have been written by his young attaché... Very probably Guido Antonio employed him as his private secretary for the more important reports he made to Florence at this time. It is more than possible that Amerigo did not merely copy such communications, but had a hand in drawing them up."[1]

---

1. G. Uzielli: *Nouveaux Manuscrits d'Americ Vespuce* (*Toscanelli*, Firenze, January 1893).

This was the first time Amerigo had been outside Italy, and it was to prove his first voyage of discovery. He would learn what the Old Continent was like. Circumstances were to enable him not only to see the surface appearance, but to know the inner workings of the first kingdom in Europe which took on the lineaments of a modern state.

The Ambassador and his suite set out for Paris via Bologna.[2] They had to cross the great ridge of the Apennines. In the valleys lay the peasants' cabins, the churches, monasteries, and hospitals, with the cities as their focal centers. As they climbed, they saw the turreted castles situated on strategic peaks, and the small villages surrounding the palace of the Podestà. They were stone citadels that flew the flag of some famous house, of a tyrant, a bold soldier, each with its history of murder and revenge to give it fame and standing, and above them the limpid Italian sky. Nobody knew the legends connected with each point of their itinerary better than Guido Antonio, and Amerigo had only to listen to him to have the vividly colored map of war and feuds unrolled before his mind's eye.

The tone of the lessons Amerigo heard differed greatly from those of his saintly uncle, Giorgio Antonio. Now it was the statesman teaching him that virtue in political life consisted in defending the liberty of Florence. Liberty was nothing more than

2. Guido Antonio's instructions are listed in A.S.F., Signori, Legazioni e Commissarie, Istruzioni, etc., Nos. 20, 4o, and 41.

the expression of power. What mattered was not
the liberty of the individual, but that of the Republic, which must maintain its supremacy even at the
cost of oppressing its citizens. It was on these terms
that Machiavelli would manage to reconcile freedom and tyranny. Guido Antonio combated the
Pope because the Pope was the enemy of Florence.
He wanted a just republic, but at the same time
order and authority. To clip the Pope's overbearing
pride, not only strength, but wiliness was needed.
Florence's secret weapon was intelligence. The
methods would be subtle, refined. The correspondence between Guido Antonio and Lorenzo and
the Signoria illustrates in detail his method of handling affairs of state. It also anticipates many of the
ideas later embodied in the doctrines of Machiavelli,
who a few years later followed in Guido Antonio's
footsteps, serving in diplomatic posts in which
Guido Antonio had preceded him. The political
difference between the two men was not in their
attitude toward foreign policy, but in Guido
Antonio's not believing in the personal dictatorship
of a prince.

The dialogues between Guido Antonio and his
giovane during the days of their journey and the
nights spent in the monasteries are gone with the
wind. There is no written record of these peripatetic lessons. But Amerigo learned the principles of
the government of princes, how to deal with them,
their weakness and their strength, how to make
profitable use of the advantages the crown can of-

fer, and how to sidestep the dangers. He was at the right age to be initiated into the study of political life. His uncle's words did not fall on deaf ears.

They reached Bologna. There Giovanni Bentivoglio incarnated the typical Italian dictator, the prince as conceived by Machiavelli. His power rested on popular prestige. The history of the Bentivoglio family stands out as one of the most dramatic of the epoch. Many times it was at the pinnacle of absolute power; at others it lay in the abyss of exile and persecution. The wiping-out of the Bentivoglios of Bologna thirty-three years before this visit of the Vespucci gives the measure of such family tragedies in the fourteenth century. In 1445 the Canetoli, powerful nobles, invited the Bentivoglios to a splendid feast. The final course at the festive board was daggers: not one Bentivoglio was left alive. To avenge them the Marescotti family, with the help of the populace, spent four days hunting down the Canetoli. They did not rest until all the Canetoli had been killed and their smoking hearts nailed to the doors of the Bentivoglio palaces. But the seed of the Bentivoglios had not been completely destroyed. With time they returned to power, and Giovanni, the ruler of Bologna at the time of the Vespuccis' visit, was the most powerful and best-loved of all the line. Machiavelli wrote that Giovanni was as popular in Bologna as Lorenzo the Magnificent in Florence, with a single difference, which in the opinion of the Florentine made the situation of Bentivoglio firmer: "In order to dominate Florence, Lorenzo de'Medici disarmed the people; to dominate Bologna, Giovanni Bentivoglio armed them." To Machiavelli, the health of the state was dependent on the power of its army.

By the terms of his instructions, Guido Antonio's mission in Bologna was to greet Bentivoglio in the name of the Republic, make sure of his friendship, and point out to him that if the Papal forces had made some advances around Chianti, this was an ephemeral, negligible victory. Lorenzo's far-flung plan of alliances made his final triumph certain. Bologna's position gave it no choice. It could not withdraw from the Florentine sphere of influence. The success of Vespucci's mission was assured beforehand. His stay at that court was very brief. In Bologna his party was joined by the Ambassador of the Duke of Ferrara to Milan, traveling on a mission identical with that of the Florentines. Now Amerigo entered the inner circle of higher diplomacy.

It was plain to Amerigo that there were other differences between Bologna and Florence than the prince's attitude toward the army. Bologna had the prestige and tradition of its university. Its young men did not need to leave the city for a higher education, as in Florence. They could be seen in the streets arguing with students who had come from other nations. Bologna's industry might not equal that of Florence, but its commercial activity was impressive. The city was laid out in a way new to Amerigo, with its galleried streets beneath whose arcades the merchants carried on their trade. Bologna was a communication center, the point of intersection of the roads through Pistoia and Florence to Rome; from Ferrara to Venice; from Piacenza to Milan, Basel, Strasbourg, Lyon, and Paris. Popes, emperors, and kings were no novelty to Bologna. The brick towers to be seen on every side told of centuries of greatness, and made a deep impression on the traveler. The Asinelli Tower, three hundred and twenty feet high, canted by the hand of time, had, like its even more tilted counterpart, the Garisenda Tower, a strange air of proud old age. Amerigo's world was growing. The now enlarged train set out for Piacenza over the mountain road.

Amerigo's position as *giovane* gave him an advantage. In his contacts with the secretaries and serving men of the Ambassador of Ferrara's party be was able to hear and see things that his Ambassador uncle might have missed. Long journeys on horseback establish a kind of democracy among travelers. In addition, as Guido Antonio's nephew and his closest subordinate, Amerigo also had direct dealings with the Ferraran Ambassador, who knew things about the war of which the Florentines themselves were not aware. The Duke of Ferrara was in command of the Florentine troops. His standing in Italy was second to none, not alone because of the merits of his family, the house of Este, but also because he was married to the incomparable Eleanora of Aragón, one of the Three Graces at the ball where the beautiful Simonetta had made her first appearance. The Duke of Ferrara was fighting against his father-in-law, the King of Naples, and his rival commander was his brother-in-law, the Duke of Calabria, Alfonso of Aragón, whom Count Riario and the King had put at the head of the armies hostile to Florence.

The party did not stop in Piacenza, but pushed on toward Milan. It was a long trip, but the imagination could feast on what it saw. They had entered the domain of the Sforza, at the time under the regency of Bona of Savoy. The greatness of the Sforza had not come about, like that of the Medici, through trade or learning. They had begun as *condottieri*. They were cruel, refined, unscrupulous, bloodthirsty, and polished. They machinated atrocious crimes, and were patrons of Leonardo da Vinci. It was for them that he painted *The Last Supper*. Like all the rest of Florence, Amerigo seven years before had seen Galeazzo Maria Sforza and Bona of Savoy when they visited Florence, displaying a splendor never before used even by kings in Italy. The number of servitors attending them was out of all proportion, as was their wealth of silks, jewels, and courtly appurtenances. Now Bona was a widow and encompassed by treachery. Some two years earlier, Galeazzo Maria had been cruelly stabbed to death in church. With this antecedent it would not be hard for Bona to grasp Lorenzo's moral right to resist the conspirators of Rome by force of arms.

Nor was this accidental circumstance the only reason. From the days of Cosimo de' Medici, the Sforza and the lords of Florence had been linked

in close friendship. The Milanese had not felt themselves on such an intimate footing with any other
ruler in Italy for the past forty years. Machiavelli
states that the visit of Galeazzo Maria and Bona to
Florence was fatal to the Republic because it led it
down the paths of luxury. But it must be borne in
mind that the Medici showed themselves so lavish
with the Sforzas on this occasion that the extrava-
gance of their gifts also has gone down in history.

Nearly all the ambassadors who favored
Lorenzo's cause had come to Milan. Amerigo's post
was that of an observer before whose eyes and
ears everything was happening. The inner workings of this assembly of diplomats, of this general
staff meeting on high strategy, unfolds through
the Ambassador's letters. The discussions of the
ambassadors covered two fronts: on the one hand,
the war in Italy, with which their mission was not
immediately concerned; on the other, how best to
approach the King of France and mobilize the opinion of Europe against the Church for its support of
Count Riario, which was their direct objective. The
inclination of the King of France could not have
been more favorable. Louis XI cordially detested
the Pope, and had for some time been threatening
to call a council censuring him. His letter of condolence to Lorenzo on the murder of Giuliano was
not that of a king, but of a brother. Moreover, Guido
Antonio, during his mission in Rome, had been a
witness to the defiant attitude of the French ambassadors toward the Pope. All the rulers of the

Western World had been receiving appeals from Louis to make common cause against Sixtus. The internal affairs of Milan presented a more delicate problem: there the regency of the Duchess Bona was under fire. But that was a matter of a different order. The ambassadors talked and exchanged ideas, and the missions proceeded on their way to France.

When they had left Italian soil, Guido Antonio's and Amerigo's route took them to cities where almost without exception there was a colony of Florentines and agents of the Medici. It was typical of Guido Antonio's missions that his correspondence with the Medici and that with the Signoria were equally voluminous. The Florentine colonies were always outposts that supplied the ambassadors with up-to-the-minute news. The Medici bank was particularly important in Lyon. Several of the Vespucci had worked there. A curious piece of information had been the letter from Giovanni Vespucci to Lorenzo the Magnificent on the occasion of the visit to Lyon of Galeazzo Maria Sforza and Bona of Savoy shortly before their visit to Florence, the Magnificent's first direct report about the couple.

Fortune smiled on Guido Antonio in Paris. The representative of the French King throughout this war was Philippe de Comines, Sieur d'Argenton, a great writer of his day and one of France's most famous historians. He was head and shoulders above the normal level of the courtiers. As a matter of fact, in those days there was no such thing as a career diplomat. The duty of representing their gov-

ernment was assigned to men who had distinguished themselves at the bar, in intellectual pur-
suits, or in business. Not one eminent man of that
period in Florence but had on some occasion undertaken an embassy. Comines's gifts as a historian
are evinced by his ability to penetrate the character
of his personages. His description of Louis XI is
one of the masterpieces of French literature. As for
the war of Florence, his support of the Florentine
cause was unqualified. He went even farther than
the King. His *Memoirs* bear testimony to his political predilection. He and Guido Antonio became
friends at once. Amerigo could have had no better
introduction to the best of France.

For the Florentines the war embraced many fronts.
Like all human affairs, it was a circumstance af-
fording many opportunities. One of its fronts was
the economic. In modern times, under middle-class
domination, this has become increasingly manifest;
it was already evident to the Florentines of the fifteenth century. On this very occasion banking interests were involved on the Pope's side. It must
not be forgotten that at that meeting in the Vatican
to plot the change of government in Florence the
four principals were the Pope, the Archbishop, the
Count, and the banker. Or that the Medici, before
becoming rulers of Florence and princes of the
Renaissance, had been, as they continued to be,
bankers and merchants. The conspiracy against
them has not gone down in history with the name
of the Archbishop, or the Count, or the Pope, but

with that of the Pazzi, the bankers. When Sixtus broke off relations with Florence, the first thing he did was to confiscate the property of the Medici in the Eternal City and hand it over to Genoese bankers, Domenico Centurione and Giovanni Doria. The first thing Lorenzo instructed Guido Antonio to request of the King of France was that he confiscate the holdings of the Pazzi and close down their banks.[3]

Guido Antonio had another commercial matter to attend to: indemnity for the attacks on Florentine shipping by the corsair Colombo. This affair, which other ambassadors had tried to settle, was still pending, though the King recognized the justice of the claim. Florence had always been proud of being regarded as a distant daughter of France; its coat of arms displayed the royal fleur-de-lis. And now a foreigner, flouting every consideration, had broken these traditional ties. Under protection of the French flag Colombo had plundered the Medici ships. Lorenzo was particularly incensed over the booty he had seized, which. included not only valuable merchandise, but works of art, masterpieces of Flemish painting which the Medici agents had bought for him at a high price. Guido Antonio had known

3. Contained in the instructions for Guido Antonio: "In keeping with the instructions you carry from the *Officiali de' Ribelli* having to do with the property of the Pazzi company in France, because of the events of April 26 and the treason of the aforesaid Pazzi, this should be confiscated by His Majesty the King," etc.

for some time about the exploits of this Colombo,
whose possible relationship to Christopher Columbus has been a matter for speculation on the part
of the Admiral's biographers. The first news of him
had arrived when Guido Antonio was Prior of the
Signoria. But this was Amerigo's first opportunity
to have any direct connection with the affairs of
the Colombos.[4]

In his letters to Lorenzo and the Signoria the Ambassador reported in detail on all these matters,
informing them of the general course of political
events, of his audiences with the King and his ministers, of what was said and left unsaid among the
ambassadors, of what could be ferreted out through
some third party, of the movements of the Pope's
legates, who were kept under careful observation.
His mission was not confined to France. It embraced
a much vaster area through the medium of correspondence, messengers, and special envoys. His
embassy was Florence's observation post for northern and central Europe.[5]

The court of Louis XI, like the courts of the other
monarchs of Europe, was ambulatory. It almost never

4. In Guido Antonio's instructions: "In France, Bernardo de Bardi
   will inform you of the complaints of our merchants who should
   be reimbursed for the losses they have suffered for over a year at
   the hands of Colombo, in connection with which some time ago
   we sent Donato Acciaiuoli who reached certain agreements with
   His Majesty the King."
5. Part of this correspondence has been published by Desjardins,
   op. cit. Other letters are contained in the State Archives of Florence.

remained in Paris. Guido Antonio had to spend a part of his time in Paris, and when be could not be there himself, he sent members of his suite there to perform minor duties. They carried on the petty espionage that was such an essential part of the program of an important mission; they took notice of changes of feeling, reactions of the ministers, movements of the other ambassadors. Amerigo, whose mission lasted almost two years, must often have had to carry out assignments of this sort, deliver oral messages for Guido Antonio, transmit to him the gossip of the court. Or go to Paris or elsewhere when the Ambassador was at court and some matter of importance required attention. But for the most part Guido Antonio and Amerigo were together, writing letters, receiving them, utilizing that network of invaluable agents which the employees of the Medici bank comprised.

If, for example, it was necessary to bring something to the attention of Edward IV of England, there in London as agent of the Medici was Gherardo Canigiani, who was held in high esteem at the court. If it was a question of establishing contacts with Duke Maximilian of Austria, wherever the Duke might be, there was sure to be a Medici agent to whom Guido Antonio could write.

In his reports to Florence, Vespucci could write: "This morning I was with the Ambassador of this Most Christian King who had been in Hungary, Poland, and Bohemia..." Then he went on to tell all that he had been able to elicit during the conversation. The mission of the Ambassador had been to persuade the kings and nobles of those countries to take part in the council with which Louis XI had been threatening the Pope. Guido Antonio had now learned what each of them was prepared to do, the objections they had raised, what support Louis could count on, and what were the weak spots in his campaign. And Amerigo came to know how this inner history operated.

Guido Antonio told of the impression made on the King or Comines when he could tell them of some triumph of Florentine arms. Comines received the news with outbursts of jubilation, as though it were a French victory. The King, no less out-spoken, took advantage of such occasions to insult both the Pope and his ally, the King of Naples. But the sad truth was that the King was less effective in deed than in word. Comines himself remarked this sadly in his *Memoirs*. But the criticism must be qualified. In the wars of the fifteenth century—as in those of other epochs—words can be as valuable as bullets and swords. It was no small triumph for Florence to have the voice of a king on her side, and that this king was the King of France.

There has been much speculation about the acquaintances Amerigo may have made in Paris. Such clues as exist are to be found only in Guido Antonio's correspondence, which gives a picture of official life, especially as it bears upon the problem of war and the affairs of the Medici. But Amerigo was twenty-six, a well-favored young man and the nephew of an ambassador. He had the attraction, the honey, and the drop of poison implied in his name; he was one of the Vespucci wasps. Guido Antonio's home was open to men of letters and learning, to diplomats. May not Amerigo on some occasion, or many, have met the Archbishop of Vienna, Angelo Catto, an Italian astrologer who was living in Paris at the time and was a great friend of Philippe de Comines? It seems only natural to assume that the Italians visiting Paris would have gone to see the representative of Lorenzo de' Medici, especially at a time when Florence was gambling its future on a war with the Holy See. The only thing that can be categorically said is that uncle and nephew moved in a select circle. Before entering the world of politics, Guido Antonio had been a man of study, a friend of the arts, a patron of painters. As for Amerigo, he was born with a trait he preserved to the end of his days: a gift for friendship. He was discreet, never brusque. Giorgio Antonio had shaped him for the Academy, with perhaps a certain bent for the religious life; Guido Antonio for the court, and, to a degree, for the worldly life; Stagio, to be a worthy citizen of Florence and to enjoy wit and poetry. Each of these teachers was a master in his field. With this patrimony Amerigo knew his way about the world. He became acquainted with the streets of Paris, or wherever the court happened to be, with its courtiers trained in the art of good living.

The political panorama of France was another story. Florence's affairs were only one among its problems. Louis was at open war with Charles the Bald, who headed the discontented nobles. Louis was, first and foremost, a bourgeois king. He had strong ties with the upper middle class and the city aristocracy, and he was heavy-handed in his treatment of the nobles and the artisans, to secure from them the funds he needed for his wars and his diplomatic intrigues.

Under his firm hand France was emerging as a powerful state. He was engaged in bringing Normandy to heel, and at the same time was working to establish a border with Spain along the line of the Pyrenees, which would bring Navarre into his realms. He had ambitions to organize a great trading company to monopolize the commerce of the Mediterranean. The episode of Colombo, who, in fact, was sailing with corsairs' letters authorizing him to attack foreign shipping, is proof of the King's endeavor to weaken the Italian maritime power in favor of France. Louis called an assembly in which all the loyal cities of his kingdom were represented–two delegates of the bourgeoisie were sent by each city–to consider ways and means of replacing all foreign currency with the national money. He quarreled with the Parlement of Paris because it resisted his absolute power.

To Amerigo all this was a new world. He knew that in Italy neither Florence nor Venice, nor even the kingdom of Naples, could make plans that went beyond the narrow limits of its own frontiers. Alliances were made and unmade with every changing circumstance, and the intelligence of princes and the practical sense of the *condottieri* were employed in miniature baronial conflicts. Amerigo was in France during Louis's last brilliant years. After them the King withdrew from the world and became almost inaccessible. But his intervention in the affairs of Italy, his support of Lodovico il Moro in making himself master of Milan, give the measure of his ambition and power, which made the scope of his influence so broad. This was the only way to enter upon the modern age and leave behind that archipelago of enchanted islands which was the Middle Ages.

Florence's war was not made or directed from Paris. Not even the great diplomatic battle took place at the court of the French King or at that of the Pope of Rome. It was Lorenzo's finest moment when, in an audacious move, the most daring he ever made, he decided to go alone, without warning, to the court of the King of Naples, and there, with the King, arrive at the decision that was not possible on the battlefield. Nobody got wind of his plans, not even the Pope. When the news leaked out, Lorenzo and the King were already sitting at table like two good comrades. It would be hard to say who enjoyed the trick more, the Neapolitan or the Florentine. That was the end of the war. The Pope never got over his surprise, nor Count Riario his chagrin. Peace was breaking out. The King of France looked upon it as a triumph for himself, and Comines congratulated himself on the outcome.

The French must have enjoyed a hearty laugh. All that was needed now was some way to bridge the gap between Lorenzo and the Pope and effect a reconciliation. For this Guido Antonio was needed, first at Florence and then in Rome. The mission to France was over.

VII

RETURN TO FLORENCE
(1481-1483)

Paris, Lyon, Milan, Bologna, Florence–the road taken two years before, but now in reverse. The same inns, the same hoary monasteries, talks with the Medici agents, state visits. All was the same, and yet all was different. It is one thing to set out at the beginning of a dubious war, another to return with assurance of a happy ending or, at any rate, as in this case, the beginning of a happy ending. At times, on the long days' travels through the beautiful valleys and mountains of France, the very walled cities, the monasteries and castles, seemed to have another air. The French words, which at first had been incomprehensible, now told Amerigo many things. Even the road seemed different because of its human associations. Paris had shown both Ambassador and his *giovane* what a modern state in process of evolution was like. Guido Antonio had found ample food for his political philosophy. He had come to feel more strongly than ever that two things were necessary to ensure good government in Florence: the maintenance of the legal order and the utilization of the abilities of its most capable citizens. It fell to Guido Antonio later on to oppose Savonarola's party. Savonarola had advocated the participation

Sandro Botticelli, Portrait of the Count Girolamo Riario from the fresco The Redeemer tempted by Satan, *in the Sistine Chapel of the Vatican.*

of the reckless, irresponsible masses in the government, and Guido Antonio displayed exceptional courage in standing firm against the demagoguery of the Friar, whose eloquence aroused the passions of the populace. His diplomatic experiences stood Vespucci in good stead.

The travelers found Florence, too, changed on their return. The grief and apprehension engendered by the assassination of Giuliano and Rome's threat had been replaced by the assurance Lorenzo's master stroke gave the city. Friends stopped Guido Antonio in the streets, carried him off to their gatherings in the loggias. In his flowing cloak of geranium red he looked like a senator of Imperial Rome. He was tall, well built, elegant. Although he did not lack sensibility, his head ruled his heart. Lorenzo the Magnificent could rest assured that the affair of Rome was in good hands. In all his dealings Guido Antonio acted with unclouded logic and a clear grasp of reality.

Was Amerigo to accompany his uncle to Rome? No, Amerigo would remain in Florence. The Ambassador took occasion, however, to commend him to Lorenzo. Amerigo was not a jurist who could head a mission, nor a notary to act as *canciller*. The court did not attract him, nor politics tempt him. Although he had no clerical inclinations, Giorgio Antonio's philosophy had taken hold of him. And the adventurous spirit of Piero, the Vespucci of the sea. Letters, science, mathematics, geography, sea voyages–these were the stuff of his ambitions. But the most cogent reason of all was that Amerigo was needed at home.

Stagio had aged very quickly; his days were numbered, and Amerigo had to become the man of the
family.

One unexpected event in the family must have
pleased Guido Antonio and Amerigo. The King of
Naples, in his talks with Lorenzo the Magnificent,
had asked him to set Piero Vespucci free.[1] Ferrante
of Aragón had a great fondness for Piero, who had
captained his galley to Constantinople and delivered
a letter from the King to the Sultan. Affection for the
Vespucci was traditional with the house of Naples.
The Magnificent granted the King's request. The release of Piero Vespucci involved no sacrifice on his
part. He opened the door of the cage, and the bird
flew off to Milan. And as Piero was no fool, in a
short time he had ingratiated himself with the house
of Sforza and was beginning a new life. It was probably never clear to the rest of the Vespucci just what
Piero's part in the conspiracy had been. But it was a
great relief that a Vespucci was no longer in prison.

In Amerigo's immediate family things were going well and badly. Stagio was ailing, but Giorgio
Antonio was more active and busy than ever. The
Church of Ognissanti had commissioned Sandro
Botticelli and Domenico Ghirlandaio to compete
in two paintings. It was a rare artistic duel. Ghirlandaio was to do a *St. Jerome*, Botticelli a *St. Augustine*. The subjects and the lines the painters should
follow were left to the suggestion of Giorgio Anto-

---

1. Uzielli, in notes to the *Life of Amerigo* by Bandini, op. cit., p. 75.

nio, who had been tonsured and was in line for a bishopric.

Botticelli's *St. Augustine* has been called the masterpiece of the virile cycle of his painting. It was the occasion on which the artist surpassed himself. Yashiro, the great Japanese critic of Botticelli, says: "The painter seems a different man, strong and commanding, as he had never been before, and was not to be again."[2] On the saint's right hand lies an open book with geometrical figures, and as chapter heading these words:

> *Where St. Martin fell into despair*
> *And went out of the Prato Cate.*[3]

The reference, according to Brockbaus, is probably to the Blessed Martin of the Camaldolite Order, who died in 1250, and had lived in the Convent of Camaldoli in Florence, near the San Fredlano Gate. The words may have had a personal reference. The Prato Gate led to the road to Peretola, the seat of the Vespucci. "Perhaps the one who arranged for the painting," Brockhaus observes, "like the saint, in this same place, settled his doubts concerning the limits of human knowledge, and took the decision to become a priest."[4]

2. Y. Yashiro: *Sandro Botticelli and the Florentine Renaissance,* p. 26.
3. *Dove San Martino è disperato e dove andato fuor della Porta al Prato.*
4. Brockhaus, op. cit., p. 98.

Giorgio Antonio's influence on Botticelli in the conception of the painting is manifest. Fifteen years later Botticelli painted another *St. Augustine*, which is in the Uffizi Gallery of Florence. The one in Ognissanti could be subtitled *St. Augustine in Toscanelli's Study*. Opposite the book with the geometrical figures is an astrolabe; beside the scholar's lamp, the armillary sphere representing the course of the planets. The head of the saint is that of a man in the throes of a struggle between light and darkness to lay hold upon the truth. Forehead, eyes, the expression of lips and hands, are equally eloquent. The St. Augustine of the Uffizi painting is a calm, simple priest in a cell without books or instruments; he is a passive copyist, not a searcher for the truth in the grip of intellectual anxiety. On the cornice of the cell of the *St. Augustine* of Ognissanti is a coat of arms, displaying a field of gules with an azure band, and on the bend a golden wasp—the arms of the Vespucci.

Ghirlandaio's painting resembles Botticelli's *St. Augustine* only in setting. St. Jerome is usually depicted as a hermit doing penance, or in the company of a lion that follows him like a dog, with the simplicity of form in which Carpaccio conceived him. Ghirlandaio has painted him as the scholar working in his study on the translation of the Vulgate. In the background are an hourglass, a rosary, a Greek inscription; on the table, a candle, sand, ink, scissors, prayerbook, and the saint's spectacles. With his noble head resting on his hand, St. Jerome is the thinker. Ghirlandaio had already painted the frescoes of their chapel for the Vespucci and *The Last Supper* for the convent refectory. In this *St. Jerome* he outdid himself in portraiture.

With Guido Antonio's appointment to the court of Pope Sixtus an exchange of courtesies between Florence and Rome began. The Pope spared no effort to efface the memory of past unpleasantnesses, and Count Riario imitated his example. At this time the plan was announced of decorating the Vatican chapel that was to become the finest legacy of Sixtus's occupancy of the chair of St. Peter: the Sistine Chapel. This was the pontiff's opportunity to show his regard for the Florentines. Guido Antonio offered to bring painters from his city to do the first frescoes. That was how Ghirlandaio and Botticelli went to Rome. Their work in the Vespucci chapel had been their preparation for the visit to the Vatican.

Ghirlandaio painted in the Sistine the scene of Jesus calling St. Peter and St. Andrew to the apostolate. The painting is half Biblical, half Florentine history. The Florentine half is completely profane. Behind the figure of Jesus appears that of Judas, at whose soul the worm of treachery is already gnawing: it is the portrait of Diotisalvi Neroni, who had plotted with Luca de' Pitti against the Magnificent's father, Piero de' Medici. In the foreground stands a group of Florentine citizens, among them the Greek philosopher Giovanni Argyropolus, whose coming to the court of the Medici was a milestone in the organization of the Academy. One of the Florentines was Giovanni de' Tornabuoni, the brother of the Magnificent's mother, the banker who looked after Lorenzo's interests in Rome. "If Sixtus IV had the tiara," says Piero Bargellini, "Giovanni de' Tornabuoni had the cash box."[5] There were many other figures, but the one who, in a corner of the painting, overshadows them all is Guido Antonio Vespucci.

Botticelli painted the miracle of the leper who had been healed as he went to hand the priest the offering Jesus had ordered him to bring. In this, too, half the scene is sacred, half profane. The watching crowd is made up of Romans and Florentines. In the corner in which Guido Antonio appears in Ghirlandaio's fresco, Botticelli has painted Count Riario. Ghirlandalo's Guido Antonio is a figure of proud dignity. The Count Riario of Botticelli is an arrogant, vain master of ceremonies who, with the baton of marshal of the Papal armies in his hand, seems about to give the signal for the performance to begin. Among the other figures Botticelli painted there is a harmless, absent-minded-looking man in clerical garb, his hands folded across his stomach after the manner of a fat, simple friar. This is Cardinal Raffaello Riario, the nephew of the Count who had officiated in the Duomo the day of the Pazzi conspiracy. Directly behind him stands a strong-featured jurist with whom we are acquainted, Guido Antonio Vespucci.

Before leaving for Rome, Botticelli had painted two more pictures for the Vespucci, in addition to his *St. Augustine.* One was a *St. George* for Ognissanti,

5. Piero Bargellini: *Il Ghirlandaio*, p. 98.

also undoubtedly commissioned by Giorgio Antonio in honor of his patron saint; and the figure of a
young man which R. Langton-Douglas has identi-
fied as the portrait of Amerigo.[6] Between the Amerigo
painted by Ghirlandaio seven years before and this
by Botticelli, the only difference is an accentuation
of the virile traits that both paintings have in common. Botticelli stresses the energetic air of the young
man who has now emerged from Giorgio Antonio's
tutelage, whereas in the Ghirlandaio fresco Amerigo
had been but the reflection of the master. Now the
clear, frank eyes look steadily ahead with the gaze
of a man who has experienced life, revealing the
calm assurance of one who can face difficulties and
not be dismayed, who feels himself the master of
his fate. He has the power of attraction. Over his
forehead and about his face fall the ringlets of his
youthful days. And he wears his princely cap with
an air that was surely not lost on the maidens of
Florence.

At the dictation of Giorgio Antonio, Amerigo had
written in his composition book:

*Arise with the morning hours and yield not to sleep,
O youth, who have passed your time in amusements,
dancing, and making music. Sit not with idle hands.
Work before age overtakes you, and your strength is
gone, and you become unhappy and discontented.*

6. R. Langton-Douglas: "The Contemporary Portraits of Amerigo
   Vespucci," *Burlington Magazine* (London), January-December
   1944.

Because if you strive to live virtuously before death comes to call you or old age is upon you, I assure you that you will die happy, and afterwards you will certainly enjoy the glory of the saints where none sickens, or grows old, or dies.

Amerigo had the example of the close of life before him in his own father. He was only fifty-six years old, and yet everyone spoke of him as "Old Stagio."

On April 24, 1482, two Franciscan friars arrived at Stagio's home. They had been called in to act as witnesses to a solemn document. Stagio was unable to work any longer. He might never leave his bed. Someone would have to assume his daily obligations; he would have to appoint someone to collect the fees due him. He named Amerigo.[7] This was the document the two friars had been summoned to witness. Stagio had not chosen Antonio, even though he was far more experienced in notarial matters than Amerigo. Antonio had a heavy burden of his own. He had been appointed trustee of the confiscated property of the Pazzi family, and was in line for an appointment as notary of the Signoria. As for the other two brothers, Girolamo and Bernardo, they were, as we have seen, difficult, unreliable, and unsettled.

Four days after giving Amerigo power of attorney, Stagio died in the house of Guido Antonio. Amerigo and Antonio took charge of settling the estate. The

7. Alceste Giorgetti published the power of attorney granted by Stagio Vespucci in *Nouveaux Documents sur Améric Vespuce et sa famille* (Toscanelli, January 1893).

house in Peretola, occupied by poor relatives, and some lands in Brozzi were sold. That was all Stagio left. The family broke up. Amerigo for the time being entered the service of Lorenzo the Magnificent, to whom Guido Antonio wrote a letter from Rome thanking him for this help. Guido Antonio was as concerned over the future of Giorgio Antonio as over Amerigo's. He was in a position to use his influence with Lorenzo, for whom he was carrying out an extremely delicate mission with great success. He was not only looking after Lorenzo's political affairs, and working closely with Tornabuoni, the banker, for his commercial interests, but at the same time was securing for Giovanni, Lorenzo's son, a series of benefices that were the first rungs in the ladder by which he rose to the throne of St. Peter as Leo X. At the age of seven and one half, Giovanni was tonsured; at thirteen he was made a Cardinal. Without Guido Antonio's efforts on his behalf, none of these incredibly early distinctions would have been possible. For these good offices Guido Antonio asked almost no return. His life was now devoted to the Magnificent and the Republic. His own affairs in Florence were completely neglected. Time and again he had to ask for brief leave to look after them. But at least he secured a post in the Signoria for his brother Simone, the advancement of Giorgio Antonio in his ecclesiastical career (obtaining for him a canonship, in the Duomo), and a helping hand for Amerigo.

It would seem that the pupil-teacher relationship between Amerigo and Giorgio Antonio had been left far behind. Now the uncle treated him as an equal and introduced him to his own group. Giorgio Antonio's group was that of the Academy of Ficino, of which Della Torre, the historian of the Platonic Academy, said: "we could repeat what has already been said of the Platonic Academy, that if Tuscany was the garden of Italy, and Florence the heart of Tuscany, the Academy was the flower of Florence."[8] Giorgio Antonio's fame had become universal. Marsilio Ficino, his close friend, had just dedicated an essay on medicine to him. A year before, Ficino had written his study on plagues, in which he gave general advice about how to avoid them. In this essay, dedicated to Giorgio Antonio and Giovan' Battista Boninsegni, he dealt principally with the problems of persons of advanced years, as a matter of particular interest to centers of study.

Undoubtedly acting on suggestions from Amerigo, Guido Antonio wrote to Lorenzo the Magnificent from Rome:

You know how eager I am to have your Giorgio Antonio receive an appointment. Think whether you feel that he should be given the see of Fiesole. I think what would be needed is a nice letter to the Count Riario. Nobody here is interested in the post except Battista Panchatichi, to whom there has been some talk of offering it, but he is away. You would give all our house, and myself, great happiness...[9]

---

8. A. della Torre, op. cit.
9. A.S.F., M.A.P., F. XXXVIII, c. 172.

But the advancement of Giorgio Antonio in his career was not owing to these recommendations alone. The man held such an important place in the intellectual life of Florence that his fame was spreading to other parts of Europe. One very logical circumstance brought Giorgio Antonio into contact with the German humanists, a circumstance that was influential in making the achievements of Amerigo known later on. This had to do with the visit of Count Eberhard of Württemberg and Johann Reuchlin to Florence in 1482.

Johann Reuchlin was, with Erasmus, one of the fathers of humanism in northern Europe, and an authority without equal in Hebrew. Aside from the fame that came to him from his Hebrew grammar and dictionary–*De rudimentis hebraicis*–he became widely known as a result of a great controversy in Germany over the suppression of writings in Hebrew, a measure put forward by certain elements to combat the Jews. Reuchlin had proposed to the Emperor that he issue an order creating two chairs of Hebrew in each German university for a period of ten years, with the Jews supplying the necessary books. To the virulent criticism aroused by this suggestion, Reuchlin replied with his *Augenspiegel*, which was banned by Imperial edict as the result of pressure brought by the Inquisition through the University of Cologne. Reuchlin replied with his *Defensio contra calumniatores.* Whereupon Paris, along with a number of other universities, ranged itself against Reuchlin, and he was ordered to stand trial. Reuchlin managed to have the hearing transferred to Rome, and Rome decided in his favor. The incident reveals the temper of the man.

From the time of his first trip to Italy with Count Eberhard, Reuchlin had been in close contact with the humanists of Florence. In his *De rudimentis hebraicis* he makes special mention of Giorgio Antonio Vespucci, Agnolo Poliziano, Marsilio Ficino, and Demetrio Cholcondylen.[10] He was strongly drawn to Giorgio Antonio. Their common interest in Greek and Hebrew was a bond. It must be borne in mind that Giorgio Antonio had instructed Ghirlandaio to paint his St. Jerome translating the Vulgate. In Reuchlin's opinion the Vulgate was a first draft that needed to be perfected. When he returned to Germany, he decided to send his brother Dionisio, in company with Johann Stràhler of Ulm, to Florence to study Greek, and he put them under the tutelage of Giorgio Antonio, who lodged them in his home. They brought letters from the Count of Württemberg.

Reuchlin's second trip to Florence was made in 1490. He made the journey to get a Bible in Hebrew, which be had not been able to find in his own country. As late as 1498 he returned to Rome, on a mission for Philip, Elector Palatine of the Rhine. Reuchlin delivered Philip's speech of obedience to Rodrigo Borgia, Pope Alexander VI, of whom the humanists had great hopes.

10. Bandini, op. cit., p. 12.

Over the years of their friendship, Giorgio Antonio's interests were not a matter of indifference to Reuchlin, whose prestige in Germany was second only to that of Erasmus. Although he was not directly interested in geographical problems, all areas of the questing Renaissance curiosity engaged his attention, and an interest in discoveries and navigation was one of the aspects this curiosity took. One of Reuchlin's most intimate friends and correspondents in Rome was Lorenzo Behaim, who was at the Vatican court for twenty-two years, receiving special marks of distinction from Sixtus IV. Behaim, who was from Nuremberg, devoted himself to collecting the inscriptions on ancient monuments, and became a tutor in the house of Rodrigo Borgia, who conferred upon him the title of Doctor of Canon Law. Lorenzo Behaim was probably the brother of Martín Behaim, also from Nuremberg, who lived at about the same time. Martín was a famous navigator who entered the service of the King of Portugal. It was he who made the Nuremberg sphere of 1492 on which, before Columbus had crossed the Atlantic, the terrestrial globe was already depicted in accordance with the theories of Toscanelli, demonstrating that sailing westward from Spain one could reach the coasts of China and Japan.

There is no doubt that, as a close associate of Giorgio Antonio Vespucci, Reuchlin must have known Amerigo, and other persons such as Zenobi Acciaiuoli, who was the center of a group in Florence which venerated the memory of Toscanelli. When, some years later, Amerigo began to inform his Florentine friends of his voyages and send them his maps, a request for this information was received from Germany, and in this way it circulated about Reuchlin's world, which was all of Württemberg and a part of Lorraine. The name "America" came into being in Lorraine, and Waldseemüller's map, which confirms this christening, was discovered in the library of Wolfegg Castle in Württemberg.

The year after Stagio's death, an unforeseen circumstance took a hand in Amerigo's destiny. Lorenzo, the son of Pier Francesco de' Medici, married Semiramide d'Appiano.[11] If the assassination of Giuliano had not brought to a tragic end his intended marriage to Semiramide, the Appiani would have been connected with the Medici of the oligarchy. As it was, their connection was with the Medici "popolani." The difference between the two branches of the family is an important one, and it is important to know how Amerigo came to serve the rival house. To be sure, the Appiani continued to look upon the Vespucci as members of the family, for the beautiful Simonetta still cast her benign shadow upon them all.

The Medici of the oligarchy and the "popolani" were descended from Cosimo de' Medici, their common grandfather. The head of those denominated the oligarchy, especially by Savonarola, was Lorenzo the Magnificent. The others were the sons of Pier Francesco, who have gone down in history with the

11. C. Pieraccini: *La Stirpe de' Medici di Cafaggiolo*, Vol. I, pp. 383 ff.;
    L. Cappelletti: *Storia della città e Stato di Piombino*, p. 113.

name of *"popolani."* When Lorenzo the Magnificent and Lorenzo the Popolano were young they were good friends. Money came between them.

The Magnificent was as bad a businessman as he was an outstanding statesman and poet, not because he neglected his affairs or mismanaged them, but because of his lavish spending. His position as one of the grandees of Italy, his patronage of artists and writers, his munificence with the guests of Florence, required a bottomless purse. Instead of increasing the family fortune, as his forefathers had done, he let it dwindle in his hands, whereas his cousins, the children of Pier Francesco, grew richer and richer. One day the Magnificent had to turn to them for a loan of sixty thousand ducats. He made over to them the house of Cafaggiolo and the lands of Mugello. This was a bitter pill for the Magnificent to swallow, and he soon began to give vent to his growing resentment in rancorous words.

From this to an open break was only a step, and the public life of Florence began to oscillate between the oligarchic Medici and the Medici of the people, on whom the name *"popolano"* had been conferred because they echoed the complaints of the discontented lower classes, who were determined to overthrow the oligarchs. In these struggles the Vespucci behaved like all the other families of Florence–the Soderini, the Acciaiuoli, or the Rucellai–some with the oligarchs, some with the *popolani*–that is to say, with a foot in each camp. Guido Antonio was in the service of the Magnificent; Giorgio Antonio was connected with the Popolano. Amerigo began his career as a member of the Magnificent's embassy to France, and he was now in the service of a member of the *popolano* group. Immediately after the marriage of Lorenzo di Pier Francesco and Semiramide, Amerigo became a member of their household.

VIII

IN THE SERVICE OF THE POPOLANO, SEVILLE
(1484-1489)

Lorenzo di Pier Francesco de' Medici spent more time in Cafaggiolo than in Florence. Semiramide, more fertile than Simonetta, who left no descendants, presented him with a child each year. The country air proved more healthful for all of them than the stuffy streets of the city. A few years after the marriage of Lorenzo di Pier Francesco and Semiramide, Amerigo took charge of their house in Florence, installing himself there. He was in charge of everything—dinner services, silver, the chests of damask, hangings, tapestries. Semiramide turned to him whenever she was planning to entertain in Cafaggiolo, or when some friend or relative wanted to borrow those articles of luxury, which made the rounds on the occasion of a marriage or festival. Amerigo looked after their business affairs, besides. He acted as agent in the sale of the crops from the Popolano's lands, and in his banking transactions. One quality that Amerigo possessed to the end of his life is essential to an understanding of his achievements: people trusted him, never hesitating to hand over to him the keys of their houses.[1]

When the threshing in Mugello was finished, Lorenzo had the wheat sent to Amerigo, who sold it on the best terms he could get, either in lots of twenty

Piero de Cosimo or Pollaiuolo, Portrait of Simonetta Vespucci, The Chantilly Simonetta, *Portrait in the Musée Condé, Chantilly.*

or thirty sacks, which the Popolano thought was the better system, or as a whole harvest. The wine of Cafaggiolo went either to Frescobaldi in Florence or to the dealers of San Friano, but it was Amerigo who kept the accounts. When Frescobaldi inquired about the price in Cafaggiolo, he was told to communicate with Amerigo: "I have told him to make his arrangements with you." The Popolano's commissions were of the most varied sort: to buy him mulberry trees for his silkworms, to offer a Spaniard as high as twenty ducats for a mule.

The banking operations were more complicated. Benedetto Paganotti, Bishop of Viason, was always in need of money, and Amerigo was his refuge in times of trouble. To increase his income the Bishop had engaged in a business transaction with the knowledge of the Popolano and Cardinal Rucellai, but the handling of the operation was left to Amerigo. When the Bishop wanted to know how things were going, he inquired by letter or invited Amerigo to have dinner with him. The following lines from a letter to Amerigo give an idea of how such business matters, in which many important persons of the day were engaged, were conducted:

Illustrious and dearly beloved friend: The bearer of this letter is Rosso de Somaglia, to whom I owe twenty-seven gold florins, which sum he loaned me

---

1. Ida Masetti-Bencini and Mary Howard-Smith published in the above-mentioned *Rivista delle Biblioteche* (October-December 1902) seventy-one letters addressed to Amerigo during these years, which are the principal source for this chapter.

some time ago. Please pay him out of the hundred and fifty you promised me. You can deduct them from the amount you are to pay me later on. Please look after this as soon as possible. My situation is terrible, and if you could see me you would be moved to compassion...

Some approached Amerigo proposing business deals; others because they needed money. From prison he received letters begging him to use his efforts to secure some unfortunate wretch's release. He was in a most favorable situation because, though he was working for the Popolano, he had kept the friendship of the Magnificent; his uncle was Lorenzo's ambassador to Rome, and he himself was the right-hand man of the rich Medici in Florence. A certain Luca de' Colti, for example, wrote to him from Piombino. He wanted to return to Pisa, his homeland. He was living in exile because he had stabbed his wife to death, and only by securing a safe-conduct from the Magnificent could he put an end to the proscription that was ruining him. If Amerigo would talk to the Popolano and the Magnificent, Luca was sure that he could accomplish his purpose. He wrote to Amerigo:

I killed her because of the wanton life she was leading, a fact that was notorious in Pisa... The government of Florence has no grounds for refusing me a safe-conduct, because I killed her in Lucca, and she was from neither Pisa nor Florence, but a Sicilian... After this had happened I went to Sicily, where I was on friendly relations with my father-in-law...

At other times the request was for a letter to the Archbishop. Chino Orlandini wrote to him:

Dearest Amerigo: I am not going to be able to see you today because important business matters have come up which I must attend to. Our Piero, the bearer of this letter, is calling for the one you promised me for the Archbishop, interceding on my behalf. Tell the Archbishop in your letter that Girolamo has written me that he, the Archbishop, has in his power things that belong to Girolamo. You must put it in such a way that the Archbishop won't take offense...

At times it was to request the extension of a debt that had come due, as in the case of Bernardo Vermigli when he was made notary of the Signoria:

Amerigo: I have ordered the sum I promised you paid to you out of the estate of Stefano Canacci... even though I have not yet received the money. But as I have just received this new appointment, I have to make some necessary expenditures. If it were possible to delay this payment until the end of my appointment, you would do me a great service... If this is really impossible, let me know, and I will try to get a loan...

There were occasions when it was Amerigo who was in default. At the request of his aunt Maddalena, Antonio Morelli's steward wrote to him:

Beloved like a son: I beg of you do not delay longer in sending me that ducat. Do not, Amerigo, make it necessary for me to send for it again. I would remind you that you wrote me that in the case of an agreement between the two of us, your word was as

*good as a notarized document. Please bear this in
mind and do not make me send people to collect from
you. Please, for the love of Christ!...*

The home of the Popolano was a gathering-place
for poets, philosophers, men of science, humanists,
painters. Giorgio Antonio Vespucci was as welcome
there as though it were his father's house. The painters who worked for the Popolano were all friends
of the Vespucci. Botticelli decorated his villa in
Castello. In her letters Semiramide reveals the deep-
est concern over the health of the painter who immortalized Simonetta.

The most famous portrait of Simonetta is attrib-
uted by some to Piero di Cosimo, by others to
Pollaiuolo. It is believed that it was commissioned
by Lorenzo the Popolano while Amerigo was in his
service. Both painters belonged to the Vespucci circle.
It was Piero di Cosimo who, with Botticelli, decorated the house of Guido Antonio Vespucci, as Vasari
states in his *Lives of the Painters.* As for Pollaiuolo,
he, together with Verrocchio, had been Botticelli's
master, and Verrocchio had lived in a house that
belonged to Guido Antonio Vespucci.

The portrait of Simonetta in question is to be seen
in France today, in the gallery of the Château of
Chantilly. Beneath the portrait runs the inscription:
"Simonetta Lanvensis Vespuccia." It shows her in
profile, her breasts bared. A snake is coiled around
her gold collar. What is the significance of this snake?
Is it, as Vasari suggests, an allusion to Cleopatra? Is it
a symbol of life, in which the serpent biting its tail

suggests man's beginning and end? Brockhaus gives this explanation, which seems more plausible: "Lorenzo di Pier Francesco de' Medici had as the emblem of his coat of arms a serpent, which, according to Psalm lvii, 'stoppeth her ear; which will not hearken to the voice of charmers.'" To Semiramide, as to Amerigo or Lorenzo the Popolano, this Simonetta of the bared breasts was the complete image of her beauty, which none of the three felt any need to veil, recalling its dazzling triumph. In nearly all Botticelli's paintings of her she appears completely nude.

During these years Amerigo may have met Michelangelo, who was working in Ghirlandaio's studio. His genius was already revealing itself. The Popolano had commissioned him to do the statue of St. John the Baptist as a child. Between Michelangelo and the two painters with whom Amerigo was most closely associated, Ghirlandaio and Botticelli, who had just returned to Florence flushed with their triumphs in the Sistine Chapel, a friendship developed which was limited only by the difference in their ages. Michelangelo was on the threshold of his career. Not even in dreams did he foresee that he would be called upon to complete the work the other two had initiated in the Vatican. Life and a community of ideals created a bond among them. It was not long before the three of them, along with Giorgio Antonio Vespucci and the Popolano, were active in the ranks of the *Piagnoni*, the party opposing the oligarchy. On the death of the Magnificent, this party, spearheaded by

Savonarola's demagoguery, dominated in Florence. By then Michelangelo was in Rome, but he communicated with the Popolano through Botticelli, thus outwitting the censorship of the oligarchy.

The Popolano was greatly drawn to literature. He wrote morality plays in verse, which were staged in Florence. At his request, Botticelli illustrated *The Divine Comedy*. Poliziano dedicated poems to him. In the Popolano's house Giorgio Antonio Vespucci and Zenobio Acciaiuoli were the moving spirits of a group that was like an intimate academy, of which Amerigo formed a part and at which Ficino and Poliziano were familiar figures. Zenobio, too, joined the *Piagnoni* party.

Zenobio Acciaiuoli was a poet, theologian, and student of Greek and Latin. His life and that of Giorgio Antonio ran parallel. Both were friends of Marsilio Ficino, both followed the same political line, both took vows. It fell to Giorgio Antonio to catalogue and save for posterity the fabulous library of the Medici of the oligarchy when it was threatened with destruction by the fury of the popular uprising Savonarola had unleashed. Zenobio ended his days as librarian of the Vatican under Leo X.

Zenobio treated Amerigo with the warmest friendship. He was interested in maps and geography. He came to know the Germans who visited Giorgio Antonio. Years later his interests and friendships were of great importance in connection with a document that was decisive for Amerigo's renown. At the moment, the poetry of Poliziano, Pulci, Ariosto,

Franco, and Zenobio himself, the philosophy of the Greeks, the teachings of Ficino, the contribution of the painters–all were mingled and interwoven in the conversations and in the life of Zenobio and his friends.

In the conversations of these men geographical matters were very much in the foreground. Geography was a theme of paramount interest to all in Florence, but especially to the two great men with whom Zenobio and Giorgio Antonio were most closely associated: Marsilio Ficino and Agnolo Poliziano. Marsilio Ficino had so marked an inclination toward geographic problems that in the fresco painted by Giorgio Vasari for the audience chamber of Cosimo de' Medici in the Palazzo della Signoria he is shown at Toscanelli's side. Geography in that day easily induced lyrical exaltation. It was the philosopher's dream, it was a mystery filled with omens that lent themselves to a kind of prophetic revelation. The existence of a fourth continent had been "admitted or prophesied by San Antonino," Archbishop of Florence, according to Uzielli. Where experimental science could not penetrate, where ships could go no farther, the imagination took over, turning theories into poetry and giving a magic touch to the limits of knowledge. In 1482 Francesco Berlinghieri concluded his *Geografia in terza rima* in Florence, where it was published with an apologue by his friend Marsilio Ficino.[2]

Evidence of Poliziano's passion for geography is the fact that when death came to him he was considering the idea of writing an account of the voyages of the Portuguese. The theme of the yet undiscovered world was the topic of the day in Florence. Between 1476 and 1480, Lorenzo Bonincontri had been discussing it in his public lessons on the *Astronomica* by the Latin poet Manilius.[3] In a word, the problem of the New World passionately interested these people of Florence before the New World had been discovered. The talk was of the antipodes, whether the regions below the equator were habitable or not, the division of the waters and the continents, the races; and concerning all this they drew imaginary maps, they wrote poems, they revived ancient theories, they discoursed in academies and meeting-places. This was the intellectual climate of Amerigo's Florence.

A gifted and noble poet of Constantinople came to Florence about this time. He was Theodoro Marullo, who dedicated his Latin epigrams to the Popolano, his "intimate and cordial friend." He had been attracted by the prestige of the capital of letters, the new Athens, and he became the friend of Poliziano, Giorgio Antonio, Zenobio, and Ghirlandaio, who painted his portrait. Marullo's ambition was to have a place in one of the small courts of humanists which gathered around the princes of the Church. He pinned

2. Berlinghieri spent twenty years writing his work, which was the first in which maps were printed. In connection with him, see Uzielli's notes in his book *Paolo dal Pozzo Toscanelli* (Florence, 1892).

3. For the *Astronomica*, see Uzielli's book referred to in the preceding note.

his hopes on Cardinal Antoniotto Palavicino, a Genoese whose star was rising in Rome and who was a great friend of Poliziano.

The Popolano wrote to the Magnificent asking him to use his good offices toward having Marullo admitted to the Cardinal's circle. For the moment nothing came of it. Days went by and nothing happened. Marullo was staying in the home of Zenobio. One day a certain Gazzerano, it seems, robbed the two men of their belongings. Amerigo learned of this first, and, through him, Zenobio, who was away from Florence at the time. In a letter from Zenobio to Amerigo we read:

By the first trustworthy messenger I shall send you the keys of my chests so you can get out underwear, shirts, handkerchiefs, or anything Marullo needs... Comfort him in my name... If Gazzerano did not steal the books after I left, he did not do it before. I am sure of this, because after I had heard a noise in my study, as though someone was trying to force the lock, I hurried to it and looked it over and there was nothing missing. Nevertheless, the investigation should not be hurried, because I have learned from Scarabotto that a book bound in red leather was found in the house of that woman...

Problems of greater transcendence were often dealt with, and Zenobio was present on all such occasions. In this fashion one learns of one of the most celebrated literary love affairs of the period. Marullo and Poliziano had both fallen in love with Alessandra, the daughter of Bartolommeo Scala.[4]

Alessandra was an extraordinary woman. Her father, though the son of a miller, was a famous scholar, and she possessed refinement and charm in the highest degree. Marullo and Poliziano wrote poems in Latin to her, and she replied using the same meters and the same language. But Oriental allure won out, and Alessandra gave herself to Marullo. Poliziano's wrath and jealousy were uncontained, and he wrote Greek epigrams, dripping with venom and obscenity, against Marullo. Zenobio was a great friend of Poliziano as well as of Marullo. Scurrilous and foul though the epigrams were, they had literary value, and on Poliziano's death Zenobio published them. They are glimpses of humanism in small clothes.

These incidents of life among the artists were common knowledge, and everybody enjoyed them and repeated them with that wit and cruelty typical of Florence. There is no record, no detailed information of the meetings of the Popolano's protégés, such as we have of the Platonic Academy or the Convivium of the Magnificent. The tone of the gatherings of the Popolano was confidential. Those who assembled there were the same ones who attended the brilliant

4. Bartolommeo Scala, who wrote a history of the First Crusade, and was chancellor of the Signoria, was considered one of the great scholars of Florence. He was of humble origin. "I came to this Republic," he writes in his memoirs, "naked of everything, like a poor beggar, of the lowest extraction, without money, without position, without connections, without relations. Cosimo, Father of the Country, brought me up, receiving me into the bosom of his family."

lectures of Ficino or Poliziano. Even in the Popolano's home in Florence, the atmosphere was rather one of secrecy, of intimacy. If it were possible to reconstruct the dialogues that took place on such occasions, we should have a living document of the Florentine merry-go-round.

Piero Vespucci, the son of Bernardo, was commander of the old fortress in Pisa, with the rank of captain. He wrote to Amerigo frequently. "If you can, lend me your Livy, or your copy of Dante with Landino's commentary…" or "If you can, send me some books in the vernacular… last year, when I was in Arezzo with Ottaviano Manfredi, I was impressed by his taste and we became friends… Now I wish you would lend me the sonnets of Pulci and those of Franco, for he told me he would like to see them, and I promised to get them for him. I promise to return them to you in a month…"

The Medici had no branch bank in Seville or Barcelona, but they did have agencies or factors who supplied them with wool, cochineal, almonds, horses, and mules, and who sold brocades and finished cloth. They arranged for shipments or chartered vessels for Mediterranean and northern European trade. The Spanish ports were key points in the great commercial network that embraced the entire Mediterranean. At first it had been the Medici of the oligarchy who had business interests there. Now it was the Popolani.

In going over the accounts of Seville, the Popolano and Amerigo discovered irregularities that needed investigation. The books of Tommaso Caponi, who had been acting as the Popolano's agent, and of late had been dealing in velvets, satins, damasks, and taffetas, were not clear or detailed. He was handling merchandise that belonged to the Popolano as though it were his own, and the interests of Francesco and Giovan' Battista Taddeo were also involved. The Popolano was a hard man when it came to money. All his dealings were characterized by a mixture of suspicion and sharp dealing. Various incidents reflect little credit on his memory. He tried to cheat his nephew, Giovanni delle Bande Nere, out of his paternal inheritance. He was indignant at the behavior of Tommaso Caponi in Seville, and he asked Amerigo to look into the matter, and not to stop until it was cleared up.

Amerigo's first step was to study the affairs of the Taddeo, one of the causes of confusion. He pointed out to Tommaso Caponi the justification that the Taddeos had for their demands and suggested a method of arbitration, for which Francesco Taddeo was very grateful. In a letter to Amerigo he said:

My best and most honorable friend... I approve everything you have done to establish the justice of our claim. I have seen that the appraisal you have made does not differ from ours, though it seems that the brocades might have been sold at a better price. In a word, I am satisfied with what you have done, not only for the advantages that will accrue to us from it, but also for the good reputation we will acquire for acting reasonably... I am amazed that

Tommaso is not satisfied with such an equitable arrangement...

But the matter was not that simple. Everything depended on what Tommaso's employees said or did, and the Popolano did not trust them. He said that all they knew how to do was to lie, and he may have been right. He was of the opinion that the only thing to do was to get the business out of their hands, give them no further commissions, and find new agents. Donato Nicolini, who also worked for the Popolano, had gone to Seville, and he suggested the name of Gianetto Berardi, whose services he was using temporarily. But who was this Berardi? It was Amerigo's job to find out. The Popolano wrote to him:

Find out what sort of person he is, and whether, in your opinion, he is trustworthy for such dealings. If you decide that he is, he could replace Tommaso.

To inform himself of this, Amerigo had to go to Seville. But for this slight irregularity in the Popolano's affairs, Amerigo would probably never have gone to Spain, and this book would not have been written.

Just to find out who Gianetto Berardi was hardly justified a trip to Seville. Seville had been an important trading center for centuries, and was much more so now. The Catholic Kings, who had been in conflict with Portugal over matters having to do with Atlantic voyages and trade with Guinea, had reached an agreement assuring them safe, easy access to Guinea. In 1479 a gold mine that had all Seville agog with excitement had been discovered there. Trading companies made up of Spaniards and foreigners made frequent voyages to Guinea and along the coast of Morocco, exchanging articles of trifling value for slaves, ivory, and gold. Europe was suffering the effects of the gold crisis of the Sudan, which took place between 1460 and 1470, and which had been such an incentive to the voyages of the Portuguese. Seville became such a beehive of activity as a result of the discovery of the mine in Guinea that the monarchs had to appoint collectors and a whole crew of officials to collect the Crown's share from these new Argonauts, and notaries to sail with the ships and keep a record of all transactions. The announcement of the discovery of a mine always touched off a train of bureaucratic hopes in any court.[5]

But another circumstance made Seville important. The Catholic Kings regarded themselves as the last crusaders of the Western World. The taking of Granada was their prime objective. Everything was organized around this campaign. In 1488 Málaga had fallen and the monarchs had entered Córdoba in triumph. A year later they were preparing to move on Baza. When speaking of the monarchs in connection with these crusades, one should really say "the Queen," for Isabella was the driving force. She was a fine horsewoman, and when she reviewed her troops, mounted on a prancing horse, even the Moors, watching from a distance, were impressed by this brightly clad figure riding before her

5. Pérez Embid: *Los Descubrimientos en el Atlántico*, etc.

arquebusiers and lancers amid the fluttering of flags, the ring of martial music, and the soldiers' cheers.

Fighting was going on not far from Seville, which had the character of a frontier city. It was ruled by an *adelantado*, not a governor. It came to the ears of the Popolano that there were good business openings in Seville. Where there's war, there's trade. But the source of this information was Tommaso, and how much stock could be put in what he said? This was another matter for Amerigo to look into.

Seville resembled nothing Amerigo had ever known before. Italy was touched by the golden enchantment of Byzantium; here there was Oriental flavor, too, but a different one, that of the Moors. The Cathedral had been a mosque. The campanile bore the name of a woman; it was called the Giralda. It was and is a graceful tower whose four flanks seem four poems of Araby. It was not so delicate and slender as Giotto's campanile in Florence, but, like the latter, it dominated the city more by its grace than by its height. In the midst of a world bristling with feudal turrets, these campaniles, that of Florence and that of Seville, were like two magic wands.

Carrying on a tradition of centuries, the Catholic Kings were determined to wrest from the Moors the parts of Spain they still held. This was their manifest destiny, and they were on the point of fulfilling it. The standard of the Cross would be the only banner to fly in their kingdom. Seville had been the first major achievement in the long crusade. Two and a half centuries earlier, Ferdinand the Saint had re-

stored it to Christendom, destroying the most pros-
perous of the Moorish kingdoms. It was said that
some four hundred thousand Moors left that thickly
settled area to take refuge elsewhere. In the Cathedral stands the tomb of the conqueror, who is venerated by the Spaniards as a saint. There his sword
hangs. He was a saint of iron, steel, combat. And yet
the Moorish influence lingered on. There were the
mudéjar palaces. At heart everyone lived a Moorish
novel, the novel of the Moorish and Christian frontier. The old Oriental world lived on in the color of
the women's skin, in their eyes, in the songs, the
tambourines, the language, the gardens, the patios,
in the realm of the subconscious, in the depths of
the soul, as though Hafsite, the last of the Almohad
princes, had not died. Women of olive skin and
coal-black almond eyes came to the church to pray,
shades of the past returning to the mosque. The
Orient of Seville was perhaps more authentic than
that of Italy: it was an Orient of the blood, in the
roots of the words, in the glances. The people of
Seville did not say "perhaps" or "maybe," but *"ojalá,"*
"May Allah so wish! May Allah permit!" their souls
soaring on the wings of the single word.

Seville was closer to the sea than Florence. It was
as though Pisa and Florence had formed a single unit.
The Guadalquivir at times flowed upstream, at times
down, depending on the tides of the Mediterranean,
which were felt as far as the port of Seville. The Mediterranean and the Guadalquivir saved Seville. Its destruction at the hand of King Ferdinand the Saint

proved to be but a salutary pruning. And the four hundred thousand Moors who had left the Kingdom of Seville ebbed back like the tide. Seville was the port of Spain, the flower of the Mediterranean. When Amerigo arrived, it was a city of multiple-faceted souls. Italians were so numerous as to constitute a community, and Jews were legion. The Jews, more compacted with Spain than with any other nation, had so much influence in court circles and with the monarchs themselves that one could already hear the angry ground-swell of the envious multitude foretelling their fall. The bankers of Genoa lent an attentive ear— who would inherit the Jews' business if they were expelled? There were Germans in Seville, too. They had just introduced the printing press there and were bringing out the first books.

Through the narrow streets moved donkeys loaded with firewood, casks of wine, and sacks of olives, and peasants whose rustic air recalled that of the folk of Peretola. The jests were less subtle than those of Florence, but aroused a franker, heartier laughter; the friars were less intelligent than those of San Marco or Ognissanti, but more human. The women were less exquisite, but more ardent. The wine of Florence was Chianti; that of Seville sweet Málaga.

And Spain had something Amerigo had already noted in France: unity. It was united states, united kingdoms. The old regional dialects remained, and peoples with typical dress and customs, but the language and the Crown of Castile were acquiring ascendancy over them all. The rivalry among the Italian republics did not exist there, nor those dukes, kings, doges, or barons who had made Italy a battleground of conflicting ambitions, of fierce struggles for power. There was no pope in Spain to encourage civil wars and take sides in them. When they went to Italy, Spaniards, like the Borgias, the kings of Naples, played the game of internal politics, striving for the pre-eminence of their small states. Machiavelli, the dreamer of Italian unity, had high praise for Ferdinand the Catholic, seeing in him the prince who worked for the unity of his kingdom.

Moreover, Spain was the land where Don Quixote and Sancho rode and talked together. The popular base there was much broader than in Italy, with a less refined upper class that preserved touches of a much more lively medieval magic. At the top were a golden King and Queen who traveled to court on muleback; below, a motley folk that rode donkeys.

This world captivated Amerigo Vespucci. He understood its language from the day he arrived. It was nothing so foreign as France had been. It had a soul both different from and akin to his.

The information Amerigo received from Gianetto Berardi could not have been better. Berardi belonged to an old Florentine family, and had been working in Spain for over fifty years. The family had had business connections with Seville and Valencia as dealers in silk. Amerigo talked with Gianetto, he talked with former agents of the Popolano, and he saw that Seville was a land of opportunity where he himself might work out a more independent life.

Gianetto Berardi offered his friendship. After all, whether or not he was to remain in Seville as Lorenzo di Pier Francesco de' Medici's business representative would depend on Amerigo.

To be sure, before the Popolano could reach a final decision, the matter would have to be studied in the account books kept in Pisa. The perfection of the Medici bookkeeping, with its double-entry ledgers, is famous in business history. Out of them came the record, written in florins, of the rise and decline of families, including that of the Medici themselves.

Amerigo's first visit to Seville must have been very brief. He left Florence at the end of September 1489, and was back in Piombino by the second half of November. His associations in Seville were almost wholly with the Italian colony. The Genoese plainly were in a favored position in the business world, but the Florentines got on well with the Genoese. Gianetto Berardi was on a particularly friendly footing with them.

Among the Genoese seeking their fortune in Seville there was one who was a friend of Gianetto Berardi and who was to become a close acquaintance of Amerigo's because of an intellectual bond between them: their admiration for Paolo dal Pozzo Toscanelli, the sage of Florence. The name of this Genoese was Christopher Columbus. There is no proof of a meeting between him and Amerigo in 1489, but it is very possible. Columbus, or Cristóbal Colón, as the Spaniards called him, had been in Spain for five years, after having lived in Portugal. He was a sailor, and was perhaps related to that Colombo the corsair about whose attacks on Florentine shipping Guido Antonio had complained to the French King. Columbus had become a passionate believer in Toscanelli's theory that by sailing west one could reach the lands of the East, the spice-producing lands described by Marco Polo in his *Book*. Moreover, he had secrets that he kept to himself. For Columbus, Seville was a more propitious medium than the court. It was a port, and he was a seafarer. There were men of learning there. Not for nothing had St. Isidore been born there, that savant whose theories concerning the parts of the world Archbishop Antonino of Florence had incorporated into his writings and Giorgio Antonio Vespucci into his knowledge.

Columbus could talk to Amerigo–if he did talk to him on this occasion–with greater assurance and intimacy than with most. Amerigo was a product of the school of Toscanelli; all his friends and teachers had been first-hand pupils of the master. Columbus, on the other hand, had managed only to get hold of a copy of his map from the canon of Lisbon. And this map alone had been enough to chart his life course.

Unfortunately for Columbus, his experience during his five years in Spain had convinced him that the people he had to win over were the friars, who did not argue on Toscanelli's own terms, but on the basis of Holy Writ. There was no way of detaching them from the world of prophecy. Columbus began to see that if he was to be successful, he would have to use a different approach, the Biblical, not the, scientific; not maps, but quotations from the Church Fathers. He had lost all faith in kings. "After many talks," Ferdinand Columbus, the Navigator's son, wrote, "and seeing that there was no hope of reaching a decision in Spain, so he said, and that his project did not take shape, he considered going to talk with the King of France, to whom he had already written in that vein, and advise him that if he paid him no heed, he would go to England to talk with his royal brother."[6]

Gianetto Berardi was sympathetic to the ideas of Columbus.

In Portugal, as in Spain, the Italian bankers were legion. There were the Pinellos, the Centurione, the Dorias, the Di Negri, the Spinolas. These, along with Berardi, were to be Columbus's bankers, as were the Cattaneos of Genoa, probably members of the same family as Simonetta Vespucci. Amerigo's brother Antonio came to act as notary in Florence for nearly all of them. Through the documents in his register runs the history of the most important establishments of Seville, Barcelona, and Lisbon.

Before leaving Seville, Amerigo carried out the commissions Semiramide had given him. He had gone to Seville not merely as an employee of the Popolano, but also as a member of the family. Semiramide's commissions had nothing to do with

6. Fernando Colombo: *Le Historie della vita e dei fatti di Cristoforo Colombo*, Vol. 1, p. 109 (ed. Alpes, Milan, 1930).

the bank, or shipping, or the sale of brocades. They were all things for the children: an ivory comb for Laldomina, a beige velvet cap with silver appliqué for little Pier Francesco. When Amerigo arrived with these gifts, the children received him with delight, like a favorite uncle.

IX

IN PIOMBINO AND IN PISA
(1490)

Amerigo left Seville for Piombino, en route to Pisa. He was stopping at the home of Semiramide's parents, the castle of the Appiani, from which Simonetta had set out for Florence.

Jacopo III, the father of Semiramide, had died several years before. He had been a man of lewd, despotic nature. He had ordered in his will that anyone who rebelled against his government should be given twenty-five turns of the screw on the rack and condemned to life imprisonment. His heir was Jacopo IV, and it was this brother of Semiramide that Amerigo was going to visit. Jacopo IV governed with the support of the King of Naples, to whose niece, the daughter of the Duke of Amalfi, he was married.

Jacopo IV was keenly interested in talking with Amerigo. The inhabitants of the island of Elba, which formed part of the dominions of Piombino, were continually being harassed by Spanish corsairs, and they had come to complain to their liege lord. Things had reached such a point that the islanders were considering emigrating from their home en masse. This meant not only the possible loss of Elba, but a direct threat to Piombino by the Spaniards. Elba was in sight of the castle. The Council of Elders of Piombino appointed four illustrious citizens to make formal representations to Jacopo IV. The situation was especially absurd in view of the relationship between the King of Naples and Ferdinand of Aragón, the Catholic King.

The Piombinans were beset by these tribulations when Jacopo IV received a letter from Ferdinand the Catholic assuring him of his protection, and ordering all officers, pilots, and masters of Spanish ships to refrain from harming in any way, on any pretext or excuse, the holdings of the Lord of Piombino or his vassals, under penalty of being fined in the amount of fifty thousand ducats and losing the favor of the King.[1]

Jacopo was anxious to have all this brought to the knowledge of the Medici, and at the same time he wanted to find out from Amerigo, whom he looked upon as a nephew, how things stood in Spain. Once again Amerigo found himself in the midst of those conflicts which exercised the sovereigns of Europe and the absolute rulers of the miniature Italian states, of which Piombino was a typical example.

Piombino had a variety of family associations for Amerigo. On the island of Elba were the iron mines that Jacopo III had given to Simonetta as part of her dowry. In the castle of the Appiani, Piero Vespucci, on his way home from his voyage to Constantinople,

---

1. L. Cappelletti: *Storia di Piombino*, p. 119.

had forged the first link in his dream of greatness by arranging the marriage of his son Marco to Simonetta. There he had stolen certain documents that would ingratiate him with Lorenzo the Magnificent; he had tried to work out with Jacopo some solution that would have spared Volterra the sacking by the Florentines, and the Magnificent the enduring stain this action left upon his name. Casting up the balance of these events brought home to Amerigo Giorgio Antonio's teachings on the mutability of fortune. Simonetta had been cut down in the flower of her youth; the mines of Elba hung between the Spanish pirate raids and Ferdinand the Catholic's pleasure; and Piero Vespucci had departed life in a tragic manner. For all his soldier-of-fortune streak, he had been the great navigator of the Vespucci family.

After his release from prison Piero Vespucci had gone to the court of Gian Galeazzo Maria Sforza in Milan. The Duke had welcomed him and made him one of his gentlemen-in-waiting. In this manner he spent nearly four peaceful years. He whiled away the time writing letters to Benedetto Dei.[2] This adventurer had renounced his travels, and kept up a vast correspondence with his friends. His letters were a forerunner of newspapers, sheets that were passed around from hand to hand, containing information on everything between heaven and earth. All the

2. In the State Archives of Florence, Collection of the Convent of Badia, there is a thick folder of letters from Piero Vespucci to Benedetto Dei.

Vespucci were happy to have Piero and his son Marco far from Florence, thus obliterating the memory of the years the former had spent in prison. From time to time Piero wrote to the Magnificent. He knew that anger does not endure forever, and he hoped to prepare the way for his eventual return to his homeland.

The Duke of Milan decided to send Piero on a mission of pacification to Alessandria. In the vast region of his duchy which lay between Tortona and Varsi, as far as Alessandria, highwaymen and thieves were making life impossible, and the conflicts between Guelphs and Ghibellines contributed to the disorder. Piero was accompanied by the nephew of Cardinal Sforza, Guidobono Cavalchini.

After making a careful study of the situation in Alessandria, Piero reached the conclusion that the cause of the disorders was a young, audacious captain of the Ghibellines, Carranto Villavecchia. Everybody was afraid of him. Piero decided to take him by surprise. One morning at daybreak his troops surrounded the fortress of this Ghibelline. The attack was completely unexpected, and in a short time the besieged had to surrender. Old Villavecchia, the father, came out and implored mercy of the commander of the troops; he was stabbed to death. The women and children fled in terror, young Carranto was captured, the castle sacked. The soldiers brought the prisoner to the house of the Podestà. Villavecchia threw himself at Piero Vespucci's feet and begged for forgiveness. Piero unleashed against him a flood of repressed passions and gave no hope of mercy.

Whereupon the Ghibelline asked the one boon any Christian had a right to expect of another in such circumstances: a priest. Piero answered: "You can make your confession in the other world!" A noose was thrown around his neck and he was hanged from the balcony of the palace.

The friends of the dead man met that night in the Church of San Marco. They swore vengeance on the cross of their dagger hilts. The next morning they forced their way into the palace of the Podestà and seized Piero Vespucci by the throat. In a choking voice he asked the one boon any Christian has a right to expect of another in such circumstances: a priest. Waving the noose before his eyes, the Ghibellines answered: "You can make your confession in the other world!" The noose was thrown around his neck and he was hanged from the balcony. What a useful thing a palace balcony is! Piero struggled in the air, and the rope broke. He fell to the street still alive, and they finished him off with daggers. The palace was sacked.[3]

In Piombino, Amerigo received a letter from the Popolano. This time a more valuable life had been in danger, that of Giorgio Antonio: he had been gravely ill. He had had a sudden hemorrhage, and the doctors were not yet sure they could save him. "We have done everything we could for him," the

---

3. The final phase of Piero Vespucci's life is described, with documents, by F. Gasparolo: *Pietro Vespucci, podestà di Alessandria* (Alessandria, 1892).

Popolano wrote, "and we are in constant attendance upon him."[4] Another letter followed shortly, this one from Zenobio Acciaiuoli. "You will have heard," he wrote, "of the attack our good father, Messer Giorgio Antonio, has suffered... Lorenzo and Giovanni (the Popolano's brother) have behaved toward him as though he were their own father..."[5]

By the grace of God, Giorgio Antonio recovered. Amerigo, his mind at rest, left Piombino for Pisa.

Pisa was, for Amerigo, a little like a prolongation of Florence, not only because the Florentines controlled its port, but also because he could move there in a family atmosphere. The commander of the old fortress was Piero Vespucci, the son of Bernardo, the one who used to write to him in Florence asking for books. He was only six years older than Amerigo. They were very close friends. We can judge the degree of friendship from his requests to Amerigo in later letters, such as those referring to Madame B., whom he mentions on several occasions:

Tell me, I beg of you, my dear Amerigo, if I can count on Madame B., whom I await with the keenest desire, I assure you, provided she is willing, otherwise I shall put it out of my mind. If the journey is postponed, let me know. If she wants to come at once, the bearer of this letter could accompany her. He is a good and trustworthy man, and he has funds for the trip. Or she could come by boat comfortably and quickly...[6]

---

4. A.S.F., M.A.P., F. LXVIII, c. 232.
5. A.S.F., M.A.P., F. LXVIII, c. 229.

Again, Piero needed a cook, or he regaled Amerigo with tidbits of Pisan gossip. This Piero was to play an important part in the history of Florence later on. Giovanni Vespucci, the older son of Guido Antonio, was also in Pisa. He was a boy of only twelve, but he was an extremely precocious lad who was already studying at the university and had such a knowledge of Latin that he was translating Sallust's *Conspiracy of Catiline* into Italian, a translation that still exists. Nor did the passage of years defraud the hopes that had been placed in this youthful prodigy. Giovanni became one of the legates Leo X employed for the most delicate diplomatic missions. At the time of this story Guido Antonio was working in Rome to open the paths to the Church for this son of Lorenzo the Magnificent, who was to occupy the Holy See. When he reached this ultimate goal, Leo X turned his eyes toward Giovanni, the son of his former advocate, and sent him as his ambassador to the King of Spain.

Pisa stood for still other things in Amerigo's world of memories. It was at Pisa that Piero Vespucci, the navigator, had arrived on his return from Constantinople, accompanied by Benedetto Dei, who astounded his friends with the live crocodile he had brought as a gift to the Medici. Amerigo talked there with old friends of Piero and Benedetto Dei. They were all interested in voyages, discoveries, and trade with the Orient. What was a remote and academic interest in Florence was the daily pabulum of Pisa.

6. A.S.F., M.A.P., F. LXVIII, c. 231.

Pisa, with its direct contact with the sea, resembled Seville. It was the natural outlet to the sea for the Republic of Florence, just as Seville was for the Kingdom of Castile. In a sense it was even more important, for it lay on the road from Rome to Genoa, and was the connecting link with Lucca. The Arno, which in Florence was nothing but a chattering stream that carried little water, emptied into the sea at Pisa. For centuries that city had been a trade barometer of commerce with the Orient. At the time of the Second Crusade, in 1099, so decisive in the history of Europe and the Orient, Pisa joined the stream of adventurers following the Cross with ships and men, setting up banks, consuls, merchants, and warehouses in the Near East. This brought about a revolution in the commercial dealings and the life of the whole Western World, but most of all in that of Pisa itself, which became a crossroad between East and West.

Two names that Amerigo had heard in his home from his earliest youth, those of Benedetto Dei and Paolo dal Pozzo Toscanelli, were closely associated with the affairs of Pisa.

For years the Toscanelli had had their bank, their business interests, their clearing-house of information in Pisa. Paolo's theories were not the result of mere speculation. From childhood he had been hearing about voyages to the Orient, problems of navigation. Paolo had died in 1482, but his nephew, Master Ludovico, and several of his most gifted disciples, among them Piero Vaglienti, were still in Pisa.

Piero Vaglienti, goldsmith, merchant, money-changer, had a small shop. In earlier years he had worked in Florence for the Dei. His relations with Benedetto had made him one of Piero Vespucci's group. Writing to Benedetto's brother, Vaglienti addressed him as "in the place of a good father." Not a good business-man–he was practically ruined when he died–he was a man of infinite curiosity. He collected accounts of voyages and wrote history. In Vaglienti's notebook, copied in his own hand, some of Amerigo's rela-tions of his voyages were found centuries later.

The discoveries initiated by Portugal were followed with the keenest interest in Pisa. Bartholomeu Dias's discovery of the Cape of Good Hope–he sailed from Lisbon in 1486, rounded the Cape in 1487, and re-turned to Lisbon in 1488–paved the way for the voy-·age completed by Vasco da Gama in 1497-9. Piero Vaglienti left two books, one the collection of voyages which included the letters of Amerigo, the other a chronicle of the notable events that took place be-tween 1492 and 1513.[7] As an example of how Vaglienti's mind worked, we have only to read what he wrote on learning that Vasco da Gama, rounding the Cape of Good Hope, had successfully reached India:

To whom do we owe this discovery? To a doctor of medicine, a Florentine, Paolo dal Pozzo Toscanelli, a most exceptional man, who announced this route to the Florentine Bartholomeo Marchioni, who was

7. The above-mentioned review, *Toscanelli*, contains a good article on *"Piero Vaglienti et l'authenticité des relations des Voyages d'Améric Vespuce."*

*at the court of Lisbon. He gave this information to
the King. And thus an enterprise has been carried
out that arouses the admiration of the whole world.
The spices that should, or used to, go to Cairo by way
of the Red Sea are now carried to Lisbon by this other
route, and with this the Sultan has lost some five or
six hundred thousand ducats a year, and the Venetians the same...*[8]

This Bartholomeo Marchioni to whom Vaglienti refers, for whom Antonio Vespucci later acted as notary
in his dealings with his fellow Florentines, was closely
associated with the maritime activities of Portugal.

As for the introduction of Toscanelli's theories in
Lisbon, it is a long story, and is linked to the discov-
ery not only of new sea routes, but also of the New
World. Toscanelli had been in touch with people of
Portugal for many years. Prince Pedro, when he vis-
ited Florence on the voyage he made to collect the
geographical data utilized by his brother, Henry the
Navigator, visited Toscanelli. In addition to Toscanelli,
the Prince made the acquaintance at that time of
Filippo Pieruzzi, Giorgio Antonio Vespucci's teacher.

In 1464 Toscanelli and the Canon of the Cathedral
of Lisbon, Fernando Martínez de Roriz, met in Rome,
at the deathbed of Cardinal Cusano. Ten years later,
the Canon in a letter recalled to Toscanelli their acquaintance and told him of the favor he enjoyed
with the King. The moment had come to introduce

---

8. P. Vaglienti: *Cronica*, which exists in manuscript in the Biblioteca
Nazionale Centrale of Florence, Codex Magliab., segn. 11, IV, 42.

the ideas of the Florentine, which cast a spell over all who listened to him. Toscanelli answered the Canon in one of the most famous letters in the history of the world. It was the cornerstone of Columbus's faith, and on the strength of it he managed to win the support of the monarchs of Spain for his enterprise. Among other things, Toscanelli said to the Canon:

I am very happy to learn of the friendship of your Serene and Magnificent King which you enjoy, and inasmuch as I have often discussed the shortest sea route from here to the Indies, where the spices are found, which is much shorter than the route you now use via Guinea, and you tell me that His Highness would like me to give him some clarification or proof in order to study and see if it is possible to use this route, I could demonstrate this to him, globe in hand, and explain to him the distribution of the world. Failing this, it has occurred to me, for the purpose of ease and understanding, that I could show him this route on a map similar to those employed by navigators, And so I am sending it to you designed and drawn by my own hand. On it you will see the limits of the Occident, from Ireland southward to Guinea, with all the islands to be found along this route. Facing this line to the west the beginning of India is drawn, with the islands and places where you could go. As for the South Pole, you can sail below the equator for a good distance. And traveling leagues you will reach marvelously fertile lands with every kind of spice and gems and precious stones. And do not wonder that I

*speak of the west referring to the lands where the spices
grow, which are commonly said to lie to the cast: for
those who sail steadily westward will find those regions to the west, and those who travel eastward over-
land will find them in the east...*[9]

In his history, Ferdinand Columbus relates that
his father heard of this letter of Toscanelli's, and wrote
to the Florentine requesting further information. According to Ferdinand, Toscanelli sent him a copy of
his letter to the Canon.

The trip to Seville, the stop in Pisa, rubbing elbows with all those people who spent half their time
on their business affairs and the other half speculat-
ing about new travel routes, all combined to determine Amerigo's destiny. At a high price, for a sum
that represented a sacrifice for a man of his means,
he bought a vellum map. This was no geographical
curiosity, but a practical navigator's chart. It had been
made, however, by a first-rate cartographer, Gabriel
de Valesca, a Mallorcan. In his own hand Amerigo
wrote on the back that he had paid one hundred
and thirty gold ducats for it: *"Questa amplia pelle de
geografia fu pagata di Arnerigho Vespucci CXXX
ducati di oro di marco."* The map had been made
in 1439: *"Gabriell de Valsqua la feta in Majorca lany
MCCCCXXXVIIIJ."*

It was a map of great accuracy in everything having
to do with the Mediterranean, the waters Valesca knew
best, and which were the most important for naviga-

9. F. Colombo, op. cit., Vol. 1, pp. 56 ff.

tors. Captain José Gómez-Imaz, of the Spanish navy, studied it in 1892, at the time of the four-hundredth anniversary of the discovery of America. A replica of Columbus's flagship, the *Santa María*, had just been launched. And Imaz wrote: "If the captain of the neo-caravel, the *Santa María*, which has just been launched, were given Valesca's map, drawn four and a half centuries ago, he could sail the Mediterranean without ever getting off course or failing to make port with greater ease than is common with sailing boats today."[10] More recently, in a book published by Salvador Garcia Franco in 1947, a modern map of the Mediterranean has been superimposed on that of Valesca, and the amazing accuracy of this map of the fifteenth century is further substantiated.

The purchase of the map, of so accurate a map, indicates that Amerigo was considering a change of occupation. In studying observations made by Amerigo during his voyages, scholars have asked themselves if he must not have had contact in Italy with the men who made such notable contributions to the study of astronomy. Only in this way can they account for the exactitude of the conclusions at which he arrived.

The map, incidentally, has a history of its own. It changed hands many times in Italy, until finally it came into the possession of Cardinal Despuig, a Catalan. In 1839 it was on display in the library of

10. Gómez-lmaz: *Monografía de una carta hidrográfica* (Revista General de Marina, Madrid, 1892).

the Count of Montenegro. Its subsequent fate may be read in *Un Hiver à Majorque* by George Sand, who was living her romantic interlude with Chopin on that island:

There is to be found in that library the beautiful navigator's chart by the Mallorcan Valesca, drawn in 1439, a masterpiece of calligraphy and topographical design... This map belonged to Amerigo Vespucci... The chaplain who was conducting us unrolled this rare and precious treasure, for which Amerigo had paid one hundred and thirty gold ducats, and Cardinal Despuig, who later acquired it, Heaven only knows what. It occurred to one of the forty-five servants of the house to place an inkwell on one corner of the map to hold it down. The inkwell was full to the top. The vellum, as though possessed of the devil, crackled, leaped into the air, and rolled up, dragging with it the inkwell, which disappeared from sight in the roll...

It was no easy task to clean off the map after the visit of the famous pair.

What had taken Amerigo to Pisa was, however, a business matter. His first duty was to study the accounts in the branch house the Popolano had there, and to do this he needed information contained in the master ledger in Florence. Frescobaldi, who may have been an employee either of the Medici bank or of the Frescobaldi enterprise, wrote to Amerigo:

Illustrious and respected Sir: The object of the present is to urge upon you the need of getting hold of the accounts of the transactions that Neri Capponi and Com-

pany have carried on in the name of Simone & Donato Nicolini, or in that of Lorenzo di Pier Francesco de' Medici. You should have no trouble in securing them.

And so that you may have full information about everything, I am here transcribing all the transactions which appear in the master ledger in the account headed Tomasso Capponi, from which it appears that the aforesaid Capponi of Pisa owes us 41 ducats, 31 soldi, 11denari. You should find out why this sum is still outstanding...[11]

Amerigo's working days were spent checking the books before he could leave for Florence.

The study of Tommaso Capponi's transactions and the general procedure of his agents led to the conclusion that the best solution would be to transfer the operations to Gianetto Berardi in Seville. More than what Amerigo said in his letters, it was what he told the Popolano on his return to Florence that decided the matter.

This business trip to Seville, to Piombino, to Pisa, was of far greater importance for Amerigo's future than his trip to Rome with Giorgio Antonio, the philosopher, or his trip to Paris with Guido Antonio, the statesman.

11.   A.S.F., M.A.P., F. LXVIII, c. 230.

X

LAST YEAR IN FLORENCE
(1491)

Amerigo was nearly thirty-seven years old. His contemporaries had taken posts to which God and Florence had been pleased to call them. Some were famous, especially the painters. Botticelli and Ghirlandaio continued their joint work; they were decorating the Chapel of St. Zenobio in the Duomo. Others occupied outstanding positions in the Signoria. Still others were merchants, bankers, notaries, members of their respective guilds. Not a few had chosen the religious life. A number of the Vespucci had become friars or nuns. But Amerigo had not yet found his calling. He might have gone on for years in the service of the Popolano, but the experience of his brief travels had filled him with the desire to liberate himself from the limitations of life in Florence. In this year the Republic was being tossed about on a sea of passions which was engulfing everybody.

From the pulpit of San Marco and from the Duomo itself, a Dominican friar, Savonarola, was beginning to fulminate against the Medici of the oligarchy. He possessed a rare eloquence, and under his spell the city was gripped by a wave of hysteria. In the name of a rigid, harsh morality he inveighed against the

Poet Poliziano with Lorenzo de Medici's son Piero, from Ghirlandaio's fresco cycle in the Sassetti Chapel, Florence.

corruption engendered by luxury, laying the responsibility at the door of the traditional masters of Florence. The city was split into two irreconcilable
factions. Friends of the day before passed one another with glances charged with hatred. The Friar
believed himself inspired by God, and so affirmed.
He accused the Magnificent of the pride he bore within
himself, intending to humiliate him. Savonarola was
really a foreigner in Florence. He was from Ferrara,
and he seemed to take special satisfaction in denounc-
ing the vices of a city to whose history he was alien,
a city that had paid little attention to him when he
had visited it for the first time. His sermons had bored
his listeners, and the church where he preached had
been empty. Now, having achieved popularity, he
was bent upon despoiling the city of the brilliance
conferred upon it by the splendors and pleasures of
the Medici rule. He wanted to see Florence in the
garb of a penitent. His speeches had the irresistible
power of all reckless demagoguery. Women screamed
and wept as they listened to him. Men shivered at the
threat of eternal punishment. Fantastic stories were
told of conversions and renunciations of the world as
the result of his spellbinding eloquence. The excited
children, whipped up and organized under his impassioned guidance, staged mass demonstrations to
purify the city, and bonfires were lighted into which
lutes, paintings, books, brocades, and jewels were
thrown. In the pulpit Girolamo Savonarola seemed
one of the wrathful prophets of the Old Testament,
possessed of a holy fury.

Much the same thing happened in the Vespucci family as in the others of Florence. Although Giorgio Antonio and Guido Antonio continued as partners in the milling enterprise of Ognissanti, and Guido Antonio was working for his brother's advancement in his ecclesiastical career, they were divided on the matter of Savonarola. Giorgio Antonio, like the others closest to the Popolano, supported the Friar. In this he was not blindly following Lorenzo di Pier Francesco's lead; he had a deep-rooted aversion to dictatorship. Guido Antonio, on the other hand, was on the side of the Magnificent.

When the threat of a civil war engendered by the Friar's preachings began to loom darkly on the horizon, leading citizens whose aim was to maintain peace and harmony decided to take steps. Five of the most eminent, among them Guido Antonio, went to San Marco to effect a conciliation. A conversation between Savonarola and the Magnificent might bridge the gap. After all, Cosimo de' Medici had been the patron of the convent; he had rebuilt it at his own expense, and the first act of a new superior was to pay a visit of respect to the Medici. In moments of leisure the Medici were in the habit of visiting the convent, strolling about the gardens, and talking with the friars. Savonarola failed to carry on the tradition. When he was elected superior, he refused to go to the house of the Magnificent. When Lorenzo called at the convent, he refused to come down to the garden to converse with him. It was a situation that called for drastic measures, so the five Florentines

went to the convent and knocked at the Friar's cell.
He did not give them a chance to say what they had
come to say. "You have come to tell me," he said
before they could open their mouths, "that you have
come here on your own initiative. You lie. You are
here because Lorenzo has sent you here. Go back
to him. Tell him to comply with the will of God. Tell
him he will go and I will remain here in Florence to
purify it!"[1] Throughout Savonarola's preaching ran
one persistent note: every word was directed against
Lorenzo the Magnificent.

Botticelli, who grasped the subtleties of painting
more clearly than those of politics, trembled at the
pictures of eternal punishment the Friar drew in his
sermons, and became his follower. Others, like the
Popolano, chuckled with satisfaction at the barrage
of stones landing on the glass house of his rival
cousin. The Popolano hoped that by embracing the
people's party he would come to power.

Amerigo was torn between the two parties, like an
outsider who has no desire to militate against one
side or the other. He lacked the political vocation. He
never aspired to be prior of the Signoria or gonfalonier,
much less a friar. To him the conflict seemed a struggle
between stoics and epicures. He had probably picked
up this terminology from Giorgio Antonio, and he
never forgot it. Savanarola demanded a life of peni-
tence, and Florence loved its pleasures. Amerigo was
neither an ascetic nor a slave of the flesh. Two politi-

1. P. Villari: *La Storia di Girolamo Savonarola*, Vol. 1, p. 139.

cal parties, basically very similar, arrayed themselves
around these two moral attitudes, which seem two
pretexts rather than two philosophies. What it boiled
down to was who would go to the stake or into exile.
Amerigo showed no inclination to follow either Guido
Antonio or Giorgio Antonio.

The end of the affair, which reached its denoue-
ment after Amerigo had left Florence, is well known.
Savonarola, enthroned in Florence, challenged not
only the Medici, but also the Pope. From the theme
of Florence's corruption, he went on to that of Rome's
and just as he had refused to talk with the Magnificent, he refused to talk with Sixtus IV. The Pontiff
sent for him, almost humbly, and the Friar refused to
take one step toward Rome. Giorgio Antonio entered
the Convent of San Marco, and his little lamp of learning shone wanly amid the licking flames of the bonfire. Guido Antonio became the leader of the
anti-Savonarola party, which finally sent the friar to
the stake. The only winners were the Popolano Medici.
Toward the end of the conflict the Magnificent died,
and it was not difficult to toss the oligarchs out of
Florence and set the Popolani in their seats.

Amerigo saw only the gathering of the storm, while
it was still possible to meet friends and discuss matters that had nothing to do with politics. Even those
who had caught the faction fever still sought moments of repose in the company of the learned.
Among Giorgio Antonio's friends, all of them admirers of Toscanelli, the theme of the discoveries was as
fascinating as to the Pisans, but in Florence it was

raised to an imaginative level on which the poets moved freely.

Nobody had followed the voyage of Bartholomeu Dias along the Cape of Good Hope with more interest than Poliziano. He wrote a letter to the King of Portugal, telling him that the hour had come for His Majesty, the sponsor of the voyage, to allow his fame to be made immortal. He requested the King to send him full information on all that the navigators of his kingdom had accomplished: he would put it down in Latin, the language of eternity. The King of Portugal ordered Poliziano's request attended to at once. If death had not come to the poet shortly afterward, he would have stood as one of the first chroniclers of the era of discovery.[2]

Poliziano's request and the King's response were the recognition of a fact nobody disputed. The setting down of an event in the letters of Florence established its place in history. A discovery that was not published in Florence was not a discovery in the fifteenth century. Florence made it official, gave it universality. Poliziano's request to the King implied all this, but there was no false pride or vanity in it. It was a fact that everybody accepted, the Portuguese King first of all.

All Toscanelli's admirers were as keenly interested as Poliziano. His letter to the King of Portugal may very well have been the outcome of a conversation

2. The letters between Poliziano and the King of Portugal appear in his *Opera Omnia*, published in Venice, Epistolœ, L. X, Nos. 1 and 2.

among the group. Cristoforo Landino wrote various
dialogues about a feigned meeting that had taken
place in the Convent of the Camaldolites. The theme
under consideration was the true nobility of man.
Who were the participants? Leon Battista Alberti,
Marsilio Ficino, Agnolo Poliziano, Giorgio Antonio
Vespucci, and Landino himself - that is to say, the
followers of Toscanelli, who were always together.
They were linked by the bonds of intellectual interest, Greek, philosophy, the question of the true nature of man, astronomy, geography, and the reports
of the new voyages.

The dialogue on the subject of the discoveries was
not included, but it is evident that the theme was
present in their minds. Nor did they all approach it
in the same way, as can be plainly seen from their
works. Poliziano considered it from the point of view
of the chronicler, the historian. His aim was to set
down the relation of the important events of his day.
It was his desire to put into Latin the Portuguese
voyages, as he had done earlier with the Pazzi conspiracy. Giorgio Antonio's interest, on the other hand,
was in the scientific and philosophic aspects. He
was eager to know whether the theories of Toscanelli
coincided with the dicta of the philosophers, whether
the two great figures of antiquity, Aristotle and Plato,
would acquire or lose luster as the far-faring ships
tore aside the veils of the earth.

Giorgio Antonio's idol was Plato. Ficino had consulted him on his translation of the *Dialogues*, and
had dedicated to him the edition brought out in

Pages 198-199: *A woodcut of Savonarola in his cell, from his* Della
semplivita della vita Christiana, *1496.*

Venice. According to Plato, of all the feats of legendary Athens none could compare with that of having destroyed a haughty power which, coming from far off in the Atlantic, had invaded part of Europe and Asia. These were the armies of the isle of Atlantis.

"There was an island," Plato says, "beyond the passage known as the Pillars of Hercules. This island (Atlantis) was larger than Libya and than Asia. The travelers of those times could cross to it, and from it to others, and reach the continent lying on the opposite shore of this sea... On the hither side of the strait there was only a narrow entrance... On the farther, this real ocean and the land surrounding it, which could truly be called a continent..." A race of bold warriors sprang up in Atlantis, hoping to extend their power beyond the sea. They conquered Libya to the frontiers of Egypt, and Europe to the Tyrrhenian Sea. Only the Greeks were able to withstand their onslaughts. But disaster overtook them. The Atlantic, which had borne the green island on its waters, shook off its burden, and Atlantis disappeared. Where it was fabled to have been, all that remained was roiled waters, the Sargasso Sea. Centuries had elapsed since then. Would the waters have carried away the mud churned up by the seaquake? Could this rippling surface now be crossed again? Toscanelli felt sure that it could.

Aristotle, for his part, presented different points of view which were no less persuasive. In the first place, he held the earth to be spherical. He scoffed at Homer's idea that it had the shape of a disk. But it was a small sphere. Those who had studied its size gauged it to have a circumference of 400,000 stadia. The antipodes, said he, existed. Possibly the distance from the Pillars of Hercules to India was not so great as was thought. The center of the universe was in the earth. Man had already voyaged to all the habitable parts of the earth.

Giorgio Antonio had to take these texts into account, but, in addition, he venerated the memory of Archbishop Antonino, whom he had had included as a member of the family in the fresco of Ognissanti. A large part of the Archbishop's papers were in his possession. So supreme was the authority of Antonino, so great his fame, so outstanding his virtue, that the Church canonized him. He, too, had been a friend of Toscanelli's; he had concerned himself with the same problems. Pursuing the idea of the earth's spherical form, he concluded that the earth could be divided into eight parts, four of water and four of land. In addition to the three known parts of the earth–Europe, Asia, and Africa–there remained another, a fourth continent to be discovered. This was the theory put forward by St. Isidore of Seville. St. Antonino repeated it in these words, recognizing the existence of the antipodes: *"Extra tres partes orbis, quarta est pars trans Oceanum interiorem in media Zona terræ posita, quæ solis ardoribus nobis incognita est: in cujus finibus Antipodes fabulose habitare dicuntur."*[3]

---

3. Quoted by Uzielli- *"Le Quatriène Continent avant la découverte de l'Amérique"* (*Toscanelli*, January 1893).

All this scientific interest was connected with the discovery and translation of Ptolemy. Claudius Ptolemæus of Alexandria, of whom we know only that he lived sometime between the years A.D. 127 and 151, summed up in his *Geography* and *Astronomy* the learning of the Greeks in those fields. His books disappeared from the memory of Europe during the Middle Ages. They were preserved, however, by the Arabs. A translation from Arabic into Latin, made in the twelfth century by Gherardo di Cremona, was not published until 1515, when it appeared without the name of the author. But another translation, made from the Greek in 1451, was published around 1462, perhaps in Florence. Ptolemy's point of departure was his first-hand observation of distances in the Mediterranean, with which he was familiar. As soon as he departed from those waters, his calculations rested on the contradictory reports of travelers. His errors, in the light of our knowledge today, were enormous. But at that time they were a stimulus to adventure; they made it more possible. A longing to know, to travel, to explore the seas, to discover, sprang up, one of the characteristics of the Renaissance. In Florence no discussion of such matters failed to go back to Ptolemy, as will be clearly seen in Amerigo's letters.

Florence produced no Columbus who should say: I will set out for the Sargasso Sea to find out if what Toscanelli says is true. The glory of daring to set out on this journey, which after Columbus was within the reach of every navigator, belongs to him.

But the Florentines possessed a series of facts on
which to base their talks and reflections which put
them beyond the realm of mere academic speculation. First, there was the *Book* of Marco Polo, which
stripped the mists of legend from the concept of
the kingdoms of the Orient. Marco Polo had begun
his career as a merchant. His travels had had a commercial objective, and the provinces he visited were
an extension of those already known to the
Florentines through the spice trade. The voyages
of Bartholomeu Dias (1487) and Vasco da Gama
(1497-1501) combined the discovery of a solution
to an economic problem with a revision of existing
scientific ideas. They shed light on a series of doubts
concerning the austral regions and the inhabited
portions of the earth which the geographers had
been arguing about since ancient times. The travels of Benedetto Dei provided abundant information concerning the routes to the interior of Africa
and Asia.

Amerigo listened, asked questions, and engraved
these lessons on his memory. But his first duty was
to look after the Popolano's business interests. He
attended to the correspondence with Spain, listened
to appeals of every sort. Among his letters there is
one that will serve as an example. It is signed
"Giovanni de Lorenzo," who may have been
Lorenzo's son, the Cardinal later to become Leo X:

*Amerigo: I would ask you to give the bearer, who is
Matteo, servant of the nuns of Ripoll, all the clothes
you can, and the nicest you have. I shall be eternally*

*grateful to you for this. I trust that you will not fail
me, for you would deprive them of a spiritual comfort. May Christ keep you.*

Giorgio Antonio, who, it would seem, also had to
look after the Popolano's affairs, was kept as busy
as Amerigo and was involved, like everyone else, in
a series of petty problems known to us only through
ambiguous allusions. He wrote to Amerigo on behalf of one Piero, who was in jail and for whom
some German friends of his had interceded. In connection with some gambling problem he said: "As
for the cloth and the gambling money, Filippo in
person will tell you about it; I shall try to do what is
expected of me and to get myself and the others out
of it, thus stopping the mouths of gossipers."

As to the state of affairs in Seville, there is a letter,
which must be from one of the Popolano's employees, alluding to Donato Nicolini, with whom Amerigo
had gone over the Spanish accounts. The conclusion of the letter seems to indicate that Amerigo now
enjoyed a measure of independence:

*A week ago we received your letter, together with a
package of those written us from Seville by Donato
Nicolini. There is nothing of which you are not already informed. From a letter of the aforesaid Donato
we have learned that he has put aboard a ship belonging to Iñigo de Sajonia, in Cádiz, thirty tons of
wax and a mule meant for Lorenzo di Pier Francesco
de' Medici, to be unloaded at the port of Pisa and con-
signed to Piero de' Medici and Company. I have no
doubt you have already had notice of this. I leave ev-*

erything in your hands, as though it were your own
merchandise. Please God that everything reaches its
destination safely. If you do not receive what is due
you on these transactions, let us know so that we can
figure the commission that should be paid you.[4]

In the course of these business developments
something of transcendent importance in Amerigo's
life was about to happen: he was going to Seville
for good. But before he leaves Florence there is one
more aspect of his life we should examine.

What of Amerigo's love life? Certainly he never
established a home of his own in Florence. Many of
his old comrades were now married. For Giorgio
Antonio the problem was clear-cut: a man either
married or took vows. It was not that he was shocked
by the illicit affairs that everyone took as a matter of
course, but that he considered the family the cornerstone of society. Among the exercises he had
dictated to Amerigo was the following:

Even though I have been unjustly exiled from my
country, where men of virtue are held in no esteem,
and where those who by night go from house to house
committing felonies receive little punishment, at least
I married a noble maiden, and thus all my children
and descendants will marry persons of good family,
even though today I must sell all my goods and leave
them without fortune.

Whatever the reason, of the members of that family which Mona Lisa ruled with her rod of iron, Anto-

4. A.S.F., M.A.P., F. LXVIII, c. 280.

nio alone founded a legitimate family. Bernardo and Girolamo left no descendants. Amerigo built a clandestine nest and had one daughter. His intimate friends knew this. Juan Tosiña wrote to him from Spain:

Tell me how your daughter and her mother are, and that woman called Francesca. Give them all a thousand regards. I should like to know if Lisandra is well. Not that I love her, but I wonder if she is dead or alive. She has a poor opinion of me, and I a worse one of her... Give my greetings to all those of Lorenzo's household, and especially to Master Giacomo, the shoemaker...[5]

Judging from the letters of Amerigo's friends, his natural daughter would seem, to have been the fruit of some romantic attachment formed in nocturnal philanderings in the lower quarters of Florence. Amerigo's brigade did not move in the upper circles of Florentine society. We do not even know the name of this consequence of his passing attachment; we know only that it was a daughter. Heaven only knows what arrangements he made for mother and daughter when he left Florence. The social recognition and responsibility of a legitimate family did not bind him to his native city.

These lines from a letter written from Rome by Jacopo di Dino shed further light on this secret aspect of Amerigo's life:

Dear brother and comrade: I believe, or, rather, I am sure you were surprised that I should leave with-

5. A.S.F., M.A.P., F. LXVIII, c. 650.

out telling you good-by, and you have probably cen-
sured me, blaming me for something that really does
not exist... I swear to you that when I did what I did,
I suffered as I have not suffered this whole year. If you
don't want to believe me, just remember that by not
coming to see you I had to leave without the dogs, and
you know how much I want them... The truth is that I
received an urgent call, and I rushed to say good-by
to you and Giovanni, but I was not able to. And if it
were not for the fact that I am so in love with
Francesca–which is mainly your fault, but in part
because of her charms–I would not have ventured out
on that dark street where strong men feel fear. I com-
mend my four dogs to you. And you, commend me to
your wife, and to Francesca... May Christ keep you... [6]

6. A.S.F., M.A.P., F. LXVIII, c. 245.

LÁM.ª XIII. T. III.

Dª. ISABEL LA CATÓLICA,
PRIMERA REYNA DE CASTILLA, ARAGON Y LAS INDIAS,
Y D. FERNANDO V. EL CATÓLICO,
REY DE ARAGON Y LAS DOS SICILIAS: EM-
PEZÁRON Á REYNAR EN 1474; MURIÓ LA
REYNA EN 1504, Y EL REY EN 1516.

XI

SEVILLE
(1492-1496)

1492, the year the Spaniards, or, to be more exact,
the Castilians, went mad. From the time of its ob-
scure medieval origins, Castile had been a nation on
the march. The villages of Old Castile kept pushing
southward, and for centuries its history was made
by the frontier. The line kept edging forward, dis-
lodging the Moors from the center, pushing them
toward the periphery. Castile advanced under the
sign of the Cross. In 1491 final victory was in sight.
All that remained to the Moors was the Kingdom of
Granada, and its fall was as certain as that of a ripe
fruit. In November of that year the capitulation articles were drawn up, allowing a term of sixty days
for complete surrender. During the final phase the
conquerors gave proof of their generosity of spirit.
After all, these frontier experiences had engendered
mutual understanding and respect. Fighting did not
preclude love. The two peoples flew different flags,
but there was intercourse between them. By the terms
of the capitulation, the inhabitants of Granada were
allowed to keep the mosques of their faith, and no
ban was put on their dress, their language, or their
traditional customs. King Abdallah might reign in
the Alpujarras as a vassal of the Crown of Castile.

Queen Isabella and King Ferdinand, the Catholic monarchs.

The victors wanted to make their triumph less bitter for the vanquished, but it was impossible for them to hide their happiness. The term of sixty days was shortened, and surrender took place on January 2, 1492.

Fundamentally, it was Isabella's victory. She represented Castile. The will to conquer had been hers. And she was an enchanting Queen, a Queen on horseback. Not that Ferdinand was a nonentity. Far from it, he was a great King. In the motto of the day–*Tanto monta, monta tanto, Isabel como Fernando*–no slur was implied on Fernando. He was not a king consort, but the living image of Aragón. In the fact of Isabella's being his equal lay her greatness.

On the day of surrender Ferdinand and Isabella, or, better, Isabella and Ferdinand, rode out of their camp in Santa Fe toward Granada at the head of a splendid procession. King Boabdil came to meet them with his knights. He was carrying the keys of the city. He kissed them and said to King Ferdinand: "Sire, these are the keys of your Alhambra and city. Take them."

Ferdinand accepted the keys and banded them to Isabella: "Your Majesty," he said, "here you have the keys of your city of Granada. Appoint its warden."

Isabella bowed her head respectfully and said: "It all belongs to Your Majesty." Then, turning to Prince Juan: "Take these keys of your city and Alhambra and in your father's name appoint the warden Granada is to have."

King Boabdil wheeled and rode off down the "Hill of Tears." He turned back for a glance at his lost kingdom, and his heart broke. His mother, stouter-hearted than he, said to him: "You do well to grieve like a woman for what you could not defend like a man." But she was unjust; Granada was doomed. The only unknown factor had been the date, which was resolved on that day.

Cardinal Mendoza rode forward with the royal guard. On the Torre de la Vela of the Alhambra he placed a great cross of silver, and below it he unfurled the banner of Santiago de Compostela and the standards of Castile and León.

Wherever there was a Spaniard anywhere in Europe, the course of the war had been followed with passionate interest. The shouts of jubilation almost drowned out the *Te Deums*. Guido Antonio in Rome described the celebrations in the Vatican. Luca Landucci, who kept a day-by-day record of events in Florence, wrote: "On the fifth day of January of 1491 (1492) the Spaniards living here in Florence lighted bonfires and held great celebrations because they had received word that their King of Spain had taken Granada, and this news did not so much serve the glory and advantage of that King as the advantage and glory of us and of all Christians and the body of the Holy Church. Good and true men held it to be a victory for the faith of Christ, and the beginning of the conquest of the infidels at the Levant and of Jerusalem."

Amerigo had left Florence for Spain on the eve of this victory. He joined Donato Nicolini in Seville.

On January 30 he wrote the Popolano a letter signed
by both:

*As it is probable that in a short time one of the two
of us will be going to Florence, he can better inform
you in person. It is hard to explain things fully by
letter... For the time being, it is impossible to do anything in the matter of the alum, as for some time we
have heard of no ship sailing from Cádiz that was
not carrying a full cargo. We regret this, but we are
looking out for your interests. Take comfort in the
thought that we shall do all we can.*

*From Donato the Elder, who wrote you from
Barcelona, you will have learned of the great good
fortune that has come to His Royal Highness, this Most
Serene Majesty. It is evident that Almighty God has
lent him aid to make himself master of the world.
There is no need for us to give you details. May God
grant the King long years of life, and may we enjoy
them with him. There is no further news. May Christ
keep you. Don't forget to let us know about the casket
and the gold braid Amerigo left with you and com-
mended to you...*[1]

On their return to Santa Fe, Their Catholic Majesties found themselves the rulers of a kingdom that
now seemed to have reached the goal it had been
pursuing for centuries. This success and glory gave
them the character of rulers predestined to carry out
a long-cherished historic mission. They had formed
the habit of pushing forward, but now they did not

1. Published by Bandini, op. cit., p. 24

see clearly how to go on. It was the psychological moment to bring new undertakings to their attention. The wave of popular feeling that, for a long time, had been rising against the Jews had now gathered enough head to bring about the edict of their expulsion. The tens of thousands of Jews living in Seville and the cities of Castile were given a term of three months in which to leave Spain. And "they exchanged a house for a donkey, or a vineyard for a piece of cloth, for they could take with them neither gold nor silver."

Another visionary who turned up in Santa Fe was Christopher Columbus. What he proposed was a continuation of the Castilian drive. Why not move the frontier beyond the Atlantic, to Asia? It was a fantastic idea. Everyone with his feet on the ground had pooh-poohed the idea, but it was the time of the harebrained. As we have already observed, the Spaniards, including the Queen, had been seized by collective madness. Even Don Ferdinand, to whom normally two and two made four, had caught the contagion. On the 31st day of March the edict expelling the Jews was signed, and in April the articles between Columbus and the Catholic monarchs were drawn up.

The discovery of America was in part an Italian enterprise. Columbus's one asset was his faith, and boldness was his bondsman. At that moment he emanated self-assurance. The sovereigns had consented to his proposals, but what they offered him was less than half the cost of three caravels. They did not have even that. Resplendent monarchs they were, magnificent, but without a penny. It is said that the Queen cozened Don Ferdinand with these words: "I don't want you to risk the resources of your kingdom of Aragón. I will undertake this as an enterprise of my crown of Castile, and if my funds fall short, I shall cover the expenses by pawning my jewels." This, of course, was a manner of speaking. Ferdinand understood her perfectly, for his whole universe was based on who could fool whom. Castile did not have a penny to bless itself with. And to make matters worse, it had expelled the Jews, who were the moneylenders. So Columbus and Isabella had to see where they could raise the money for three tuppenny-ha'penny caravels, three little craft of planks and rags.

Columbus managed to scrape up his share from the Italians. The Genoese and Gianetto Berardi believed in him, and advanced the money. "He was aided," writes Fray Antonio de Aspa, "by three Genoese merchants, one of them called Jacobo de Negro, who had a high rating in Seville at the time, another called Capatel, who lived in Jérez, and the other, Luis Dorio, who resided in Cádiz." Father Antonio knew only about the Genoese; but Gianetto Berardi gambled 180,000 maravedís on the venture.This sum may be considered an earnest of faith resting on the conversations that undoubtedly took place among Berardi, Amerigo, and Columbus, presided over by the memory of Toscanelli. Of far greater value than the 180.000 maravedís was the advance Berardi made to Columbus of his friendship, a long-term friendship, for life, as was that of Amerigo.

The Queen's share was provided by a loan made to her by Luis de Santángel and Francesco Pinello. Pinello was a Genoese. Santángel, of Jewish origin, was a friend and associate of Pinello and was linked to the Genoese merchants by family tradition. His father was a farmer of the tolls and customs to which the Genoese in Valencia were subject, and on his death his son succeeded him in this post.[2]

It was decided that the expedition should set out from Palos de Moguer. Columbus went there to arrange for the ships, crew, and supplies. Though a small port, Palos was already important in the Guinea trade. Moreover, the main center of the Italians, the people with the money, was Seville, not far distant from Palos and, after Madrid, the second city in Spain. Columbus shuttled back and forth between Palos and Seville during the months needed to collect funds and fit out the expedition. During this period his friendship with the Italians grew—or if not friendship, at any rate, business associations.

The ships that had been chartered were three, and their complement was ninety men. One was the *Santa María*, owned and commanded by Juan de la Cosa; another *La Pinta*, under the command of Martín Alonso Pinzón; and the third the *Santa Clara*, which

2. Concerning this detail, see *Il Finanziamento del primo viaggio e l'opera dei capitalisti italiani in Spagna* by Rinaldo Caddeo in appendix to the Life of Columbus by Fernando Colombo (*supra cit.*).

Pages 216-217: *The* Niña, *the* Santa María *and the* Pinta.

came to be called *Niña*, whose captain was Vicente Yáñez Pinzón. Gianetto Berardi and Amerigo Vespucci were associated with all these men and became their friends.

Amerigo, who had come to Seville in part to look after the affairs of the Popolano and in part to engage in trade independently, now found that the first important decision confronting him involved a journey across a sea that had not been crossed since the fabled days of Atlantis.

The streets of Seville were such a rumor-factory, the shape of things unseen so filled the air, that Columbus's projects were threshed out in the back rooms of Italian business agents rather than in public.

The celebrations over the fall of Granada had hardly ended before the roads of Spain became the scene of the exodus of the Jews, making their way to the sea with cries and lamentations. Stripped of all they had once possessed, they clogged the gates of the cities, waiting to take ship. Some had not sold their homes, but carried the keys with them. It was hard to think that they would not return. Times would change, the less pessimistic thought.

Columbus had to talk a great deal to convince a very few. He had been denied the capacity for frank, easygoing, straightforward friendship. One thing was in his favor: it was no great feat to persuade ninety Spaniards to sit in on a game with death. Spaniards are given to acting without thinking, without reckoning the costs; the longer the odds, the better they like it. As between the lottery and a sound, low-return investment they will always choose the lottery. And those ninety visionaries of Palos who set out on the first journey would later become legion under the Pied Piper spell of men who could not be compared to Columbus.

The caravels weighed anchor.

Seven long months elapsed. In their office Gianetto and Amerigo must have asked themselves over and over: "Will he come back? Won't he come back?" If Columbus had ventured one million maravedís in the affair, a fifth of this million had been put up by Berardi on the security of Amerigo, who knew more than he about Toscanelli's theories. The roulette wheel had never spun so long. It was not that Gianetto was a miser; on the contrary, he was of generous spirit and always willing to give a helping hand. But any way you looked at it, the problem presented frightening aspects. What if they had been shipwrecked? Could they chart their course? Was there really a sea of mud between Spain and Asia?

No Holy Week in Seville ever had such a happy ending as that of 1493. The Genoese had returned! Many had forgotten all about him. But not the Italians. He entered Seville on Palm Sunday with ten live Indians, red and green parrots, and nuggets of gold. He had been to distant islands, lying, so he said, in the Sea of Japan, of Cipango–of India–and in proof there were the ten Indians. He paraded the streets like the manager of a circus, and he was an Admiral.

He had returned as he had set out, by the port of Palos, after calling at Lisbon, where he had been forced to put in by a storm. In Palos, or at the nearby Convent of La Rábida, he had laid to for a week or so to get himself in shape and make a fitting entrance. From the moment they landed, there had been a breach between him and Martín Alonso Pinzón, the captain of the *Pinta*. Some said that Pinzón took refuge in a monastery because he was afraid of Columbus; others, because he felt he had been unfairly treated. At any rate, he died in a few days. Columbus was still a difficult person. The tales spread by the sailors aroused the curiosity of all, and the Admiral's appearance was eagerly awaited. Everybody wanted to see the Indians. There they were, naked, with their glossy cinnamon-colored skin, not yellow as was said of those of Cipango. It was hard to say which was the greater attraction, the Indians or the parrots. People gathered all along the Admiral's route, pouring out of inns and taverns. In Seville, whither the festivities of Holy Week had brought a larger crowd than a fair, the spectacle was truly imposing.

A love of color was characteristic of the period. All the effort Columbus put into making his show as brilliant as possible was hardly enough to compete with reality. Nobles, knights, rich burghers, and guild masters decked themselves out in velvet, brocade, silks, fur, lace, with a ring on every finger, necklaces, earrings. Then there was the infinite variety of religious habits, and on high festival days the famous chasubles, the bishops' vestments, the robes of the Virgins who were carried in the processions. This was common throughout Europe. And all this wealth of color descended to the folk and took on an even livelier hue among them. The simple peasants driving their donkeys loaded with baskets of olives or wineskins wore green and blue jackets, and red or yellow bandannas around their heads. Just like the parrots. The processions wound through the narrow streets, whose balconies were gay with hangings of velvet and brocade and displayed silken banners and tall silver crucifixes. They moved as on a tide of droning Latin prayers, lighted candles, liturgical pomp.

No flags, hangings, or standards were displayed for Columbus, but he did himself well. He took his place in the Gobelin with his exotic fauna, and his triumph gave him a superiority complex. His reddish hair, now going gray, shone about his high, proud forehead. No smile moved his tightly compressed lips. Bartolomé de Las Casas compared him to a Roman senator. The bewildered Indians and the parrots afforded the spectators food for noisy comments and the jokes the Andalusians love. The necklaces of gold lay motionless on the Indian flesh, and the sound of their bare feet on the cobblestones was as muted as the swish of velvet.

Never had Columbus seen brighter sun, more diaphanous light, greener trees than those of Andalusia on that Palm Sunday in the month of April 1493.

Point and counterpoint. The ten Indians had made a voyage of discovery to Europe. What they saw about them was a host of bearded men. And horses, dogs, pigs, cats, chickens, donkeys, cows, feathered animals that did not fly, men on horseback and men astride donkeys, men with their legs covered with hairless leather and men wearing skirts, and everyone covered up–not even the commonest women baring their breasts to the air. There were houses of stone, iron gratings, swords, men clad in iron, the smell of garlic, wine, sausages. Not a substance or a color or a sound did they recognize. They were given bread and onions, olives, chick-pea soup. And the delicious surprise of oranges. In the churches they saw strange medicine men performing their rites amidst clouds of perfumed smoke. They heard such a wealth of words as they had never dreamed of. Hunger made them eat food their bowels rejected. They shuddered as the cold tongue of a sword licked their flesh. It was the chill of a wild moon and fear. The sea crossing in the caravels had taught them certain things, but it was as nothing compared with the flood of new experiences that impinged on their five senses. They were the first American tourists to Europe.

The Indians were lodged close by the Arch of the Images. Bartolomé de Las Casas, a boy at the time, and one of the most avid spectators, saw them. "I saw them then in Seville," he wrote later. Those who can fathom the inner recesses of the heart can try to figure out what went on in the souls–if they had souls–of those poor devils; or in the senses-and these they had, and keen–of those innocents. Their tongues being useless, they were all eyes. Until a few months before, their world, like their fathers' and their fa-

thers' fathers', had been the rustling trees, the restless sea, the fiery sun, the coconut-fleshed moon. A
strange man had come out of the sea, had taken
them prisoner, had put them in huge ships with sails
of cloth, which danced on the waves of the sea.
They ran into the worst storm the sailors had ever
seen, and before they reached the shores of Portugal, the Atlantic was like the Caribbean in the hurricane season. The Indians had never experienced a
hurricane on the high seas. The pitching of the ships
made them sick unto death. And when they had
come through that, Columbus handled them like an
animal-trainer. The world seemed to have turned
into a hand with thousands of fingers, all eager to
touch their flesh, eyes examining their teeth or scru-
tinizing their rears for a tail that was not there. Even
in the still of the night they hardly dared talk to one
another. Their only escape, their only flight, was to
huddle together, to touch each other as though they
formed a single cluster of human flesh. The only
moment of relief was when sleep overpowered them.
And even then what nightmares must have ridden
them!

The King and Queen were in Barcelona, and it
was there that Columbus had to go. It was a long
trip. Not all the Indians were strong enough to make
the journey. Columbus chose the sturdiest six, leaving the others in Berardi's care. Berardi's house,
which was where Amerigo also lived, became a de-
pot for this human flesh of the Antilles. This was the
only group of the new visitors which enjoyed a

measure of repose, and Berardi and Amerigo were able to observe them at leisure. It is curious to note that in matters of trust Columbus preferred the Florentines to the Genoese.

Amerigo was now in business for himself. A letter of his addressed to Corradolo Stanza (December 1492), in the archives of Mantua, is signed: "Ser Amerigho Vespucci, Florentine merchant, Sybilia."[3] He was, in fact, in partnership with Berardi. And from the very first moment it fell to them to look after many of Columbus's affairs—Berardi as the person who had put up money for the first voyage, and as head of the establishment, Amerigo as his partner, and as a man of greater intellectual preparation.

Columbus trusted few people. His first letter was to Luis de Santángel, who had been the promoter of the expedition. He stayed with the friars of the Monastery in La Rábida for less than a week. When he reached Seville he must have spent long hours in Berardi's house talking of the voyage he had just completed and of his future plans. Berardi was like his partner. Columbus had already received a communication from the monarchs in which they addressed him as "Admiral of the Ocean Sea and Viceroy and Governor of the islands that have been discovered in the Indies." And they summoned him to court: "It is our wish that your coming should be soon, therefore, for our service, that you make all

3. Reproduced in facsimile in R. Levillier: *El Nuevo Mundo*, p. 63.

the haste you can in your coming." And they spoke of a second expedition: "See if anything can be arranged in Seville." From then on, Seville was to be the central office of the voyages. Amerigo was at the very heart of all that was taking place and of Columbus's private affairs and interests.

The Europeans who were most stirred by the discovery were the Spaniards and the Italians. Destiny had joined their fortunes. The Portuguese on this occasion had reacted somewhat slowly. Nobody took the trouble at first to relay the news to France, England, Germany, Hungary, Poland, or the lands of the Sultan. Through Columbus's letter to Santángel, the news reached the Genoese and Santángel's associate, Pinello, as soon as it did the King and Queen. The other letter Columbus wrote was to Gabriel Sánchez, treasurer of Aragón. This letter appeared in print simultaneously in Barcelona and in Rome. Leandro Cosco made the translation into Latin of the version that appeared in Rome in the very year 1493. It went through four editions.

The news was swiftly received in Milan by the ambassador of the Duke of Ferrara. It had been sent to him from Spain by his brother, Anibal de Zennaro. "In the past month of August," Anibal wrote, "Their Majesties, the sovereigns, in response to the petitions of one by the name of Colomba, acceded to his request to be allowed to fit out four caravels and sail westward on the ocean sea in a straight line until he should reach the east, inasmuch as, the earth being round, he would perforce by so voyaging come to the eastern part, and so it was." From Milan, Giacomo de Trotti transmitted the tale to Ercole d'Este.

In Genoa the Doge, Battista Fregoso, recorded the news in the notes he kept on memorable happenings.

But the person who showed the keenest interest in bringing the news to the ears of Rome was Don Ferdinand the Catholic. Even more than the Queen–and in this he was already showing the zeal with which he defended the interests of Spain–he realized that by the discovery of these islands, which Columbus had taken possession of in the name of Their Catholic Majesties, the question of Portugal's claims would arise again. It was urgent to secure the sanction of the Pope for these new conquests. Rodrigo Boria or Borgia, Alexander VI, was a Spaniard, born in Xátiva, Valencia, a man of the world, and a friend of the King. Another Spaniard, Cardinal Bernardino de Carvajal, had been instrumental in his election. It was to Carvajal that Ferdinand entrusted the securing of the necessary bulls. In the month of May–that is to say, barely two months after Columbus's return–the first two bulls were issued. And immediately afterwards the demarcation along "the line that you say should be specified in the Pope's bull," as Ferdinand wrote to Columbus. Like Ferdinand, Columbus knew that the question should be aired first in Rome. If there was one person who grasped the scope of Portugal's ambitions, it was Columbus. When he had had to put in at Lisbon on his return to Spain, he had been terrified at what the Portuguese might be plotting in those few hours.

The news was received in Florence in a letter to the Signoria. It must have come from Gianetto or Amerigo or Donato, who were in close touch with the Medici. The information contained in the letter is more nearly complete than that from other sources. The original text has never come to light, but its contents are known from the notes contained in the book of Tribaldo de' Rossi, to which he undoubtedly added touches of his own.

I recall (he says) that in the month of March 1493 a letter arrived for the Signoria telling how the King of Spain had sent certain young men out in some caravels to look for new lands. They had not been able to do it before for the King of Portugal. They sailed in three caravels, carrying provisions for three years. It is said that they sailed for twenty-three days until they came to a very large island, where no nation of men had ever reached before, inhabited by men as well as women, all naked, with only their private parts covered, who had never before seen Christians. They came out to meet them with sharp sticks tipped with porcupine quills instead of iron, for they had no knowledge of any kind of iron... The letter stated that there was gold in abundance, and a river whose bed is mixed with gold; that there are grains that they eat without bread, and cotton and pines and cypresses of great size, and rich spices. This seemed to all a wonderful thing. They say that the King of Spain gave a greater celebration for their re-

turn than for the capture of Granada. It is said by many there that a considerable number of ships will be dispatched again... They say that all those who sailed came back rich...[4]

As in Florence poetry followed geography as the night the day, Giuliano Deti quickly dashed off a poem: "This is the history of the discovery of the Canary Islands..."

Rossi's version of the letter received by the Signoria is a classic example of the transformation of fact into fable. Not all who set out with Columbus returned, and those who came back brought no other wealth than their tall tales, further heightened by Spanish hyperbole. Columbus said nothing in public. He was satisfied to display his Indians, his birds, his native jewelry, and let the spectators' imagination grow by what it fed on. The glitter of his eyes, blown bright by glory, seemed to say that anything was possible. Ten days were employed in the journey from Seville to Barcelona, ten days during which the gaping crowds parted to make way for him and then closed ranks, standing on tiptoe to catch yet another glance.

He made a triumphal entry into Barcelona. The streets were unable to hold the onlookers. The sovereigns awaited him seated on a dais and surrounded by the court. Columbus, at this moment, must have allowed himself a laugh—Las Casas mentions a "modest smile." It was the smile of self-satisfaction and embarrassment. Columbus fell to his knees before

4. T. de' Rossi: *Ricordanze* (*Delizie degli eruditi toscani,* Vol. XXIII).

the King and Queen; he kissed the royal bands. To use the metaphor of playing cards, Isabella was the queen of hearts, Ferdinand the king of clubs. They seated him at their side, and then the three rode through the streets on horseback. The Queen liked to have her subjects see her mounted. It was a great day for everybody. Coming on top of the conquest of Granada, this leap across the Atlantic to its opposite shore, to the Far East, was like a divine blessing. Without need of the Jews, the sovereigns could now find gold in other confines, extract it from mines far richer than those of Guinea. Columbus showed them his jewels.

When alone with them, Columbus threw aside caution and told them things he revealed to no one else. Especially to the Queen he gave secret information. But he warned both Isabella and Ferdinand against the ambitions of Portugal. His words carried authority. Everything he had said before, which no one had believed, had come true. The friars of Salamanca had said that it was impossible for him to reach the other side of the Atlantic, and here he was, back from the round trip. The next step would be to corroborate the accounts of Marco Polo. If the outlying islands of Japan had been reached, directly behind them would be the mainland, with its marble-bridged cities and its forests of cinnamon and logwood. All the exploits of the Venetian could now be duplicated by this easy route, without need to cross the vast steppes and dangerous uplands of Asia. The Queen's answer was undoubtedly yes, Ferdinand's, yes, no, maybe. In the last analysis, God was on their side. They conferred a coat of arms upon Columbus: a castle of gold on a field of vert, a lion rampant with two azure anchors. He was a grandee of grandees: his arms those of Castile and León, the realms of Isabella, and the emblems of the sea he had serenely mastered. Aragón, Ferdinand's patrimony, was not represented. The truth of the matter was that Spain was Castile and León; Aragón, whose outpost was the Kingdom of Naples, weighed less heavily in the balance. Yet it was Ferdinand rather than Isabella who had the concept of Spanish national sovereignty.

There was no time to lose on the second expedition. Lock the door on the seas and give Columbus the keys! Keep a close watch on the Portuguese and tie them short with the authority of the Pope! And utilize the Italians in Seville, call upon Pinello the Genoese and Berardi the Florentine. Pinello, as treasurer, would honor payments ordered by Columbus or Bishop Juan Rodríguez de Fonseca, royal representative for matters pertaining to the Indies. Berardi was in charge of matters bearing directly on the expedition, and along with him Amerigo. One of Berardi's first orders was to charter a ship of one hundred to two hundred tonnage and to supply 203,000 arrobas of sea biscuit.[5]

Bishop Fonseca was an important figure. Patriarch of the Indies, as he was called, he watched all that went on with his shrewd, suspicious glance, which had been sharpened by dealings with sinners, and

---

5. F. de Navarrete: *Colección diplomática*, II, Document XXV.

had the self-assurance that some acquire with the power of binding and loosening which Christ conferred on his vicars. He was a loud-voiced, rigorous man, untempered in his justice, and fundamentally devout. The meetings between him and Columbus were those of flint and steel–the sparks flew.

Columbus was the captain of the armada, Admiral, Viceroy, and "Don" Christopher Columbus. By virtue of the titles he had received, he had been transformed into a Spaniard. The justices of Aragón and Castile were ordered to provide lodgings for him wherever he arrived, with his five servants, and to supply him with pocket money. Seville was to be the financial center of operations, of official contacts. Bishop Fonseca was in Seville. But Columbus, Berardi, and Amerigo had to keep moving from Seville to Cádiz, to Málaga, to Palos, and to spend perhaps more of their time in Triana than in Seville proper. Triana, which lay across the Guadalquivir, was the sailors' quarter of Seville, the school where cabin boys and captains were trained by listening to old salts, hanging about the taverns, talking with the women who received and spread the inside stories of voyages, the tall tales, the sea chanteys. Seventeen ships were to sail on Columbus's second voyage.

"If you haven't the money," the sovereigns wrote to Pinello, "find it." Pinello had to pay cash on the barrelhead. The Holy Brotherhood was ordered to give him fifteen hundred gold ducats, but that was only a drop in the bucket of Columbus's demands. Pinello got a loan of five million maravedís from the

Duke of Medina-Sidonia, which was guaranteed by the gold and jewels the Crown had confiscated from the Jews.

Berardi was a kind of liaison officer between Columbus and the monarchs, and this was a great help to the Admiral. Ferdinand and Isabella approved his choice. They had known Berardi for a long time as a good and trustworthy person. They had issued him a safe-conduct seven years before in Córdoba, and another three years earlier in Seville. Moreover, he had the advantage, in the eyes of the Crown, of being in the habit of handling funds. The ship they had ordered him to fit out for Columbus was to be paid for only when it was turned over to the Admiral. And the monarchs were so satisfied with the way he handled the ship negotiations, and especially its provisioning, that they wrote a letter thanking him and asking him to continue to act as purchasing agent for the sea biscuit.[6]

It is fair to assume that from that time forward neither Berardi nor Amerigo had time for anything but looking after Columbus's needs. They could devote very little attention to the Popolano's interests. Four months went into the preparations for the voyage, and these preparations included talking with people, signing on the crew, chartering ships, arming them with cannon, supplying lances, swords, sea biscuit, wine, flour, oil, vinegar, and cheese. The object of this trip was not the discovery of new routes,

6. F. de Navarette: *Viajes*, Vol. III, p. 321.

but the establishment of a colony; so masons, carpenters, smiths, workmen, and farmers were needed, and tools and seeds. A church would have to be erected, and the first priests sent out. Pinello bought vestments for the priests, as well as altar, chalice, and all the liturgical objects required. The majority of the crew were Andalusians and Basques, but it also included three Genoese and one Venetian.

Many things were clear and straightforward, but others more difficult to discern could only be conjectured. The mystery had not been fully revealed. People asked one another where Columbus got his ideas, his information, and what it was he knew and did not tell, but whispered into the ear of the Queen, perhaps to his confessor, and probably to his fellow Italians, such as Gianetto Berardi and those who had lent him money. If they were advancing funds to him, he was not telling a cock-and-bull story. Asia must be within grasp. The Italians grew in importance. They had agents in Portugal as well as in Spain; they had voyaged to the East; they had information of all sorts; they had read books of science; and there was Columbus opening the horizon for Spain. The greatest source of information was the correspondence carried on by Italian merchants and ambassadors.

News in Italian flew from Portugal to Spain, from Spain to all the states of Italy.

The Queen of Hearts accepted the good news and Columbus's prophetic forecasts with mystical enthusiasm. Naturally, she enjoyed being in the Admiral's confidence and knowing his secrets. "By this post," she wrote him, "I am sending you a copy of the book you left me, and the delay has been caused by the fact that it had to be written secretly, so none of those who are here from Portugal, or anyone else, should know anything about it..."

The King of Clubs, guided by his subconscious craftiness, was careful not to take the Italian too much to his bosom, for he intended that the exploits he performed should be for the sole advantage of Spain.

On September 25, 1493 the fleet set sail from Cádiz. Gianetto Berardi received powers of attorney from Columbus. In a letter of the sovereigns to Bishop Fonseca, they informed him that Gianetto was going to discuss with him the sending out of the caravels "in the name of the Admiral of the aforesaid islands, for he has been so empowered by him."[7]

7. Ibid., p. 293, Document II.

Cover for the Latin version of Columbus' letter to King Ferdinand announcing the discovery, 1493.

Oceanica Classis

XII

ABSENCE AND PRESENCE
OF COLUMBUS
(1493-1498)

The activities of the house of Gianetto Berardi
and Amerigo Vespucci did not end with Columbus's
departure. The spark of discovery had touched off a
flame. Many longed to set out on voyages under
Spanish command. Seville was becoming the great
school, the Babel of adventurers it was throughout
the sixteenth century. And Gianetto's and Amerigo's
establishment was an important center of interest
and information, for Gianetto was handling the
Admiral's affairs.

Columbus was away from Spain for two years and
nine months. He moved about the islands of Cuba
and Hispaniola, sometimes discovering glowing Caribbean landscapes, at others running aground on the
reefs of his fellow Christians, whose hearts were hard-
ened against him. He governed his settlements in an
arbitrary, maladroit fashion. His soul was roweled by
complexes. The sovereigns had conferred on him the
title of Viceroy and Governor; therefore, according to
his logic, the colonists must obey his orders, and that
was all there was to it. Objectors, in his opinion, should
receive such condign punishment as having their noses
or ears cut off or being strung up. The colonists, on
the other hand, had a different idea. As Spaniards,

Columbus on his ship with an astrolabe in his hand.

they were accustomed to carrying their heads high and to putting their personal dignity above every other consideration–Spaniards who knew how to say no to a king of whom each felt himself the equal. The government of the settlers in the West Indies is one of the most illuminating chapters in history on the difficulty of ruling men.

As for the Indians, from Columbus's point of view the matter could not be more simple: they should be slaves. There was the gold mine of America. Did not everyone in Italy and Spain have slaves? Who that could afford it did not buy beautiful white slave girls? Was he not conquering in the Roman manner?

In no time the islands had become a hornets' nest. The ocean became a two-way lane of bickering, gossip, and complaints that blackened the name of Columbus in Spain and undermined his government. His dreams of the fortune to be made in slaves failed to come true. He began sending them as merchandise to be credited to his account by Gianetto Berardi, who was to turn them over to Bishop Fonseca for sale. At first there seemed to be no difficulties in the way. The monarchs were concerned only that this merchandise should bring as good a return as possible.[1] The Indians were an exotic product; they seemed docile–their ways were

---

1. On April 12 the sovereigns wrote to Bishop Fonseca: "With respect to what you wrote us about the Indians coming in the caravels, it seems to us that they could be sold better there in Andalusia than anywhere else. You should sell them as seems best to you." (Navarrete: *Colección diplomática*, p. 199.)

as yet unknown–and there was every reason to think they would fetch a good price. It had never crossed the mind of Columbus or of Ferdinand, Isabella, Berardi, or Fonseca that they did not have the right to do as they liked with their savages. Not five years before, King Ferdinand had sent Pope Innocent VIII a gift of one hundred Moors. The Pope had thanked him warmly and had shared them with cardinals and close friends. His Catholic Majesty had also sent his sister Juana thirty Moorish girls. But now an unforeseen doubt raised its head. Some confessor must have whispered it into the Queen's ear or insinuated it to the King. Or it may have been one of those sophists who love to spin new theories. It began to be said that those people Columbus was sending in, not being captives taken in a just war, could not be treated as slaves. War was a much better source of revenue than peaceful conquest. Columbus had not earned the right to enslave at sword's point. He had employed astuteness and craftiness, which create no juridical status.

The position taken by the monarchs must have caused a financial panic in the house of Berardi. They instructed Bishop Fonseca that there were to be no outright sales, but that he should work out some formula that would leave the door open until the problem had been examined in the light of the doctrines of the Church Fathers. If it turned out that the Indians could not be legally enslaved, then the sales would have to be canceled and the Indians returned to their native land. It would be a slow business. Before the theologians and the experts in canon law could reach a decision, they needed to hear Columbus's allegations.[2] They asked him for them. The Admiral's point of view must have caused dismay. It was his opinion that to take slaves was a thing that redounded to the prestige of the sovereigns, and he based his opinion on a maxim of universal history. "We would gain great credit," Don Christopher reasoned, "if it is seen that we take them and make them captives." And discussing the matter of securing funds to provide livestock for the colony, he outlined with complete clarity a plan that basically consisted in exchanging men for animals: "They could be paid for in these cannibal slaves, beings strong and capable and well made and of good understanding, who, once cured of that barbarous practice, will, we believe, make better slaves than any others."

In a debate of this sort, opposing arguments served only to fatten the files. A long-drawn-out suit was worth more to a litigant, clerical or lay, than a continent. The sales were halted. Berardi could hardly

2. In the leter in which the sovereings instructed the Bishop to make the sales in such a form that they could later be invalidated, they wrote him: "We have written you that should put up for sale the Indians sent by the admral D. Cristopher Columbus arriving in the caravels, and because we wish to consult the matter with lawyers, theologians, and specialists in canon law to see whether they may be sold in good conscience... and this cannot be decided until we see the letters that the admiral sends us to learn the reason why he sends them here as captives..." (Navarrete: op. cit., p.193.)

find the time to attend to all the things the Admiral wanted done in Seville, but he was determined to help him to the best of his ability, and with Amerigo's aid he set about seeing how he could solve Columbus's problems. He and Amerigo went to see Donato Nicolini, Amerigo's old friend, and Donato lent them money. Berardi wrote to the sovereigns, and they supported him in such requests as did not involve a problem of conscience for them.

With regard to what you say (they wrote to him on one occasion) about the Admiral sending nine slaves to be given to certain persons to learn the language, and whom the Bishop of Badajoz had not handed over to you, We are writing him that he is to give them to you at once. And with regard to what you say about the logwood and fustet and copper in the cargo from the islands, We are pleased to learn of it, and as soon as We have finished the letters written by the Admiral, We shall write you about this. And with regard to the eighth part of the gold you request in the name of the Admiral, We have ordered the Bishop to give you the eighth part of the gold of the last shipment, because as for that which came the other time, the money given for the things requested by the Admiral amounted to much more than the value of that eighth. And as for the share of the slaves that you request for the Admiral, We are writing to the Bishop of Badajoz to talk to you about this matter; give him complete faith and credence...[3]

3. Ibid., p. 199.

Despite the natural risks inherent in these voyages to distant islands, and the failure to reach a decision on the Indian slave trade, many visionaries and adventurers began to feel the lure of these mysterious discoveries. This happened not only to Sevillians, but also to Catalans, Basques, and Valencians–to all the Spaniards who heard the news. There was talk of islands strewn with nuggets of gold. Some wanted to sail ships, others to engage in business. Despite their promises, the sovereigns were reluctant to give Columbus a monopoly. Not seven months had elapsed after his second voyage when a royal edict was issued providing that anyone who wished to go to discover islands or mainland in the Indies might do so. Exception was made only of Hispaniola. Barter was permitted for everything except gold. The ships were to set out from Cádiz and return to Cádiz. On the outgoing voyage they were to carry one tenth of their cargo free of freight charges for Hispaniola; on their return they would pay to the royal treasury one tenth of what they had received in barter.[4]

This was the first attack on Columbus's claim to exclusive rights. Thanks to the wedge opened by this edict, anyone was at liberty to cross the sea, and not only to scoff at the Admiral's pretensions, but also, by contraband methods, to ignore the several provisos the monarchs had stipulated. One needed only to be shrewd and sly. Gianetto Berardi at once saw the changes the new ruling would bring about,

4. Ibid., p. 186.

and he decided to take a bold step. His aim was, first of all, to protect Columbus's interests. He requested the exclusive right to freight all the ships under royal charter. By the terms of the contract that was drawn up, it was agreed that Berardi would cut the prevailing rate of three thousand maravedís per ton to two thousand. And if anyone offered freightage at a lower rate, he would underbid the offer by one thousand maravedís. Berardi immediately proceeded to assemble a fleet of twelve ships. During the same month that the contract was signed, he agreed to have four of nine hundred tonnage each ready to sail in the harbor of Cádiz. The remaining eight, in two groups of four, would be at Their Majesties' orders in the same port in the course of six months.[5]

The Bishop of Badajoz, true to his nature and his office, did his best to thwart the plan. He wrote to the monarchs, telling them that Berardi would give them ships that were not seaworthy: what was saved on freightage would be paid out in extra expenses. And he made haste to charter other ships. Berardi had to employ all his wits to defend himself. He wrote to the monarchs, and they listened to him. They answered that he was to carry out his contract in good faith, observing the obligations he had agreed to. And they added: "The Bishop will use your caravels and not others, and We have so instructed him, even though he has them loaded."[6]

5. Ibid., pp. 180, 191.
6. Ibid., p. 199.

The person who bore the brunt of outfitting these fleets must have been Amerigo. Berardi did not have long to live. To secure ships, crews, provisions, pilots, on such short notice, involved constant effort, and running back and forth to Triana, across the river. While still on land, Amerigo began to lead the life of a sailor. He had to decide technical problems, chart the route with the pilots, and secure information on the sea and the islands from those returning from Hispaniola.

Subsequent developments proved that Berardi was not actuated by the desire for personal gain in this undertaking. The terms of his contract were too generous. He was doing what Columbus would have wished him to do to protect his interests. And Amerigo's share in the work was a part of it.

Berardi had not yet finished fitting out the fleet when he dictated his will on December 14, 1495. The following day, shortly before the Ave María, notary, clerks, and witnesses gathered around his sickbed. He had sent for them to draw up his testament and ratify the fact that the Admiral Don Christopher Columbus owed him the amount of 180,000 maravedís, as set forth in the ledgers, without including services he had performed on his behalf and that of his brothers and sons. For the space of three years, he said, he had served them with zeal, industry, and good will, neglecting his own affairs, making trips to look after the Admiral's interests, and often calling on his friends for help when unable to attend to them himself because of ill health.

His hand was too weak to hold the pen, but all present would bear witness that he charged the notary, Bartolomé Sánchez Porras, to urge the Admiral to pay him what was due him and give it to the executors of his will, Jerónimo Rufaldo and Amerigo Vespucci. They would make themselves responsible for looking after his daughter's legacy, a trust he put in their hands for the peace of his soul and satisfaction of his conscience. They were to pay the debt he owed to Donato Nicolini, with whom Amerigo Vespucci, his agent, would deal, and the same was to be done with the moneys due César lbarci. Everything depended on Columbus's paying his debt: otherwise there were no funds to repay what he had borrowed on his own responsiblity. But Berardi knew the Admiral would not fail him. He felt sure that payment would be made, and as his representatives to receive such payment he left his close friends, Jerónimo Rufaldo, Amerigo Vespucci, and Diego de Ocaña. All of them, he said, had worked for Columbus, and, in the measure of their abilities, had served his interests.[7]

Shortly afterward Gianetto Berardi departed this world of schemes and hopes. Some six months later Columbus returned to Spain.

The Admiral of the Ocean Sea, Viceroy Don Christopher Columbus, arrived in Cádiz in June 1496. He no longer looked the Roman senator. He was a poor,

7. *Autógrafos de Colón y papeles de América*, published by the Duchess of Berwick and Alba, pp. 7, 9.

bewildered old man. He wore the habit of a Franciscan. No sword hung from his waist, which was girded by a penitent's cord.

To discover the sea route, to cross the ocean for the first time, had not been difficult for him. The initial voyage had lasted only one month and six days, and only during the last two weeks had there been days of dramatic tension. On September 6 he had set out from Gomera in the Canary Islands filled with illusion, and on October 12 he had stepped ashore on the golden strand of his dreams. But two years and nine months of trying to deal with men with whom he was never able to reach an understanding had made a wreck of him. The struggle had been one between despair and indomitable will. On his return to Hispaniola all he had found of the colony established on his first voyage was the whitened bones of his former comrades. To replace this lost colony he laid the foundations of Isabela–the name was a tribute to his Queen–and the christening had not yet been completed when all the settlers fell ill. A bad omen. Seeking the lands of gold he sailed from Isabela with flags unfurled, the trumpets of a conqueror, and four or five hundred covetous adventurers. But all they found were naked Indians, good only for slaves. They took them to be sold in Seville, and what happened? Along came the theologians. The monarchs developed scruples, and the business came to a halt. He set out with three ships for the mainland. He reached Cuba. He declared that this was the Kingdom of Cathay, and

everyone had to believe him. He made the entire
crew swear before a notary that this was the continent. According to him, they had reached Asia, the
Asia he had dreamed of, the Asia of Marco Polo. Did
he find the marble-bridge cities? The rich lands? The
kings attired in tunics of silk? None of that. He found
spreading trees, parrots, lowlands steaming in the
sun. The cinnamon he sought was in the color of
the Indians' skin, and smelled of sweat. The nuggets
of gold were nowhere to be seen, only hammered
ornaments of poor quality. For four months he
threaded the coasts of Cuba and Jamaica. He returned to Hispaniola. There were no arches of flowers to receive him, but only the settlers, pale with
hunger and shaking with fever. And a piece of news:
the royal steward, Juan Aguado, was arriving. Would
he bring the Admiral Ferdinand's unequivocal support, Isabella's gentle encouragement? Nothing of
the sort. He was coming to investigate Columbus's
conduct in office. A steady stream of complaints had
arrived in Spain, and the crown officials cared little
about what happened to the willful Admiral. Their
concern was with the people, with the humble folk
who had crossed the ocean under the spell of the
Italian, with the colony they had set up. The steward was not a man of vision and soaring imagination; he was a crown official with a job to do.

Confronted by the steward, confronted by the dimensions of his own drama, Columbus did not behave like a man sure of himself. His self-assurance
deserted him, and all that remained was the fear

engendered by his complexes. He felt that if the royal steward returned to Spain by himself, everything would be lost, so he decided to accompany him. Instead of his usual hauteur, he would employ humility. His own friends were disconcerted to see him return in the habit of a penitent. There was something strange, disordered, in his behavior and in the objects he had brought with him. "The Admiral brought many things from there which the Indians employ: crowns, masks, belts, necklaces, and many other things woven out of cotton and the image of the Devil on all of them, or the face of an owl, and other worse figures..."

What this confused, suspicious brother of the Third Order of St. Francis needed was a mainland, solid ground under his feet. Possibly he would have found this in Gianetto Berardi, but Gianetto was dead. All that Amerigo could do was wind up Berardi's affairs and give up being a merchant. He had no capital of his own, and the idea of voyages was attracting him more and more. Columbus had to turn to the Genoese for money and find someone else to represent him, if he was to arrange a third voyage.

Undoubtedly he talked with Amerigo, but all he could say was what he believed: that he had reached the shores of Asia. How could the Florentine reconcile the descriptions of Columbus's discoveries with what he had read in the *Book* of Marco Polo and the relations of the merchants of his own city? Where were the pearls, the forests of logwood, and the spiceries?

Columbus spent four months in penance and conference before the monarchs consented to receive
him. They were in no hurry to hear his story. They
wrote to him, saying that they were sure he must be
tired, that the best thing for him to do was to rest.
And he was not to worry about coming to see them.
As a matter of fact, they were very busy at the moment with an important state affair, which was the
marriage of their dughter Doña Joanna to Philip of
Austria. Doña Joanna was later to be known as Joanna
the Mad; Philip was already Philip the Handsome.
The celebrations were as splendid as they were out
of keeping with the royal purse. Isabella had to pawn
her crown. This is the bald truth: she did not pawn
it for the voyage of discovery, but for the marriage.
Luis de Santángel later lent her the money to re-
deem it.

Toward the end of October or the beginning of
November, Their Majesties received Columbus, who
had arrived in June. The apprehension he had felt
about his reception was well justified. The atmosphere was one of benevolence on the part of the
monarchs and suspicion on the part of the court.
"The Admiral had many enemies who could not
swallow him because he was a foreigner, and because his rule had been so high-handed..." But the
struggle restored his powers of speech. He talked at
great length. He spread out the gold he had brought
with him, and gold smooths everything. He spoke
of Asia. By the end of the year the idea of a third
voyage had been accepted. Nevertheless, he waited

for an event that took place in the year 1497 to put him in a more favorable position. Columbus knew very well that in dealings with royalty one must always choose the psychological moment. And this moment was another family marriage, that of Prince Juan to Princess Margharita of Austria. The hopes of all were centered in this alliance. It seemed to Columbus that the wheel of fortune was raising him up once more. But before the end of the year the wheel had turned full circle, and Columbus was in the depths. Margharita had had a miscarriage, and the court was in mourning. Nothing could be done until the following year.

But marriages and mourning finally came to an end, and the third journey was decided upon. Columbus returned to Seville, where he lodged in a monastery. Father Gaspar de Gorricio gave him encouragement, and so did the sovereigns. But he lacked the firm, high-headed stride and the attraction that win the support of the people. He saw that neither the bold, devil-may-care sons of the people were signing on as for the first voyage nor the hope-lured visionaries of the second. The monarchs issued an edict authorizing prisoners so desiring to exchange their fetters for a voyage to the Indies with Columbus. Everything went cross-grained. But finally, commending himself to the Blessed Trinity, Columbus set out on his third voyage on May 3, 1498, from Sanlúcar de Barrameda. He had been weaving and unraveling the web of his dreams in Spain since June 11, 1496.

Christopher Columbus.

ANDA·   COLVMBVS
                         ORBEM

XIII

AMERIGO'S FIRST VOYAGE
(1497)

While Columbus was seeking royal favor at the
court, Amerigo was sailing along the coasts of
Mexico. What had happened, and when had he
become a mariner?

"As Your Magnificence must know," Amerigo
wrote to the new gonfalonier of Florence, Piero
Soderini,

*The reason for my coming to this Kingdom of Spain
was to engage in trade, and during the four years I
pursued this purpose I had occasion to observe and
experience the vicissitudes of fortune, which alters
these perishable and transitory worldly goods. At one
moment Fortune places a man at the top of her wheel,
and at another casts him down and strips him of the
possessions we may call borrowed. And so, knowing
the unremitting effort man puts into securing such
goods, suffering so many distresses and dangers, I
decided to give up trade and devote myself to more
praiseworthy and firmer things. I prepared myself to
go and observe a part of the world and its wonders.
The opportunity to do so was afforded me at a most
timely moment and conjunction, for the King, Don
Ferdinand of Castile, needing to send out four ships
to discover new lands to the west, I was chosen by*

La bella Popula, *Engraving from* Voyages dans L'Amerique de Sud.

His Highness to go with the fleet and help in the discovery. We set out from Cádiz on the 10th of May 1497...

The trip in question was a small, four-ship expedition like those Gianetto Berardi had outfitted during the last year of his life. This had become the regular method of communication between Spain and the colony Columbus had established. But in May 1497 new factors had laid a new obligation on the expedition Amerigo sailed with: to "assist in the discovery." The initiative had now been assumed by King Ferdinand. He had to weigh the indisputable merits of Columbus, with whom he had just had his first interviews after the second voyage, against the possible justice in the colonists' complaints, which arrived by every boat. Possibly the information brought back by the King's steward, Juan Aguado, did not coincide with Columbus's version of the facts. Moreover, there was an aspect of the situation on which the steward was not empowered to act. Columbus defended his conduct in office with the news of new discoveries and his affirmation that he had definitely touched the mainland of Asia. How far was the King prepared to back the claims of the Genoese? The Crown never relinquished control over its functionaries. At times it exercised this secretly, through spies; at times openly, through judges. The lack of precedent for these overseas governments made it necessary for the sovereigns to double their vigilance. They had spies in Portugal to report on the activities of the Portuguese rulers and all the mariners. Within Spain the number of officials who, like Bishop Fonseca, watched, touched, examined everything, was growing. Bishop Fonseca, whom historians have harshly criticized, was simply a man who had to choose between serving his King or serving Columbus. He chose the service of the King and brought to it the singleness of purpose and the stubbornness of his zealous temperament.

Columbus, to whom the monarchs owed the circumstance of finding themselves at the head of the most uncertain, fabulous, and tantalizing of ventures, was a foreigner. The islands and mainland he talked of might be the route to the riches of the Orient, or just a breeding-ground of anthropophagous Indians and complicated colonial problems. Columbus claimed that he had reached Cathay, but he had brought back from that fabled kingdom only bagatelles. Hard-headed, down-to-earth Ferdinand was not easily dazzled. He was willing to confirm Columbus in many of his privileges; he offered the Admiral lands, an entailment, but he took the precautionary measure of delaying permission for the third voyage until after he had dispatched an expedition to check the situation. This was in no sense a hostile move. Columbus's best friend, Amerigo Vespucci, was to sail with it. It had no authority to make conquests, and it carried no governor aboard. It was to set out without fanfare of any sort, and. its mission was "to discover and help to discover," thus aiding the King toward reaching an impartial judgment.

Until that moment Amerigo had done all his sailing vicariously–in taverns, scholars' studies, merchants' warehouses. He had talked with the pilots in Triana, in Berardi's office. He had often gone aboard the caravels with the shipmasters, taking note of preparations, making careful inspection of the ships being outfitted. He had been buying ships, examining them with the most calculating eye, that of the purchaser. He was relating these new experiences to his recollections of Piero Vespucci's voyage to the Near East, to the discussions of Toscanelli's thesis in the gatherings at his uncle Giorgio Antonio's, to the Valesca map of the Mediterranean routes, which he had sold before leaving Florence for Spain. He was relating his experiences to those of Columbus, whom be admired. Columbus had talked with him about his voyages, possibly more intimately and sincerely than to the King and Queen, for his obligation to the monarchs was limited to defending his prerogatives.

But never before had Amerigo joined a ship sailing the Atlantic. His knowledge of nautical instruments was theoretical. He had been familiar with the astrolabe since the time his uncle Giorgio Antonio had ordered one included in the portrait of St. Augustine; but his knowledge was only that–pictorial. Or outlined in books. All land-side information. To be sure, he was not in any post of command, but was going as an observer. If the sailors watched and listened to him with respect, it was because he had helped to fit out other ships, and they knew him as a merchant and banker, a man with a knowledge of geography. He had come from Florence with the prestige of its learning, and he knew those great geographers to whom Columbus owed so much.

Who was in command of the four caravels on this voyage, and who were the captains of the different ships? The information with regard to this is as vague and unreliable as that having to do with the earlier four-ship fleets Berardi had fitted out. The monarchs were not going to make public the fact that they were setting up controls on Columbus in the very field of the discoveries. For the most part, the first expeditions of this sort became a matter of record only by exception, and never in full detail.[1] There are those who believe that Vicente Yáñez Pinzón was in command; others suggest Juan Díaz de Solís, and some Juan de la Cosa. All of them were already friends of Amerigo, and in time would become his trusted comrades. But, as a matter of fact, the question of who commanded the fleet is of no importance to us, and there is no indication that it mattered much at the time. The crossing was not made on the initiative of an outstanding explorer. It was a step

---

1. López de Gómara writes: "Comprehending how great were the lands discovered by Christopher Columbus, many set out to complete the discovery of all, some at their own expense, others at the expense of the King, and all thinking to enrich themselves, win fame, and gain favor with the monarchs. But as most of them did nothing but discover or exhaust themselves, there is no recollection of them, so far as I know." (*Historia general de las Indias*, Chapter liii.)

taken by the King, and nothing more. It could be said with all exactitude that this was the expedition of Don Ferdinand the Catholic. It was natural that a king should wish to know what was going on. And a fleet of four caravels was necessary to make a complete geographical investigation.

There is one interesting detail. One of the first topics discussed by the monarchs and Columbus had been that of allowing anyone so desiring to go out to the new lands. This had been a blow at the Admiral's privileges. As a matter of fact, the monarchs had no right to do this, and they reached an understanding with the Admiral to do away with this liberty. But they did not carry out the understanding until they had sent out the fleet Amerigo accompanied.

This was an epoch-making voyage. More than any other it strengthened faith in the idea of a mainland. It discovered that the land of Cathay Columbus had talked of was not Cathay at all, but an island, Cuba. Beyond this island stretched the vast coast of Mexico, an arc holding unlimited promise, which began to make its appearance on the early maps as a result of this voyage.

The ships sailed from Cádiz. For the first time Amerigo found himself gazing upon the broadest sea men of the Western World had ever crossed. He did not think of Columbus; his imagination turned to Dante, to the memory of his readings under the guidance of Giorgio Antonio. Along the route Amerigo was traveling, the ships of Ulysses had passed!

In his letter to Gonfalonier Soderini he wrote: "If I remember rightly, I have read somewhere that this ocean sea was held to be an unpeopled sea, and this was the opinion of our poet, Dante, in Canto XXVI of the *Inferno*, where he tells of the death of Ulysses..." An unpeopled sea? This was no longer true. Amerigo felt the salt breezes swell his heart. The daring of his youth was returning, and he felt the intoxication of a bold dream. Here Ulysses had sailed out to meet death; Amerigo was sailing out to meet life. Where Ulysses had ended, Amerigo would begin.

There was another reason why Amerigo's thoughts turned to Dante. Canto XXVI of the *Inferno*, to which he refers, begins with an apostrophe to Florence. If Florence was already famous in the days of the poet because its flag was to be found on land and sea, in hell its name was on the lips of the damned.

Florence, exult! for thou so mightily
Hast thriven, that o'er land and sea thy wings
Thou beatest, and thy name spreads over hell.[2]

Dante spoke of the shame he felt to see five illustrious citizens of his native land in hell. The Florence of his day, riven by warring political factions,

2. *Godi, Fiorenza, pio che se'si grande,*
   che per mare e per terra batti l'ali,
   e per lo inferno tuo nome si spande!
   Translation by Henry Francis Cary (1814).

resembled the Florence of Amerigo, blazing with the conflict between Savonarola and the Medici. Dante may have seemed to Amerigo the symbol of the wandering Florentine, the exile who seeks under alien skies the inspiration for his higher ambitions. Amerigo, was a voluntary exile, but an exile. The political situation of Florence had sent him to seek fortune elsewhere.

Perhaps as he recounted his voyages Amerigo may have thought that with him the name of Florence was once more circling the globe. In the days of Dante, according to Francesco da Buti, "The Florentines were scattered everywhere outside of Florence in the most diverse parts of the world, and they traveled the same over land as by sea, and took pride in this." Above the entrance to the palace of the Podesta they had carved this inscription: *"Quæ mare, quæ terram, quæ totum possidet orbem."* It was Amerigo's great good fortune to be moving now over lands and seas, and not through hell, to be proclaiming the name of his city not in shame but in glory.

Dante had been the great visionary. He had foreseen the stars of the other pole. He had dreamed of the enchanted highlands of paradise. But his evocation of the death of Ulysses was a parable of the punishments that lie in wait for the bold. The traveler should bear in mind not only the concrete facts that shape the experiences of other travelers, but the magic signs of myth, the forecast of the stars, the voice of the astrologers. Ulysses, sailing toward the

Pillars of Hercules, was not restrained by fondness for his young son, or the filial piety he owed his father's white hairs, or the caressing arms of Penelope. He wished to "explore the world and search the ways of life." It was not the glory of discovery that he sought, but the pleasures of power. As his ship plowed onward, he saw through the spray the golden sands of Morocco, Sardinia like a basket of greenery set in the sea. Then Cádiz to the right, Ceuta to the left, and ahead the pillars of the strait. Exactly where Amerigo now found himself. Driven by his desire, Ulysses urged his rowers to ply their oars ever faster, to unfurl the tense, scudding sails. He was making for the island that lies at the antipodes of Jerusalem. "And now he saw the stars of the other pole!" And then came his undoing. The unknown sea rose in fury, lifted the Greek vessel into the air, and hurled it three times against the sea. Then the "booming billow" closed in over the wreckage.

Those were the adverse signs. Defying them, Amerigo had set out upon the unknown sea, over the frail bridge Columbus had laid, for the islands inhabited by men of the bronze race. Indians with their chains of gold, unknown trees abloom with parrots.

Amerigo was now forty-three years old, and had been working in Spain for more than five years.

The fleet's first call was the Canary Islands. According to Ptolemy, the earth was divided into twenty-one climates, and the Canary Islands were in the third division: During the fifteenth century these

islands changed hands several times. At one time
Henry the Navigator had bought them for Portugal;
then Ferdinand and Isabella acquired them from a
certain Peraza. The island of Palma had been conquered six years before, and Tenerife barely two.
They were all volcanic peaks and sounding boards
for news and gossip. There, better than anywhere
else, one could pick up information concerning the
voyages of the Portuguese and of free-lance expeditions. On both his outbound voyages Columbus had
put in at Gomera. It was an ideal spot to reprovision
and take on a fresh supply of wood, water, beef,
pigs, and chickens. There the crew took their fare-
well of women of their own race, though it was not
always easy to break the ties that had been created
in a week, in a night.

Amerigo's ships put in at Gomera for eight days.
Officers and sailors felt themselves freer, more their
own masters, in the Canaries than in Seville. These
islands were the pivotal point between the two hemispheres. The orders of the King did not reach them
so directly or swiftly, nor the intrigues of the court,
nor the inquisitorial scrutiny of Bishop Fonseca. They
were an anteroom of adventure.

The moment of departure came. Great uproar and
confusion, and then the creaking of timbers and the
lapping of waves against the prow. The sailors' oaths
and vows were stilled as they knelt on the deck,
and the salt breeze picked up the many-voiced
prayer. On shore the women followed the prayer.
Rude hands sketched the sign of the cross on broad,

manly breasts. Then, as though awakened from a dream, the shouting and oaths were resumed. Haul up the sails! The wind shook the canvas, and the rolling of the caravels increased, the creaking of the timbers sounding louder. How rich the Spanish tongue in colorful interjections! How satisfying the Spanish laughter! Anchors aweigh! "And we sailed so far that at the end of thirty-seven days we reached a land we held to be the mainland."

Deliberately or by chance they had not made for Hispaniola or Cuba, but had set a more southerly course. They passed the chain of the Virgin Islands without seeing them, and entered the Caribbean Sea. They may have touched Costa Rica or Honduras, or possibly Nicaragua.[3] In any case, they soon saw that it was impossible to proceed farther westward, and that these were not islands. Could it be Asia? Most certainly. These were the first Spanish ships that had really reached the mainland. Columbus had not gone beyond the shores of Cuba; not until his third voyage did he reach Venezuela.

3. The doubt with regard to the point of the coast they reached comes from the fact that Amerigo says only that their position was 16° north latitude. In Harrisse's opinion, this should read 10°. The information is contained in the letter to Soderini, which has reached us through various translations. Levillier (*El Nuevo Mundo*, p. 18) says: "The co-ordinate (16° north latitude and 75° west longitude from the Canary Islands) is wrong because it would fall in the interior of the Honduras. Substituting 68° for 75° would bring it on the coast. Harrisse suggests the reading of 10°, which would have the fleet anchoring off Costa Rica..."

The only report we have of this voyage of exploration is Amerigo's. His account is confirmed by the
maps that followed. On them the complete outline
of the Gulf of Mexico appears, the contours of the
peninsula of Florida, and the profile of the coast to
the north. Cuba is completely separated from the
continent, and ceases to be the mainland Columbus
proclaimed it. It was not fifteen years after Vespucci's
voyage that Ponce de León landed in Florida. Twenty
elapsed before Hernandez de Córdoba explored the
coast of Yucatán, Grijalva that of Veracruz.

The discovery was, above all, maritime and coast-
wise. But it was sufficiently comprehensive to supply Juan de la Cosa with the information necessary
to draw up his map in 1500, showing Cuba as an
island, and between Cuba and the Mexican coast
the *"mar oceanus."* The coastline of the mainland
is prolonged on this map to a point to the north
where De la Cosa places the "sea of the English,"
which is where John Cabot carried on his exploration in 1497 under the English flag. De la Cosa tilts
the entire coast of North America westward. In 1502,
again using Amerigo's voyage as his source, some
unknown cosmographer at the orders of the Duke
of Ferrara drew up the map known as the Cantino.
On this, in addition to the island of Cuba, Florida
appears as a peninsula, with fewer errors than on
the map of Juan de la Cosa. That same year a Genoese
cartographer, Canerio, designed a planisphere with
a Gulf of Mexico dotted with imaginary islands. After these came the maps of Waldseemüller (1507),

that of the German Johann Ruysch, and that which Bishop Peter Martyr of Anghiera managed to secure in Spain, all showing the mainland in the background. Their errors seem fabulous to us now, but all had in common that they established the bases of what we today call North America.

Inasmuch as no other recorded voyage would account for the new features of these maps, they bear out the veracity of Vespucci's report, and show that fate was already leading him and Columbus in different directions. In 1503 Bartholomew Columbus, the Admiral's confidant and brother, and the better cartographer of the two, drew the map representing the sum of Columbus's experiences. On it Florida is conspicuous by its absence. The mainland, as conceived by Bartholomew and Christopher Columbus, was square; at its base were the coastlines of the Guianas and Venezuela–the land of Paria– as far as Panama; from there to the north, Asia–that is to say, Cuba–stretched like a solid block joined to the Oriental continent. In 1513 there lived in the city of Gallipoli a Turk, "poor Piri ben Hagi Muhammed, known as the son of Kemal Reis," who designed a planisphere based, among other sources, "on a map Columbus had drawn of the region of the West." On it Cuba does not appear as an island, either, but as part of the mainland.

The first literary description of the new continent is that of Amerigo. Columbus had set down an account of the islands. With these documents a new literature came into being. It was the awakening of

European tongues at the magic contact with men, lands, trees, birds, never beheld before. We know the exact date, the very moment, at which American literature was born, and it happened that the two writers who brought it into being–Columbus and Vespucci–had the gift of transmitting to their pages the morning freshness and the miraculous quality that marked the discovery.

Although Amerigo makes reference to this first voyage in two of his letters to Lorenzo di Pier Francesco de' Medici and in a letter to a friend, of which only excerpts exist, the entire relation has come down to us in the letter he wrote to Piero Soderini in 1504, seven years after the journey. But it is evident that his findings were known to Their Catholic Majesties and to all those who were in touch with the discoverers from the first day.

From the letter to Soderini it is clear that Amerigo's two interests were in satisfying his scientific curiosity and in acquiring the navigator's art. He would seem to have spent most of his time on the voyage in the company of the pilots. He speaks of the degrees of the globe's circumference, measures distances by leagues, knows the names of all the winds, and the quarter from which they blew. His abilities, as a pilot, which came to surpass those of all his contemporaries, were developing rapidly.

Like the good Florentine he was, he had a gift for words, an eye for detail, and the ability to evoke what he saw. He sings the praises of the hammock, one of the wonders of the new lands:

"These big nets, made of cotton and swung in the air... Although this fashion of sleeping may seem uncomfortable, I tell you it is pleasant to sleep in them, and we preferred them to our blankets."

After the delights of the hammock comes the astonishment over the iguanas:

They roasted a certain animal that looked like a dragon except that it has no wings, and it is so horrid of aspect that we were amazed at its deformity. We went through their houses, or, better, their cabins, and we found many of these animals alive and tied by the feet and with a rope around their snouts so they could not open their mouths, as is done with mastiffs to keep them from biting; their appearance was so fierce that none of us ventured to touch them, for fear they were poisonous; they are the size of a kid, and, a fathom and a half long; their paws are long and fleshy and armed with powerful claws; the skin is thick and of different colors; the snout and face are those of a dragon, and from the nose a crest rises like a saw, which runs down the back to the end of the tail; in conclusion, we thought them to be dragons, and poisonous, and they eat them...

The four-legged serpent that Benedetto Dei had brought back from his voyage to the East when he returned with Piero Vespucci had aroused admiration first in Pisa, and then in Florence. But Amerigo's iguana seemed even more astonishing to the Florentines. Many remembered the crocodile, but nobody had ever heard of an iguana.

The instant success of Amerigo's letters was the result, in part, of his literary art. He wrote with a liveliness and forthrightness that verges on the shameless. He intended his letters to be not only informative, but also entertaining. His description of the new women he saw and knew was complete and unabashed. In his early years he had read the epigrams of Martial, the tales of the *Decameron*, the intimate letters of the gay blades of the Florentine brigades. He knew by heart Lorenzo the Magnificent's carnival songs. "They do not," he said of the Indians,

employ the custom of marriage. Each one takes the women he wants, and when he wants to repudiate them, he does so without this constituting an offense or shame for the woman, for in this the women are as free as the men. They are not very jealous, but they are lascivious… and the women much more so than the men, and out of decency I refrain from telling of the expedients they employ to satisfy their inordinate lust. They are very fertile, and during their pregnancy they do not fail to carry on their work; and their delivery is so easy that the day after giving birth they go about everywhere, especially to bathe in the rivers, and they are as healthy as fish. They are so hardhearted and cruel that if they become angry with their husbands they at once use a device to kill the infant in their womb… They are women graceful of body, very well proportioned, whose bodies reveal no defect or malformed member; and although they go completely naked, they are firmfleshed. It is the exception to see a woman with sagging breasts,

*or flabby, wrinkled belly... They showed a great de-
sire to have carnal knowledge of us Christians...*

On other occasions Amerigo uses even more highly
colored language in his reporting, which may be
said to anticipate the journalism of the twentieth
century. He had been sent out "to help discover,"
and he was doing his duty. He collected information and presented it for his readers' delectation: this
was his mission, not trading or governing. As he
spent many months exploring the coasts of Tabasco,
Taumaulipas or "Lariab," and also islands where the
inhabitants were less docile, his observations afforded
him a store of material, and he felt in a position to
make ingenious interpretations of the domestic life,
the ideas of government, and the reactions of the
Indians in contrast to those of the Europeans.

There is a very real and human quality in Amerigo's
accounts. Columbus, for example, had said–and nearly
all the conquistadors repeated–that the Indians at sight
of them had worshipped them as gods. Amerigo's
version is more natural, more plausible, and probably truer. "Many people came to see us, and they
were astonished at our whiteness, and we gave them
to understand that we had come from heaven and
were going about observing the world, and they believed it."

"At the end of thirty-seven days," he writes, "we
reached a land we held to be the mainland..." This,
as we have seen, was the beginning of his relation.
Then came the details–the beaches of white sand,
the parrot-green foliage that gleamed in the tropical

sun. They dropped anchor a league and a half off shore. They put the boats over the side and got into them, these new discoverers, more eager than frightened. The beach was thick with natives, who by shouts had communicated the news of the arrival of ships never seen before. When they caught sight of the Christians, their faces covered with hair and carrying blades the color of moonbeams in their hands, they took to their heels. It was useless to call to them or wave presents in the air. From their forest hiding-places their black, unwinking eyes followed every move of the intruders, but they did not even dare to shoot arrows at them.

As night came on, the fleet sailed northward. By the light of dawn they could see the growing throng that followed their progress along the shore. And so for two days. When they came to a sheltered cove, they dropped anchor, and Amerigo and forty of his companions got into boats. The natives here seemed less suspicious. They accepted the first gifts of mirrors, hawkbells. The edge of their fear was wearing off. The Spaniards had never seen such swimmers as those who sported like fish around the caravels. Their straight black hair glistened like sealskin. Their white teeth and small eyes, black as jet, gleamed in the water. The color of their skin reminded Amerigo of the mane of the caged lions in Florence, a tawny hue. But, he added: "If they wore clothing they would be as white as we." The only hair on their bodies was that of their heads, long and black, and adding greatly to the beauty of the women.

With the passing of the months they had made
contacts with the people all along the Gulf and had
penetrated a short distance inland. The insight of their
observations grew. Amerigo learned that both men
and women were great runners. The Indians Columbus had brought to Seville had seemed benumbed,
but how agile and graceful they were here in their
forests and streams! Far superior to the Christians, he
noted. The way the women swam was incredible.
Two leagues out at sea they played like a school of
fish. And the women could draw a bow like the men
and put the arrow where they liked. The use of iron
or other hard metals was unknown among them; they
gave their weapons a deadly point of animal teeth or
fish bones. They had no captain; each one was lord
of himself. "And the cause of their wars is not the
ambition to rule… but an ancient enmity between
them in times long past… They go to war because
the oldest member of the tribe arises and goes through
the streets haranguing them…"

Amerigo found them shrewd and sly. They talked
little, and in low voices. Their habits were barbarous because they ate at irregular times, on the
ground, without cloths. He observed that they spoke
a diversity of tongues, and that their enunciation
was like that of the Europeans for "they form their
words with either the teeth or the lips." They seemed
to him clean of person because of the frequency
with which they washed. "When they evacuate their
bowels–if I may be excused for saying so–they make
every effort to do so without being seen." He found

them generous: "It is rare for them to refuse anything"; but at the same time "they are liberal in asking." Death was like a lullaby: they put the dead person in a hammock swung between two trees and danced about the corpse for a whole day. The deceased was provided with food and drink for his journey.

Aside from human flesh, they ate little meat. Their wealth consisted of bird feathers of many colors, bone necklaces, white or green stones that they set in their cheeks, lips, or ears. "Wealth such as we use in our Europe or other parts, like gold, jewels, pearls, and other treasures, they hold in no esteem."

One aspect of Amerigo's relation differs basically from that of his contemporaries, and is in sharp contrast with the diary of Columbus. Amerigo has almost no interest in gold. He scarcely mentions it. He gives no thought to finding mountains of it. In his letter to Soderini he makes a passing reference to it: "At first we saw nothing of much value in the land except an occasional sample of gold. I think this was because we did not know the language, for the location of the place and the lay of the land could not be better."

On one occasion Amerigo and a handful of Christians, twenty-eight all told, made their way inland. They came to villages, where they were received with dances, singing, festivities. The natives regaled them with lavish meals. They offered them women, "and we could not defend ourselves against them." The old men begged the Spaniards to go with them to other settlements. And if one of the visitors wearied on the way, they carried him in a hammock. "Many of them carried presents they had given us in their sleeping-nets: rich feathers, bows and arrows, innumerable parrots of many colors..."

Once they had a skirmish before a rustic Venice. Forty-four houses, like cabins, were built on piles above the water. Canoes full of people surrounded them, carrying sixteen girls, a present of four for each caravel. Suddenly old women appeared in the houses and began to give loud cries. The girls who were in the caravels leaped overboard and swam swiftly to shore. A vast number of canoes appeared carrying men armed with lances and arrows. Fighting was joined, and the arms of the Europeans mowed down the attackers. There were only five wounded among the Christians. The defeat of the natives was absolute. When the explorers went ashore to see the houses, they found them deserted, "and we did not want to set them on fire because it seemed a cruel thing to do." They took five prisoners, fastening a bar of iron to the feet of each one so he could not run away–except the girls, who when it grew dark fled "in the most subtle manner in the world."

By this time they had journeyed far. Their food supplies were exhausted, and they had no goods left to barter. They had seen more than they had dared hope. King Ferdinand was waiting for them in Castile. They prepared for the return voyage. They made one last call at the island of Iti (Haiti?) where they encountered resistance by the Indians. They terrified the natives with their cannon fire, and after a hard fight took twenty-two prisoners (the letter to Soderini says 222, but this is undoubtedly an error), and with this prize set their course for Spain. "We reached the port of Cádiz on the 15th day of October 1498, where we were welcomed and where we sold our slaves…" It is questionable that the fight Amerigo describes really took place: if they had arrived in Spain with prisoners whom they did not describe as taken in war, they would have lost them, as happened to Columbus through lack of experience.

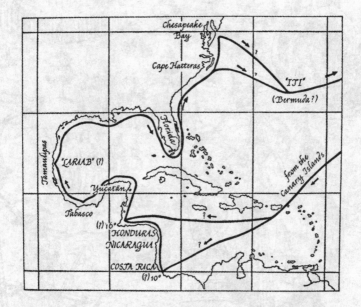

Route of Amerigo's first voyage, 1497-1498.

Route of Amerigo's second voyage, 1499-1500.

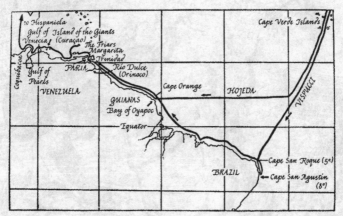

XIV

FROM BRAZIL TO VENEZUELA
(1499-1500)

Amerigo was back in Seville, among his friends.
Among these was a María, María Cerezo, whom he
was going to marry. He inquired about Columbus
and learned that the Admiral had set out to sea again
without awaiting the return of Amerigo's expedition. He had been gone for five and one half months,
seeking once more his dreamed-of Asia. The last
thing he had done was to establish with the royal
consent an entailment for his legitimate son, Diego,
who would inherit his privileges. The document in
which all this was drawn up and set forth had been
a labor of months. Columbus had the passion for
legal hairsplitting typical of many Spaniards; he was
a litigant by nature.

This writ of entailment represented more than simply the desire to perpetuate the holdings of the Admiral, which in itself was of keen interest to him. It
was also a profession of faith that he had reached
Asia and that Cuba was the mainland. "And it pleased
our Almighty Lord that in the year of '92 I should
discover the mainland of the Indies and many islands, among which is Hispaniola, which the Indians call Ayte, and the Monicongos of Cipango." The
geographical concepts of Columbus were rectified

by subsequent voyages, but the Admiral established
the word Indians for the inhabitants of the New
World, and so it has remained *in sæcula sæculorum.*
   News of Columbus's third voyage began to come
in. This time he had really touched the mainland.
Following a more southerly course, he had come
not to the latitude of the Bahamas, as on the first
trip, but to Trinidad and Venezuela, the coast known
as Paria. The Orinoco, whose multiple mouths
poured a huge body of fresh water well out to sea,
indicated the presence of a continent. Whereupon
the Admiral's imagination soared off to lofty mountains in the background, vast plains, the mighty
Asia of his circumscribed world. On the island of
Margarita he saw a mountain in the form of a young
woman's breast, and he said: "This is the Garden
of Eden." He flatly contradicted all the traditional
speculations as to where the Garden of Eden might
be located: this was it, and this was its form. He
found pearls, and for that reason gave the island
the name of Margarita and called the water the Gulf
of Pearls. There was no doubt in his mind that these
were Oriental pearls, and he left quickly, as though
he did not wish to expose this treasure to the cu-
pidity of his men. This gave rise to complaints
against him. His astuteness fell short of the malice
of the others. The story of the pearls was the first to
reach Spain.
   Columbus left the Garden of Eden and the enchanted world of pearls for the hell of Santo
Domingo. He arrived sick of body and distraught of

mind. The island had risen against him. Francisco
Roldán, his former servant, had refused to recognize his authority, and Columbus did not know how
to handle him. He wavered between harshness and
humility, and this encouraged the rebel. Columbus
wrote him conciliatory letters and glared daggers at
him when they met. He needed the backing of Spain
to regain his authority, and he sent off five caravels
loaded with slaves and other less valuable products.
"From here," he wrote, "in the name of the Blessed
Trinity, we can send all the slaves that can be sold.
Four thousand, which, at the lowest figure, will bring
twenty contos. And four thousand hundredweight
of logwood, which is worth about the same amount.
And the cost here would be about six contos. And
so, if this were effected, it would mean in the neighborhood of forty contos... Castile and Aragón and
Portugal and Italy and Sicily... use many slaves, and
I do not think so many come from Guinea... Of
logwood... there is a great supply."

All this news, and the guarded information about
the pearls, and the word-of-mouth reports, which
were the most numerous, spread through Seville,
were broadcast over Castile, and came to Amerigo's
ears when he returned from his trip. It seemed to
the Florentine that the world pictured by Columbus's
supporters was very different from that which he
had seen. The rank and file of Seville, who had
showed slight enthusiasm when Columbus set out,
now felt the stirrings of curiosity and avarice. Although the Admiral was given to flights of fancy,

there were hardheaded, landlocked folk who had followed him and had seen really promising possibilities in the islands. There were even those who saw good fishing in the troubled government waters of Hispaniola. From the throne King Ferdinand followed these developments with attention and a calculating eye. Once more he wanted an impartial report of just what was happening. Once more the question of how Columbus was dealing with the rebels and the truth of what these new lands had to offer needed investigation. With resolution and caution he prepared to send out two commissions, one to look into the matter of government, the other into the discoveries.[1]

There were by now pilots and mariners experienced in transoceanic voyages. Ferdinand or his agents selected three. One, who had the bearing of a good captain, was a Castilian living in Seville; another was a Basque seaman with a knowledge of maps; the third a Florentine who had just returned from the sea beyond Cuba. They were respectively Alonso de Hojeda, Juan de la Cosa, and Amerigo Vespucci. They were to constitute the vigilance committee of the discoveries.

Alonso de Hojeda had accompanied Columbus on his second voyage. He was brave to the point

1. Kathleen Romoli in *"Hojeda, el hombre de confianza de los Reyes Católicos"* (*Revista de América*, Bogotá, April 1945) has made a careful, well-informed study to prove that the voyage here referred to was organized by King Ferdinand to check on the reports of Columbus.

of temerity, shrewd, witty, and penniless. Short, strong, and well knit, "handsome of bearing, with a goodly countenance, and very large eyes," a thoroughbred Castilian, he had attracted the attention of the Queen with his acrobatic feats. One day Isabella was at the top of the Giralda. At her feet Seville, snug within its walls, with its red roofs and green gardens, lay like a bed of strawberries. The Alcázar seemed a child's toy. It made the Queen's head swim. From the tower of the Giralda a beam projected some twenty feet into space. Hojeda was standing beside her. Their eyes met; he smiled and pointed to the beam. Without a word he walked out to the end of it, described a circle in the air with his foot, and returned to kneel proudly before Her Majesty. If she had not been the Queen, she would probably have rewarded him with a kiss. She shivered and smiled.

In the voyage on which he accompanied Columbus, Hojeda was his right arm at certain of the most difficult moments. One of these was when they reached the island of Guadeloupe. There they found parrots, delicious fruits, and exciting Indian girls. Some of the crew went ashore and forgot to come back. Columbus was outraged and worried at this flouting of his authority and the possible loss of men. Hojeda smilingly reassured him and asked for forty men. Columbus gave his permission, and Hojeda set off inland. He returned with the missing comrades and a string of stories. He claimed to have found sandalwood, ginger, aloes, and myrrh; and falcons, herons, doves, and nightingales. Not that these existed–but he had seen them. And he saw the houses of the natives, rustically adorned, with the heads of enemies taken in battle hanging from the eaves like dark lanterns. The victims' haunches were roasting over the fire.

Columbus and Hojeda sailed on to Hispaniola, where Columbus encountered the ruins of his first settlement. The massacre of the Christians had been ordered by the indomitable chief, Caonabó. There would be no peace as long as he lived: the Indians followed him with blind fidelity. Any day, the Spaniards thought apprehensively, Caonabó would have them browning on a spit or cured and smoked like ham. But Columbus did not see how he was to lay hands on Caonabó except by means of some stratagem. It was said that the Indian had been greatly taken by the talking metal–the bells. That, thought Columbus, might be the bait. It was as though Hojeda had read his thoughts. They talked together, and Hojeda set out to find Caonabó. He flattered the chief, showered attentions on him, conveyed to him that he wanted to make him a present of a bell. It was his dove of peace. The Indian swallowed the bait. But he wanted to be clean to receive this homage, so they went to the river together. There Hojeda offered him a novel pair of bracelets. Caonabó put them on. They snapped shut: he was handcuffed. Hojeda threw him across his horse, and handed him over to the Admiral, who, needless to say, was delighted.

These stories went the rounds of Seville. When someone asked Hojeda if they were true, he smiled and said nothing. Juan de la Cosa, who had accompanied Hojeda on this same voyage, confirmed them. Their Majesties chuckled over them. For his own reasons Hojeda had not wished to accompany Columbus on his third voyage. And the monarchs, taking into account his knowledge and information, his cool-headedness, chose him to head the follow-up expedition. Naturally, this was not Hojeda's expedition; he did not have a cent. It was the King's.

Juan de la Cosa had sailed with Columbus on his second voyage as a practically anonymous member of *Niña's* crew. He was one of those who, at the orders of Columbus, had had to swear that Cuba was the mainland. He learned from Amerigo that this had no basis in fact. He did not accompany Columbus on his third voyage for reasons of his own, but not because he had not developed a taste for transatlantic navigation. Quite the contrary. He wanted to see everything and put it on maps. His was the first map of the New World, and he sailed up and down the coasts of Paria until an Indian arrow killed him. De la Cosa, being a Basque, was more of a mariner than Hojeda. He undoubtedly looked upon Columbus as a man of unbridled imagination, driven by his desire to sail farther and farther west. Referring to the exploration of the Island of Margarita, De la Cosa said: "I went ashore on the island of Margarita and explored it on foot because

I knew that all the Admiral knew about it was that he had seen it as he sailed by..."

Amerigo's first voyage, of seventeen months, had conferred on him an authority recognized by all. Public opinion awarded him the degree of pilot, and these degrees *honoris causa* given by men who went down to the sea were worth far more than those of any school. When Hojeda was making his report about those who had accompanied him to the mainland, Amerigo's name came second, preceded only by that of Juan de la Cosa. His statement was set down in these words: "He took with him Juan de la Cosa, pilot, and Morigo Vespuche and other pilots."[2] Amerigo was called Despuche, Espuche, Vespuche, in Seville; foreign names were repeated as they sounded to the ears of those who could neither read nor write. He accompanied Hojeda in the same capacity as on his first voyage: that of impartial observer who would not allow false reports to be brought against Columbus. Hojeda's friendship for the Admiral was cooling, and in the end he would become his declared enemy. Not so Amerigo. Columbus was a fellow countryman, almost his partner. By sending both Amerigo and Hojeda on the voyage of investigation, the King was displaying toward Columbus neither hostility nor blind support. The explorers were not going for purposes of con-

---

2. *Colección de documentos inéditos relativos al descubrimiento, conquista y organización de las antiguas posesiones de ultramar.* Vol. VII: *Los Pleitos de Colón,* pp. 205-6.

quest or trade, nor at the service of some rich adventurer whose name served as the figurehead of his ambition. They were simply the eyes of the monarch gazing on the pearl sea, the hands of the monarch caressing the new land to find out if it was really the Garden of Eden. King Ferdinand's prudence and shrewdness moved quietly, cautiously, in the wake of the visionary Admiral of the Ocean Sea.

On May 16, 1499–that is to say, a year after Columbus sailed–three or four caravels set out to sea from the port of Cádiz. Juan de la Cosa was master mariner of the flagship, which was Hojeda's vessel. Among the outstanding pilots who accompanied them were Amerigo Vespucci; Diego Martín Chamorro, the brother-in-law of Vicente Yáñez Pinzón; Juan Sánchez; José López of Seville; and Francisco Morales. All were to make names for themselves in maritime history.

At first the caravels kept within sight of each other, skirting the coast of Africa. The sailors could communicate from ship to ship and leap overboard for a swim when the sea was calm and the sun beat down. Hojeda followed a navigator's chart that Columbus had sent to the authorities from Hispaniola. Steering this course, they sailed south of the Canaries until they reached the Cape Verde Islands, lying below the Tropic of Cancer and near to the equator. "We sailed so far," says Amerigo, "that we came to an island known as Fire Island, and after taking aboard water and wood, we sailed with the *libeccio*" (a strong southwest wind that blows off Africa).

The fleet then split up. One group, among them Hojeda's ship, followed Columbus's route. Vespucci set his course more southward, crossing the equator and skirting the coast of Brazil, in the neighborhood of Cape St. Vincent, where the continent bulges out toward Africa. This was the first European expedition to cross the equator in the New World sea, though the Portuguese had been crossing it on the African side since 1471. And it was the first to touch the territory of Brazil. Around June 27 they stepped ashore on what was to become Lisbon's greatest colony and the largest Portuguese-speaking country in the world. Not until ten months later did Pedro Alvares Cabral, an aristocratic young mariner in the service of the King of Portugal, reach these same coasts in command of a fleet of thirteen ships whose destination was India. Cabral explored only a portion of the coast and made his way to India round the Cape of Good Hope, turning his back on Brazil. All he did was to send news of his discovery to Lisbon by messenger. The historians of Portugal have been jealous of Amerigo's priority in the discovery of Brazil, but this is unjustified. One of Amerigo's companions was an anonymous Portuguese sailor, whose name has been swallowed up like a drop of water in the sand.[3]

3. T. 0. Marcondes de Souza: *Amerigo Vespucci e suas Viagens* (1949) sums up present-day opinion concerning Amerigo's voyage: "Modern historical criticism admits that having separated from Hojeda, and sailing southwest, he at last reached Cape St. Roque, at which point he turned north... This being the case, the priority of the discovery of Brazil goes to him."

What discoveries did Amerigo make along these coasts? "We learned that these were a people called cannibals, very fierce, who eat human flesh." One of the legends that spread quickest and farthest, and one of the most difficult to verify, was that of the man-eating men of the New World. It began with the earliest voyages to the Antilles. Amerigo was mainly responsible for its extension to Brazil. Waldseemüller, whose maps are a riot of color and of fact and fancy, limits to three lines his description of Brazil on his planisphere of 1516. He says first that its lands are inhabited by anthropophagi, and adds: *"Brasilia sive Terra Papagalli."* Amerigo is responsible for this observation too. As with Hojeda in Guadeloupe, the first thing that caught his eye along these new coasts was the parrots, the most decorative and striking he had ever beheld. Some were scarlet, or green and scarlet, or lemon yellow, or pure green, or black and red. For a long time Brazil was known as "the Land of Parrots."

In addition to the.parrots there were the songbirds. "It was a thing so soft and melodious that it often happened that we were suspended by its sweetness." In this Amerigo was completely accurate, and was not carried away like Columbus into thinking he heard nightingales. Of the trees he wrote: "Its trees are so beautiful and so soft that we thought we were in the Garden of Eden." Was it Columbus's Garden of Eden that Amerigo saw? No. That of Columbus was based on the early Church

Pages 288-289: *A detail of Ribeiro's "Universal Chart" of 1529, the Caribbean and Pacific coasts of Colombia.*

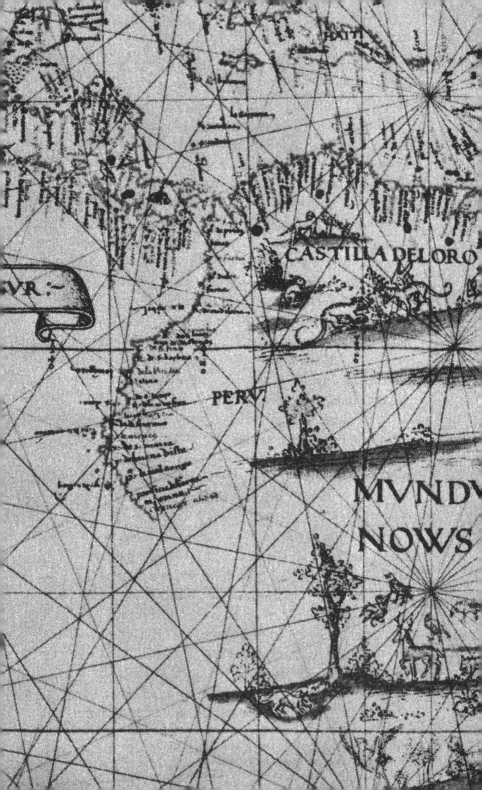

CASTILLA DELORO

VR.~

PERV

MVNDV

NOWS

OCCEANVS

TERA BRASILIS:

Fathers and certain contentious geographers. Their
descriptions were highflown, violent, full of tech-
nicalities. Amerigo's conception was more poetic,
more Florentine. It recalls the paradise of Dante
and Poliziano. It is the enchanted wood, the flower-
scented air wafted through the trees filled with sky-
soaring birds. Amerigo had in mind Dante's vision:

> *A pleasant air*
> *That intermitted never, never veer'd,*
> *Smote on my temples, gently, as a wind*
> *Of softest influence: at which the sprays,*
> *Obedient all, lean'd trembling to that part*
> *Where first the holy mountain casts his shade;*
> *Yet were not so disorder'd, but that still*
> *Upon their top the feather'd quiristers*
> *Applied their wonted art, and with full joy*
> *Welcomed those hours of prime, and warbled shrill*
> *Amid the leaves, that to their jocund lays*
> *Kept tenor.*[4]

4. *Un' aura dolce, sanza mutamento*
   avere in sé, mi feria per la fronte
   non di più colpo che soave vento;
   per cui le fronde, tremolando, pronte
   tutte quante piegavano alla parte
   u' la prim' ombra gitta il santo monte;
   non pero dal loro esser dritto sparte
   tanto, che li augelleti per le cime
   lasciasser d'operare ogni lor arte;
   ma con piena letizia l'ore prime,
   cantando, ricevìeno intra le foglie,
   che tenevan bordone alle sue rime.
   Translated by Henry Francis Cary (New York, 1834).

Even today every Florentine carries in his mind a mental image of these visions of Dante, and in Amerigo's day the memory was still more vivid. But Amerigo was cognizant of the new version of paradise in Poliziano's verses to Simonetta and that of Botticelli's painting. The verses echoed in his ears, and the pictures arose before his eyes. All Botticelli's portraits of Simonetta had been painted during the period when Amerigo was in Florence. He saw the *Primavera*, painted shortly after Giuliano de' Medici's assassination, on his return from France. It was the plastic version of Poliziano's paradise. And this paradise was the very Garden of Eden of tropical Brazil, where the trees never lose their leaves and myriad flowers combine to form a garland that circles the waist of the globe and garbs it in eternal youth. What was the difference between this paradise his eyes were beholding and that which Sandro had painted for Simonetta? Or Agnolo had sung for her?

There comes nor hoar frost light nor chilling snow
To dim the eternal garden's locks to white.
Therein the frozen Winter dare not go,
That grass, those trees, no blasts unfriendly blight.
There the revolving years no changes show
Since joyous Spring takes never hence her flight
But loosens her bright hair upon the winds
And myriad blossoms into garlands binds.[5]

5. *Ne mai le chiome del giardino eterno*
   tenera brina o fresca neve imbianca;

Compare these passages in which Amerigo found his inspiration with the words of Columbus: "Holy Writ testifies that Our Lord made the earthly paradise... I have found nóthing in Greek or Latin writings that trustworthily states the site in this world of the earthly paradise, nor seen it actually located on any mappemonde with authoritative proof... All sound theologians agree that it is in the East... I have stated what I found on this hemisphere... I believe the earthly paradise is there, where nobody can arrive... I do not hold that it is of the form of a craggy mountain... The world is of the shape of a pear, which is all round except at the stem end... as though it was a round ball, or like the breast of a woman..." Without having read Columbus's report, and certainly having in mind not Eve, but some local beauty, the fishermen of Margarita had given the hill shaped like the breast of a woman the name of "María Guevara's teat." Both Hojeda and De la Cosa state that Columbus merely glimpsed the island of Margarita, that he did not go inland, and passed it by without exploring its mysteries. This is not entirely true. He saw in it the Hill of Paradise; its form

ivi non osa entrar ghiacciato verno;
non vento o l'erbe o gli arbuscelli stanca;
ivi no volgon gli anni lor quaderno;
ma leita Primavera mai non manca,
ch' e' suoi crin biondi a crespi all' aura spiega
e mille fibri in ghirlandetta lega.
Translated by Nesca A. Robb in *Neoplatonism of the Italian Renaissance* (London, 1935).

caught his fancy, and he dreamed of ropes of pearls. But as he knew that it was advisable that everything in his relations be served up with theological doubletalk and geographical patter, he based his ideas on St. Isidore's and St. Ambrose's concept of paradise and on a variety of fabulous mappemondes.[6]

Of the three principal mariners on this expedition, we could say that Hojeda was the landman, Juan de la Cosa the seaman, and Amerigo the stargazer. He was a Florentine, and the sight most discernible from Florence was the firmament. This was the divining glass. A businessman like Strozzi, when the foundations of his palace were to be laid, consulted an astrologer to learn the propitious moment to begin the work. Lorenzo the Magnificent, the night he learned of Simonetta's death, saw in the new star he had just discovered the dead girl's soul. In drawing up his maps and working out the shape of the earth, Toscanelli always studied the stars. When Amerigo crossed the equator he was overcome with emotion as he contemplated the heavens. He felt that fortune had indeed smiled on him, for he was now sailing between the two poles, within sight of two heavens. The division of the hours was a marvelous thing: twelve in the light of the sun, twelve under the winking of the stars.

6. L. Olschki: *Storia letteraria della Scoperte geôgrafice* (p. 17) says: "Columbus may never have read a line of Dante, but the idea of the Earthly Paradise was never out of his mind on his voyages, to the point where he may finally have believed that he had reached the very site."

We can barely discern the Little Dipper (he writes),
which is the watchman that revolves about the fir-
mament... I, longing to be the one to devise the other
polestar, lost my sleep many nights contemplating the
movement of the stars of the other pole to discover
when their orbit became shortened and they were
closer to the firmament. But I was unable to do so,
despite the many wakeful nights I spent and all the
instruments I employed, which were the quadrant
and the astrolabe. I discovered no star having less
than ten degrees of movement in its orbit, so I did
not feel justified in naming any one as pointing to
the South Pole because of the great circle they de-
scribed about the firmament. And while I was doing
this I recalled a saying of our poet Dante...

Dante and Virgil had been wandering through the
circles of Hell, when suddenly, at dawn, they saw the
morning star gleaming, like a magnet guiding their
steps toward the birthplace of Paradise. Dante supposed that in the antipodes of Jerusalem a magic island raised its breast out of the water, the isle of Paradise.
And as a harbinger of this wonder, he saw the four
stars of the Southern Cross. He does not say that it was
a cross, but "four stars ne'er seen before save by the
ken of our first parents." The verses that came to
Amerigo's mind, and which he copies in his letter to
Lorenzo di Pier Francesco de' Medici were these:

To the right hand I turn'd and fix'd my mind
On the other pole attentive, where I saw
Four stars ne'er seen before save by the ken

Of our first parents. Heaven of their rays
Seem'd joyous. Oh thou northern site! bereft
Indeed, and widow'd, since of these deprived.[7]

And Amerigo saw the four stars. This was the discovery of the sky. It was such things that made the Florentine a poet, that recalled verses to his mind, that filled him with the urge to travel. Others were moved by the waves or drawn to the land, but he to the stars, by the stars, for the stars. But the lyrical quality in him was seasoned with wit. "I have seen," Amerigo observed, "four stars... that have little motion, and if God grants me life and health... I hope not to return without seeing the other pole." But it did not occur to him to think of the new constellation in terms of a cross. The music of the spheres had made him romantic: "Four stars," he says, "that have the shape of a mandolin."

He felt himself truly a discoverer as he rectified old ideas established by scholars on the basis of theory. He refuted the fantasies of Columbus himself about the subtropical climatic zones. Columbus held the belief that only Negroes lived there or that they were regions which the divine will had made

7. *Io me volsi a man destra, e puosi mente*
   all'altro polo, e vidi quattro stelle
   non vista mai fuor ch'alla prima gente.
   Goder pareva il ciel di lor flammelle:
   oh settentrional vedovo sito,
   poi che privato se' di mirar quelle!
   Translated by Henry Francis Cary (New York, 1814).

unfit for human habitation. "It seems to me," wrote Amerigo, "that most of the philosophers stand confounded by this voyage of mine, because they say that the torrid zone is uninhabitable because of the great heat, and on this journey of mine I have found it to be quite the contrary, for the air is cooler and more tempered in this region than outside it..."

Although the pilots' orders were to meet off the coast of Venezuela, the ship in which Amerigo was traveling, either at his suggestion or by agreement among the sailors, advanced a little farther south, to Cape St. Vincent, in an attempt to explore the southern coast. They descended to a point 8° below the equator. They were now hundreds of leagues to the south of the coast that Columbus had explored, and it was time to rejoin Hojeda. They turned north, skirting the coast, setting their course toward the Caribbean. They passed the mouths of the Amazon without making any attempt to enter, and arrived at the island of Trinidad, which had already been discovered by Columbus. Amerigo described its inhabitants as cannibals, of friendly disposition and goodly stature. "They took us to one of their settlements, located some two leagues inland, and invited us to eat. Anything that was asked of them they gave us, more, I think, from fear than from good will."

After this they sailed by the mouth of the Orinoco and continued skirting the coast of Paria. The natives received them affectionately. They saw lions, deer, wild pigs–fauna not present on the islands. They sailed, said Amerigo, four hundred leagues along the coast. It had not yet occurred to him that this was a new continent. Like Columbus, he still believed it to be Asia.

The thing that set him apart from Columbus and all the others was his lack of concern for gold. He neither mentioned it nor sought it. He had no dreams of finding it in fabulous quantities. When he did see it used by the Indians as ornaments, he was not at all impressed with it. But pearls were another story. In Florence the word *Orient* was associated with pearls. One of the best pledges of love was a necklace of pearls. We have seen how knights entered the lists with caps, capes, and doublets embroidered with pearls. Botticelli's, Lippi's, and Piero di Cosimo's portraits of Simonetta all show her hair intertwined with strings of pearls. Now, as Amerigo sailed the Pearl Gulf, he stopped at the island of Margarita, where he traded articles of barter for pearls, and the natives explained by signs how the fishermen brought them up from the bottom of the sea. "We found," he writes, "that they had great quantities of Orient pearls, and very good ones, and we secured the weight of 119 marks of them in exchange for a small amount of merchandise. I think they cost us the equivalent of 40 ducats, because all we gave them were bells, mirrors and beads... Each of them was willing to give all the pearls he had for a bell."

When, on Amerigo's return to Spain, he showed the pearls to the Queen, a fine passage of wits ensued between the two. Isabella was a woman as well as a queen. The Florentine has set down the scene with all his astuteness: "They gave us in barter many oysters of those which bear the pearls, one containing a hundred and thirty, and others less. The one with a hundred and thirty the Queen took from me. I took care that she should not see the others…"

From the Pearl Gulf they sailed to the island now known as Curaçao. According to Amerigo, its name should have been the Island of the Giants, and it was so called for some time. In his letter to Gonfalonier Soderini he told him the inhabitants were the size of Francesco degli Albizzi, though better proportioned. This Francesco degli Albizzi was a gigantic Florentine whom Amerigo and Soderini had known in their youth, and whom Amerigo probably imagined the gonfalonier still saw. The phrasing of the letter would seem to indicate that neither Amerigo nor Soderini had liked him. Albizzi evidently returned the gonfalonier's feelings, for not long afterwards he took part in a conspiracy against him.

What impressed Amerigo about the men was their size. As for the women, he tells that they saw hideous old hags first, and then some truly beautiful young girls. They decided to kidnap one of them to take to Queen Isabella and Don Ferdinand as a present. As they were on the point of putting this plan into effect, a group of young warriors appeared, carrying big clubs and bows and arrows. Amerigo and his comrades felt their blood turn to water, and it may have been their terror that made them see giants. They explained as well as they could that they had not come with warlike intent, but as messengers of peace. "In conclusion, we decided to get away from them without trouble, and we took the same road back by which we had come, and they accompanied us as far as the sea." As is evident from this passage, which is typical of his style, Amerigo did not cultivate the heroic manner.[8]

The ship next set out toward the mainland, and a new name was added to the geography of this hemisphere, a name as Italian in its origin as in its irony: Venezuela, Little Venice. The travelers had seen a settlement built over the sea, whose houses were of reeds and poles. Amerigo had described something of the sort he had seen off the coast of Mexico, but this one was more impressive. The houses were skillfully constructed, and filled with finely woven cotton cloth; the beams were of logwood. The inhabitants tried to keep the voyagers from entering, but, swords being unknown to them, they made their acquaintance to their grief. The explorers, too, had got off on the wrong foot. As there had been sword blows, there was war.

The ships continued along the coast, and parallel to the coast stalked war. The Indians were naked and brave. The white men protected themselves with shields and attacked with lance and sword. The sands were covered with tawny Indians left lying in their blood. Amerigo and his companions entered one

---

8. In De Bry's famous *Grands Voyages* there is a woodcut of the scene of Amerigo and the giant maidens.

settlement, found the houses deserted, and sacked them. To one like Amerigo, familiar with the looting that took place in Italy, this was a mere bagatelle.

But the Europeans did not always have things their own way:

One day we saw a host of people, all armed to defend themselves and prevent us from landing. Twenty-six of us armed ourselves well, and we covered the boats to keep the arrows from finding us. Nevertheless, they wounded several of us before we could leap ashore... We fought hard... but they rushed upon us in such numbers and with so many arrows that we were unable to resist them. Losing almost all hope, we turned our backs... and as we were falling back and fleeing in this way, a Portuguese sailor who had been left in charge of the boat... leaped ashore, shouting: "Sons, stand and fight and God will give you victory!" With this he knelt and began to pray. Then he charged the Indians... and we scattered them... We killed one hundred and fifty of them and burned a hundred and eighty of their houses. We were badly wounded and weary. We returned to the ships and took refuge in a harbor, where we remained twenty days for the doctor to treat us. We were all saved except one...

Years after Amerigo's death his nephew, Giovanni Vespucci, who was appointed official map-maker of Spain, designed a large, beautiful planisphere. By this time there was knowledge of the new continent, and as such it appears on this map. Giovanni did not use the name America, which was already being employed by others, but he did insert three names on the coast of Venezuela which are in the nature of a résumé of his uncle's relation: Aldea Grande (Big Village), Val d'Amerigo (Amerigo's Valley), and Aldea Quemada (Burned Village).[9]

It is not clear from Amerigo's account or from contemporary allusions to the expedition just where the ships rejoined one another or where they separated again. It would seem that, though they formed part of the same expedition, they were free to operate independently, like groups of policemen running down every clue. But all of the leaders–Hojeda, De la Cosa, and Amerigo–were in agreement that it was time to get back. They had seen what they had come to see, and a little more. They had spent many fatiguing months: the men were tired. The ships were badly in need of repair, and the pumps could not keep them dry. They made for Hispaniola, "the island," says Amerigo, "which Admiral Columbus discovered." Hojeda, who had more to do with administrative matters, soon learned that the situation between Columbus and Roldán had become one of open quarrel and intrigue. Amerigo set out

9. A. Magnaghi: *Il Planisfere del 1523 de lla Biblioteca del Re in Torino*, assumes that Aldea Grande corresponds to the present Puerto Cabello. With regard to Puerto Frechato, which Navarrete identifies with Chiriviquí, he points out that today this spot is to the west of Golfo Triste. Val d'Amerigo, he says, also appears on the undated map of Count Ottomano Freducci (Biblioteca Comunale of Mantua) and on that known as the Salviati Map (Biblioteca Mediceo-Laurenziana, Florence), p. 56.

through an archipelago where the islands were thick as flies. "We discovered more than a thousand islands." An exaggeration, but not too great. Columbus had baptized them with a name of even greater plurality: the Eleven Thousand Virgins. "All the natives were timid," wrote Amerigo, "...and we did as we pleased with them. We decided to take slaves, load the ships with them, and return to Spain."

Amerigo's greatest profit from this voyage was his study of the heavens. He made an extraordinary discovery bearing upon the co-ordinates of longitude. This occurred on a night that was memorable for him, August 23, 1499. This is how he describes his discovery:

With regard to the longitude I say that I had such difficulty in ascertaining it that it was very hard for me to know with certainty the route I had followed along the meridian, and I was so perplexed that finally I found nothing better to do than to observe and see the conjunction of one planet with another, and the movement of the moon with regard to the other planets, because the moon is of all planets the one traveling most swiftly in its orbit, and I proved this by the almanac of Giovanni de Monteregio (Regiomontanus), which was based on the meridian of the city of Ferrara, brought into agreement with the calculations of the Alphonsine Tables; and after many nights of observation, one of these nights when we were at the 23rd of August 1499, and the moon was in conjunction with Mars, which, according to the almanac, was to take place at midnight or half an hour earlier, I found that when the moon rose on our horizon, which was an hour and a half after the setting of the sun, the planet had moved to the east; that is to say, the moon was one degree and several minutes to the east of Mars, and by midnight it was fifteen and one half degrees, more or less, to the east, so that putting it in the form of a proportion, if 24 hours give 360 degrees, what would 5 ½ hours give? I found that it gave me 82 degrees, and I found that, allowing 16 ²/₃ leagues to each degree, my position in longitude from the meridian of the city of Cádiz was 1,366 ²/₃ leagues to the west of the city of Cádiz. My reason for allowing 16 ²/₃ leagues to each degree is that according to Ptolemy and Alfagrán the earth has a circumference of 6,000, leagues, and dividing this by 360 degrees gives each degree 16 ²/₃ leagues, and I have checked this many times with the pilots' readings and have found it true and accurate.

Whereas problems of this sort were insoluble mysteries for Amerigo's comrades, he concentrated far into the night to discover the solution. An atmosphere of admiration grew up about him. How much of a part did luck play in his findings? Were the conclusions at which he arrived accurate? When Amerigo's letter became known, not many of its readers paid any attention to this part of it, or at least there is no record that they did. It is possible that this information was not so much for the Popolano as for the scholars of the group: Giorgio Antonio Vespucci, Zenobio Acciaiuoli, and the others. At any rate, two or three centuries elapsed. Scholars found the most accurate copy of Amerigo's letters in the notebooks of that Piero Vaglienti who had a small business in Pisa. A Florentine astronomer, Stanislao Canovai, professor of mathematics in Cortona and later in Padua, was the first to study the matter, in 1791. He presented a paper before the Etruscan Academy of Cortona on the progress of observations on longitude from the time of Augustus to that of Charles V. He said: "Should we not regard as a manifestation of genius this unique insight of Vespucci, which brought him in one instant to a point no astronomer had reached in twelve centuries?"

The method employed by Amerigo seemed to Canovai inspired by genius. But he found in the calculations errors which, analyzed by others, gave rise to doubts of the authenticity of the letter copied by Vaglienti. The matter was debated for a century and a half by scholars. It was not until 1950 that the astronomer of the Vatican Observatory, Professor J. W. Stein, a learned Jesuit, studied the matter thoroughly. "I am amazed," he wrote, "that up to the present, so far as I have been able to discover, nobody has checked the observations of Vespucci of August 23, 1499, calculating the relative positions of Mars and the moon on that date. With the object of so doing, I have made use of the tables of Neugebauer's chronology." After verifying Amerigo's remarks point by point, Stein reached this conclusion: "Until there is proof to the contrary, we must consider Vespucci as the inventor of the method of lunar distances. He was the first to employ it, measuring the distance between the moon and Mars at midnight of August 23, 1499. He lacked only exact information to have given an exact longitude."[10]

What was the source of this knowledge that from the first moment gave Amerigo a position of pre-eminence on a voyage on which there was a man like Juan de la Cosa? How did he come to be regarded as a master of pilots by Spaniards and Portuguese alike, his services sought by the rulers of both kingdoms? Had he been studying while he was working for the Popolano in Florence, or had he been his own university while in Spain, assembling information from almanacs and astronomical treatises? Did he possess a natural genius such as we have seen in other members of the Vespucci family? It might be remarked in passing that his nephew, Bartolommeo, doctor in astrology and mathematics, was highly esteemed in Italy at this time by reason of his own merits. These questions are raised by the Vatican astronomer, who, without stopping to answer them, goes on to say:

What remains to be determined is whether Vespucci was the discoverer of the method of lunar distances. It is true that prior to 1499 we find no mention of him... Canovai definitely defends Vespucci's priority, and von Zach clearly takes the same position in

---

10. J. W. Stein, S.J.: *Esame critico intorno alla scoperta di Vespucci circa la determinazione delle longitudine in mare mediante le distanze lunari (Memorie della Società Astronomica Italiana*, Vol. XXI, No. 4 (1950) pp. 345-53).

his Monatliche Correspondenz *(1810), when he states that it remained for Amerigo Vespucci to hit upon, formulate, and apply the new method for calculating longtitude at sea. Nevertheless, the possibility must not be excluded that in Florence Vespucci had received some hint from Toscanelli or Regiomontanus, bearing in mind the fact that the process of reasoning employed by Regiomontanus to calculate the distance of comets is practically the same.*

From determining geographic bearings to making maps was only a step. And Amerigo took this step as soon as he returned to Spain. He wrote to Lorenzo di Pier Francesco:

I have decided, Magnificent Lorenzo, to send you two drawings with a description of the world, drawn up and prepared with my own hands and knowledge. And these will be a flat map and a mappemonde in the shape of a sphere which I plan to send you by boat with one Francesco Lotti, a Florentine who is here. I think you will like them, especially the sphere. Not long ago I made another for Their Majesties, and they prize it very much...

Amerigo brought the monarchs, not parrots, but a globe of the world. Hojeda brought them a sheaf of complaints and intrigues. Their Catholic Majesties realized that no time should be lost in sending out Bobadilla, the judge they had appointed to investigate the situation and restore order in Hispaniola. On his arrival he listened to all parties, drew his conclusions, put Columbus under arrest, and sent him back to Spain in irons. If Hojeda had not brought back any gold, he had accomplished a mission of great importance. Ferdinand and Isabella were so grateful to him that they showered him with attentions, gave him unusual marks of royal favor.

Juan de la Cosa and Amerigo took on difficult assignments. Amerigo went to Portugal; De la Cosa set out with Bastidas to explore the coast of Venezuela farther. On his return, De la Cosa went to Portugal too, as a secret agent of the Catholic Majesties, paid by them. His duty was to secure maps and information. Later he returned once more to the coasts of Venezuela, where he died from the wounds of Indian arrows.

Amerigo's second voyage had been of greater utility than any other in orienting the general policy of the discoveries. And for those who had made the voyage it was a training school whose effects would have an immediate repercussion in the subsequent chapters of Hispano-Portuguese history.

XV

THE PORTUGUESE IN AFRICA
(1501)

Recounting his voyages, Amerigo wrote to Piero Soderini, the gonfalonier:

I was in Seville, resting and recovering from the many hardships we had suffered on the last two voyages, and desirous of returning to the land of the pearls, when Fortune, not yet satisfied with my sufferings, in some fashion that I do not know, put it into the mind of the Most Serene King of Portugal to make use of me; and while I was there in Seville, without the remotest thought of going to Portugal, a messenger arrived bearing a letter from the Crown, begging me to come to Lisbon to talk with His Highness, promising me reward. There were those who advised me not to go. I sent back the messenger saying that I was ill and that when my health was restored, if His Highness still wanted to make use of me, I would do whatever he wished. Seeing that he could not win me over, he decided to send Giuliano di Bartholomeo del Giocondo, who was in Lisbon, with instructions to take me with him by any means. The aforesaid Giuliano arrived in Seville, and as a result of his coming and entreaties I found myself forced to go; and my going was eyed askance by all who knew me, because I left Castile, where I had

Nuño Gonçalves, Políptico de San Vicente. Detail of the lower right-hand corner, showing Henry the Navigator, ca. 1465.

been honored and where the King held me in high regard. And the worst of it was that I left without taking leave of anyone.

The fact was that Amerigo had nothing and everything in Seville. It was not business interests that held him there; it was his friends. He could no longer sign himself "merchant." He held no official post. He was not a citizen of Castile. He had abandoned trade for the lure of the sea, but he had neither the money nor the temperament to command voyages. His dream of returning to the land of pearls was a nebulous idea. It might have been a way of earning a living, like any other. What bound him to Seville were the ties of human relationships. He had established a home there. The fire that burned in María Cerezo's Andalusian eyes was for him. This was no hole-and-corner affair like that of his early Florentine days. María Cerezo was his wife by bell, book, and candle. The only explanation of his leaving for Portugal was that he envisaged a voyage of brief duration. Fernando, the brother of María Cerezo, was left in charge of several matters pending in connection with Gianetto Berardi's will. He was to collect 2,340 maravedís from Pedro Ortiz, who had gone security for an Englishman who left owing that sum to Berardi, an Englishman known as "Guillen Asteloy."[1]

---

1. *Colección de documentos inéditos relativos al descubrimiento,* Document No. 5.

Amerigo's closest friends were Hojeda, De la Cosa, and the sailors who had been his mates on the two preceding voyages. All of them admired him, and not a few owed him favors. His rating with the Spanish monarchs could not have been higher. He had served Ferdinand in particular on two delicate missions without any *quid pro quo*, without feeling that he had claims upon the King's bounty, withholding from Queen Isabella's eyes only a few pearls, and taking for his reward his experiences, which were of benefit to all. Few expeditions left such pleasant memories with the Crown and with those who carried them out. It is of no consequence that they are not mentioned in the records: they gave rise to no litigation.

But Amerigo's connections with his fellow Italians were still an important feature of his life. There was an uninterrupted communication with one another among the Italian colonies of Lisbon, Seville, and Barcelona and with Genoa, Milan, Venice, Ferrara, and Florence. The activities of Italian merchants in the Iberian Peninsula were of singular importance. They constituted a widespread burgher family in these commercially underdeveloped kingdoms. There was an understanding among them all; they exchanged information; they helped one another in difficulties. King Manuel's efforts alone might not have sufficed to persuade Amerigo; but a message carried by Bartholomeo del Giocondo from the Italians in Lisbon had an immediate effect. As soon as Amerigo received it, his infirmities and sloth vanished. He left Seville posthaste, without even saying good-bye to his friends.

Portugal was Europe's natural frontier on the Atlantic. It had the port from which Columbus should have sailed; it was the logical point from which to launch the search for the new route to Asia. A student of the period cannot fail to be surprised that navigators as bold and skilled as the Portuguese should have hung back, leaving the crossing of the Atlantic to the initiative of Columbus. All the information Columbus possessed he had come by in Portugal. He knew nothing not already known to the Lusitanians. Only inexplicable delay deprived King Manuel of the glory and profits of the discovery, leaving the prize to the other kingdom of the peninsula.

The Italians drew no distinction between Spain and Portugal, carrying on their activities in both kingdoms. The Florentine house of Marchioni in Lisbon played at least as important a part in the Portuguese expeditions as that of Berardi in the Spanish voyages from Seville. It was Marchioni who received the maps of Toscanelli, which encouraged the Portuguese King to send Vasco da Gama on the expedition that rounded the Cape of Good Hope. Marchioni underwrote part of the cost of Cabral's fleet in March 1500. A Florentine clerk of Marchioni's commanded one of the ships of João da Nova, who inaugurated the yearly flotillas sent out by the Portuguese to the Indies. In 1503 Giovanni da Empoli, also in the employ of Marchioni, accompanied Albuquerque to

India and drew up for the gonfalonier Soderini the best account of the voyage.[2] The ship of Cabral's expedition which first returned bringing the news of Brazil was that fitted out by the Italians.

As far as the King of Portugal was concerned, he would as lief have sent for Hojeda or De la Cosa or any other Spanish seaman. It was in the eyes of the Italians that Amerigo was a person of importance. Up to that time Amerigo had felt himself under no obligations to Spain beyond the duties he had been assigned on the missions he carried out. The accounts of his voyages were first for Lorenzo di Pier Francesco de' Medici and later for Soderini. In July 1500, before leaving Seville for Portugal, he wrote the Medici a long letter concerning his second voyage. In the year 1501 he wrote to him: "You will have learned, Lorenzo, from my letter, as from that of our Florentines in Lisbon, how, while I was in Seville, the King of Portugal sent for me."

There is a highly plausible but unverified report to the effect that before going to Portugal, Amerigo made a flying trip to Florence, where he enrolled in

2. Duarte Leite: *O mais antiguo mapa do Brasil, Historia da colonizacão potugueza do Brasil*, Vol. II, P. 253, assumes that the expedition with which Amerigo sailed was underwritten by Marchioni. Jaime Cortesão (*Revista Portuguesa*, São Paulo, 1930, Vol. I, F. I.), says: "The outstanding adviser and financial backer of the enterprise of the discoveries and the organization of trade with the Indies... was the Florentine Bartolomeu Marchioni." The notary who drew up the documents of Marchioni in Florence was Antonio Vespucci (Masetti-Bencini, op. cit., p. 182).

the spice-dealers' and apothecaries' guild, the group most keenly interested in the development of navigation to the Orient.

Two widely differing interpretations have grown up of this trip to Portugal. According to one, Amerigo behaved disloyally toward Spain. According to the other, he may have been engaged in spying. Both versions are farfetched. What was the state of affairs in the year 1500? What was Amerigo's personal situation?

King Ferdinand's choice of Amerigo to accompany the Spaniards on the two fact-finding voyages can be explained by the need of including a friend of Columbus's to remove any hint of enmity toward a man whom the monarchs did not wish to injure. What Amerigo was given, rather than obligations to Ferdinand, was an opportunity to make a place for himself in the King's court. Serving different kings in turn, even leaving the service of one king for that of his adversary, was not only frequent in Italy, but traditional routine. The profession of condottiere, a man who raised troops to offer them for hire to anyone who wanted his services, was based on this practice. Illustrious figures of those days were condottieri, beginning with the Sforza. But even this was not the case of Amerigo, nor of the crowns of Spain and Portugal.

A natural suspicion and unsettled grievances may well have existed between Spain and Portugal as an aftermath of the conflicting claims of Isabella and Juana la Beltraneja to the throne of Castile, but such jealousy and distrust had been softened by time and dispelled by the treaty of 1479. The dubious daughter of the unchaste Queen Joanna of Portugal and Henry the Impotent of Castile was living in the Convent of St. Claire in Coimbra, removed from all political intrigue. The better to weld the friendship between the two kingdoms, King Manuel of Portugal had married Doña Isabella, the daughter of Their Catholic Majesties. There was a pleasant relationship of father-in-law and son-in-law between Don Ferdinand and Don Manuel, with touches even of friendship and collaboration.

This does not imply that the two nations were not rivals or did not spy on each other. Ministers, statesmen, and bishops argued over each nation's rights within the line of demarcation of their respective conquests as established by the Pope. But, for example, when Cabral's expedition returned from India, Don Manuel made haste to notify his father-in-law; and just as Don Ferdinand employed such Portuguese pilots as Díaz de Solís and Magellan, so Spanish mariners sailed with Portuguese expeditions. On that of Cabral, to mention only one, Master Mariner Juan, Pedro López de Padilla, and Sánchez de Tovar were Spaniards.

To the Italians of Lisbon, as to the Portuguese, Amerigo was the man who up to that time had most fully explored the coasts of Brazil. He had first-hand knowledge of all the expeditions Castile had sent out, beginning with those of Columbus. No one else was known to have voyaged so extensively along the coasts of the new lands, from Costa Rica northward to Florida, and from Venezuela southward to Cape San Roque. He had visited the Canary Islands and had sailed by the map drawn up by Columbus.

Amerigo did not feel himself a stranger in Lisbon. Portugal was not an unknown land in the tradition of his family; he was not the first Vespucci to visit it. The Vespucci had been more closely associated with the court of Lisbon than with that of Castile. The circumstances of Piero Vespucci the Elder's stay there are worth recalling.

In the first half of the fifteenth century the sons of King John the Great, Pedro and Henry, began that cycle of exploration which paved the way for Portugal's colonizing activities. One of the brothers, Henry, known as the Navigator, has gone down in history as the father of the Portuguese navy. Nobody else in his day conceived and developed so vast a plan of maritime endeavors. Pedro is less well known, but equally important. He voyaged to many lands. In 1428, on his way back from Venice, he visited Florence, and in Florence called upon Toscanelli. The Republic showered attentions upon him, and, when returning his visit, made good use of the opportunity to strengthen the ties of friendship and trade between the two nations. Portugal was a key point in the mercantile expansion of Florence. The Florentine ships bound for England and Flanders called at Lisbon. The Signoria hoped to obtain from the Portuguese Crown the same privileges it had granted to the Venetians. To this end it sent one of its most skillful diplomats, Luca di Maso degli

Albizzi. He was accompanied by Piero Vespucci and Bernardo Carnesecchi as galley captains. The King paid the visitors great honor, and Florence achieved its aim. During the visit the privileges that Luca degli Albizzi enjoyed were extended to Vespucci and Carnesecchi.[3]

The history of this Piero Vespucci, whom Amerigo never knew (he died four years before Amerigo was born), formed a part of the travel annals of the family. He had been a man of even more business experience than Albizzi himself. As a young man he was in Flanders as an agent of the Medici. He was one of the company of Giovanni Orlandini, and had a share in his banking operations. He is known to have bought grain in Ghent for resale in Bruges. On his return to Florence he was made sea consul. He was called upon to assist in drawing up the statutes for the Florentine community of Bruges, an extremely interesting document that shows how the merchants of the Italian colonies organized a government of their own in foreign countries. Following his mission to Lisbon, Piero Vespucci was appointed port authority of Pisa.

Another link of the Vespucci to Portgual was through Giuliano, sea consul in 1447, who had a hand in drafting the regulations establishing the routes of the Florentine fleets engaged in trade with

3. G. Canestrini: *Intorno alle relazione cornmerciale de' Fiorentini co'Portoghesi avanti e dopo la scoperta del capo di Buona Speranza* (A.S.I., Ser. 1, App. III (1846), pp. 93-5).

Pages 318-319: *Western Africa from a Portuguese sailing book, 16th century.*

northern Europe and the Orient, determining their ports of call.

"And when I presented myself before this King," writes Amerigo, "he showed himself pleased at my coming, and asked me to accompany the three ships he had ready to go to discover new lands. As a king's request is a command, I had to agree to everything he asked of me." They sailed from Lisbon during the first fortnight of May 1501.

The voyage was to follow an opposite route to that which the ships of Spain had taken. Its purpose was not to trespass on the zone in which Their Catholic Majesties had taken the initiative. As Columbus had sailed away from the equator, bearing northward, Portugal would set its course south. It was trying to duplicate on the western coast of the Atlantic the feats it had alrcady accomplished on the eastern. The southernmost point Amerigo had reached on his voyages for the King of Castile had been Cape St. Augustine. Now he would take off from approximately that same spot, pushing south as far as possible. Perhaps he might find a passage that would enable him to round the mainland and sail farther west, such a route as Vasco da Gama had found eastward around the Cape of Good Hope in Africa.

To be sure, Amerigo was not in command of the expedition. His authority did not go beyond that of adviser. He was probably the only one, however, who had made the trip before. Portuguese experience had been limited to Cabral's voyage, but Cabral had turned back toward India, and a single caravel had been dispatched to Portugal carrying the news of Brazil. "We remained in ignorance," said Cabral, "of whether it was an island or the mainland, though we were inclined to the latter opinion."

The voyage, at first, followed the route with which the Portuguese were most familiar. They sighted the Canary Islands without calling, and continued along the coast of Africa to the Cape Verde Islands. Instead of putting in at the islands, they made port at Bezebeghe (Dakar), on the African coast. "The promontory called Ethiope by Ptolemy," says Amerigo, "which we now call Cape Verde, and the Ethiopians Biseghier, and that country Mandraga." They laid over there for eleven days. "My plan," writes Amerigo, "was to sail southward through the Atlantic gulf." His words indicate that his opinion carried weight with the pilots.

An unforeseen incident occurred in Bezebeghe: a meeting with Cabral's fleet homeward bound from India. In this way Amerigo learned the results of the latest exploration in the other hemisphere. Cabral's men had seen many lands, those of greatest interest for dealers in spices. Amerigo realized the importance of this information for his compatriots. It did not occur to him to write to Spain, but he wrote to Florence, to Lorenzo di Pier Francesco de' Medici. He sent his letter by Gherardo Verdi, brother of Simon, who worked in Cádiz. Gherardo had come out with Amerigo, but they decided that the matter was of such importance that Gherardo ought to return at once. Amerigo would have wished to include in his report certain scientific data but, so far as he was able to learn, Cabral's fleet had traveled "without a cosmographer or mathematician, which was a grave mistake."

Amerigo's source of information was a converted Jew, Gaspar by name, who spoke many languages, and who had traveled more extensively than all the others. He had twice accompanied the Portuguese through the Indian Ocean. He had gone from Cairo to Malacca, visiting the interior of India and the island of Sumatra. Destiny had led him from one spot to another. Alexander von Humboldt reconstructed his life in his study of Amerigo's voyages.[4] Gaspar was descended from a family of Poles who had fled from Poland to Palestine and Egypt. He was born in Alexandria, and went later to India. Vasco da Gama encountered him in 1498 on the island of Ankediva, off the coast of Kanara. Having to deal with the rajah, with whose language Gaspar was familiar, Da Gama took him on as interpreter. The Portuguese were suspicious of him, believing him to be a spy. When put to the torture and ordered to make confession, he told them the story of his life and asked to be baptized a Christian. He was christened Gaspar da Gama. He had remained in India and was now traveling with Cabral. He was an incomparable source of information for Amerigo, who could discuss hundreds of things with him in Italian, and a storehouse

4. A. von Humboldt: *Histoire de la géographie du Nouveau Continent*, Vol. V, pp. 82 ff.

of geographical data. In his letter Amerigo did not even mention Cabral. This is typical of his letters, and even of the man. He never bothered to name the commander of the fleet when telling of his own voyages or those of others. He had no ambition to hold the post himself. He sailed on official voyages of discovery, and never on those which adventurers who had struck it rich outfitted at their own expense to make lucrative conquests or for the purpose of trade. In the case of the fleet encountered at Bezebeghe, the most important person as far as Amerigo was concerned was the one who could supply him with information: Gaspar. It was he who turned Amerigo's eyes to the east once more.

Gaspar confirmed the news of Cabral's touching Brazil. There "he found white, naked people." Amerigo set down in his letter: "This is the same land that I discovered for the King of Castile." Cabral had turned his back on Brazil, making for India by the Cape of Good Hope route. He had run into a storm; five of his ships had foundered with all aboard. "May God have had mercy on their souls," is Amerigo's comment. The other ships, to escape the fury of the gale, traveled with furled sails. It took them forty-eight days to make the Cape of Good Hope. From there they had set their course for Arabia Felix and the lands of Prester John. The explorers still had a lively memory of that priest, who was held to be a descendant of the Magi, and who in the twelfth century was believed to govern with clemency and wisdom the lands reaching to the three Indies. In his realm the Amazons dwelt; there were the shrine of St. Thomas the apostle and the fountain of eternal youth. The rivers ran over sands of gold. All these stories were transferred to America and bloomed anew in the relations of the chroniclers, firing the imagination of the conquerors. Cabral bore east, thinking of the realms of Prester John. He reached the nearby lands of the Nile, finding there great cities like Cairo, which paid rich tribute of gold to its King. In Mozambique he found aloes, lacquers, and silk cloth. He was in Quilca, Mombasa, Dimodaza, Melinde, Mogadisho, Camperuia, Zendach, Animab Abadul, Albarcon, cities rich in treasure of gold, jewels, cloth, spices, drugs. "If the provinces, kingdoms, and names of the cities and islands do not correspond with those used by the ancient writers," Amerigo comments, "it is a sign that they have been changed, as we see in Europe, where only exceptionally does one hear an ancient name."

Continuing with Gaspar's narration, Amerigo writes that in addition to the five ships lost in the storm, another went down with a cargo valued at one hundred thousand ducats. But those which survived the hazards of the trip carried incalculable riches to Portugal. In Ceylon–Amerigo was of the belief that this was the island of Taprobana–they found pearls and precious stones, drugs, elephants, horses. Equally valuable were the products they found in Sumatra. They saw great ships, junks, bearing this wealth. To please the King of Calicut on one occasion they captured a ship loaded with elephants and rice, and carrying three hundred men. On another they sank twelve ships. Among the items in the cargo the Portuguese were carrying, Amerigo noted cinnamon, ginger, pepper, cloves, nutmeg, mastic, musk, civet, storax, cassia, resin, incense, myrrh, benzoin, sandalwood, aloes, camphor, amber, cane, lacquer, indigo, opium, and many other drugs, not to mention a kind of porcelain which King Manuel referred to in his letter to King Ferdinand by the name Amerigo had used in his.

Information of this nature explains the urge that possessed everyone to undertake the hazards of discovering new routes. As Amerigo observed: "The King of Portugal has a powerful trade and great wealth in his hands. May God increase it. I believe the spices will go from these parts to Germany and Italy, in view of their quality and price. That's the way the world goes."

In Pisa, Piero Vaglienti had already written in his book: "The spices that should go or formerly went to Cairo by way of the Red Sea are now carried the other way round to Lisbon."

Ptolemy's geography had become a living reality.

Amerigo wrote: "I consider this voyage I am now undertaking dangerous from the point of view of this our human existence. Nevertheless, I set out upon it with resolute heart to serve God and the world. And if God has been pleased with me, he will give me strength provided that I am prepared to do his will in all, and will give eternal repose to my soul."

Amerigo's letter is important for the light it throws upon his character. With the information he had received from Gaspar, with the knowledge he had acquired of the Orient, another man would have invented a voyage of his own. There was a tendency in Amerigo to give things their rightful values. He was following a family tradition in transmitting strictly accurate information to the Medici or the Signoria of Florence. His experience on the mission to Paris with his uncle Guido Antonio had provided excellent training in reporting news. The formula was to see all and tell all with maximum fidelity. To invent a voyage would have been out of character, an act of puerile foolishness. A touch of imagination was permissible in the interpretation of the facts; in the facts themselves, never. Amerigo formed part of an Italian colony, the Florentine, which was continually writing. Without proposing it, they acted as a check on one another. Every letter from Spain or Portugal to Florence, Genoa, Ferrara, or Milan was a link in a vast intelligence system within which any falsity would have become apparent instantly. Gherardo Verdi, who was carrying the letter, and any one of the crew members whom the Italians in Lisbon would question about the voyage, would have showed up any lie as a clumsy attempt at deception.

Theodoro de Bry, Amerigo Vespucci believes that crocodiles are dragons.

XVI

FROM BRAZIL TO PATAGONIA
(1501-1502)

In 1502 Amerigo wrote a letter to Lorenzo di Pier Francesco de' Medici which began: "The last letter I sent you was from a place on the coast of Guinea called Cape Verde. At that time I informed you of the beginning of my voyage. The present will adivse you briefly how we accomplished it and what its results were… We set out from Cape Verde without difficulty, equipped with everything we needed, such as water, wood, and the indispensable articles for embarking on the gulf of the ocean sea to seek new lands…"

The early experiences were not encouraging. The crossing dragged on interminably. Columbus on his first voyage had taken one month and six days to cross the Atlantic from the Canary Islands to Guanahani. He had sailed in a straight line across the widest part. Amerigo employed sixty-four or sixty-seven days, crossing the same ocean at its narrowest point. "From the promontory of Cape Verde to the beginning of the continent is about 700 leagues, though I calculate that we sailed over 1,800." The distance was not caused by the sea, but by the bad weather and, above all, as Amerigo says, by the ignorance of the pilots. The roughest storm the sailors

Ilustration for Vespucci's letter to Pier Sorderini on his second trip, 1509. Engraving on wood, 19 x 13,4 cm. The British Library, London.

had ever encountered buffeted their ships unmercifully. They had to tack and beat to windward.

One thing helped them through–Amerigo's knowledge, a knowledge that shone not only by its own light, but by the ignorance of the others. "My companions recognized my courage and the fact that I knew cosmography, for there was not a pilot or any real navigational guide who could chart our bearings within five hundred leagues. We were lost and off course, and only by the instruments–the quadrant and the astrolabe, as we all know–could we ascertain the exact position of the heavenly bodies. Since then they have honored me greatly." Amerigo made the ship his classroom. He taught the men cosmography. He gave his classes with the clouds touching the waters and the wind whipping the waves and howling through the rigging. Day after day of overcast sky, and not a single calm night. The only one who knew with certainty that they were moving toward the mainland was Amerigo. He talked of navigation charts, of the astrolabe and the quadrant. The crew knew, besides, that he had explored the distant coast, had seen its trees, its inhabitants, its animals, its wealth. They were not sailing toward the unknown.

When they finally made landfall, Amerigo's statements were confirmed. On that day science received a vote of confidence from the unlettered crew members. Amerigo had not bamboozled them, he had not alluded to mysterious writings or assumed the role of a seer. What he knew, anybody could know. Science was another terra firma.

Amerigo's first glances were directed toward the stars. After them came the landscape and the people. The heavens continued to teach him new things. The landscape made him think again of Paradise. In the four months and twenty-seven days he sailed south of the equator he did not see either the Big or Little Dipper. But he discovered many stars that he had not observed in the Northern Hemisphere. He took notes for a book. "I noted the marvelous workings of their revolutions and their grandeur, calculating the diameter of their orbits and setting them down with geometrical figures, and I marked other movements of the heavenly bodies. It would be dangerous to write of this. All the notable things I observed on this voyage I have collected for a little book I have in mind. When I have leisure, I shall devote myself to it, and thus, after my death I shall achieve some fame..."

Giorgio Antonio had taught him that the only thing that justifies man's earthly existence is the association of his name with some endeavor that contributes to increase the store of human knowledge. "Alas for those," his uncle had told him, "who leave behind the sorry memory of a life given over to the chase, dancing, pleasure!"

The landscape was not new to Amerigo, but, as always, he took it in with all his senses. So many different trees, always in leaf, with exotic odors; flowers of a thousand shapes and colors; fruits of new flavor. The only thing the crew had smelled for two months had been the damp breeze impregnated with salt and iodine, musty sails and leather, rain-soaked wood, the reek of the barrels of hardtack and olives, sweat and soiled clothing, all the components of that typical ship's odor which assails the nostrils and turns the stomach queasy. A caravel was like a cellar, a better habitat for rats than for men. And now to sail into the clear, diaphanous light, leaving the tempest behind! A gentle breeze brought them the perfume of the foliage, the flowers, and fruits of the tropical forests. While they were still aboard the ships their eyes and their nostrils found solace. "Many times," writes Amerigo, "I have been amazed at the sweet perfume of the grass and flowers, and the flavor of the fruits and tubers made me think of the earthly paradise."

A description of the animals follows:

What shall I say of the number of the birds, and their plumage, colors, and songs, the manifold species, and their beauty? I shall not extend myself, because you will not believe me. Who could enumerate the myriad wild animals, the abundance of lions and ounces and cats, not those of Spain any longer, but of the antipodes? All the wolves, baboons, monkeys of many kinds, some of them so large? Such a variety of animals we saw that I think it would have been hard to get them all in the ark... And the wild boar, the goats, and deer, and stags, and hares, and rabbits. We did not see any domestic animals.

The land was all inhabited, the people going about naked as the day they were born. Amerigo lived in close intimacy with them for twenty-seven days. He ate and slept in their villages and stretched out in their hammocks at the siesta hour. With many of these newly discovered nations relations were completely friendly. Once the strangeness and the initial fear had worn off, the natives, filled with admiration and curiosity, showed a desire to have closer knowledge of these hairy, bearded men who gave them bells, little mirrors, glass beads.

While the natives were discovering the Europeans, Amerigo was trying to discover the natives. He attempted to make certain generalizations about the traits it seemed to him the different tribes had in common. He thought that they had neither religion nor law of any kind, that they lived in keeping with nature. They had no conception of the immortality of the soul. They had no kings. Each was his own master. They were not moved by covetousness. The fact that they did not eat at table, but seated on the ground, seemed barbarous to Amerigo. Their food impressed him as being excellent, except for the last item he lists: tubers, delicious fruits, a great variety of fish, seafood such as crabs, oysters, lobsters, and turtles—and human flesh.

One day the travelers saw a great crowd assembled on the ridge of a mountain and made signs to them to come down to the shore, but the people were distrustful, and there was no way to persuade them. Evening was coming on, and the Portuguese decided to lay bells, mirrors, and knickknacks on the sand and return to the ships. When they did this, the natives approached. Uneasily they shook the bells, and finally they laughed as they saw themselves in the mirrors. The next morning the sailors went ashore to see how their scheme had worked. The natives had withdrawn to the woods, where they had lighted a great bonfire. Now they made signs to the Christians to approach. Two of the sailors asked permission of their captain to go into the forest to learn whether they could establish relations with them. Permission was given, and they were told to return within five days.

A week went by. Every day groups of women came down to the shore to call out provocatively to the ships. It was decided to send a young sailor to talk with them. He was a handsome, brawny Portuguese. As soon as he stepped ashore the women gathered around him in a circle. They observed him, they touched him. He seemed to please them. Suddenly a woman emerged from the woods carrying a great club, which she brought down on the sailor's head with such force that he dropped dead where he stood. The women swiftly dragged his body into the woods. The men came out with bows and arrows. The ships' crews did not venture to leave their vessels, but discharged four cannon balls, which did no harm, but cleared the beach as by magic. Back on the hill, the women piled more wood on the fire and roasted the Portuguese over the flames with shouts of glee. When they judged that he was done, they carved him up, and everyone grabbed a piece of the delicious meat, waving the gnawed bones triumphantly.

This passage in Amerigo's letter impressed his readers more than any other. Sometime between 1502 and 1503 a planisphere was designed which remained unpublished until 1859, when Father Kunstmann brought it out in a famous atlas in which the most important sixteenth-century Spanish and Portuguese maps were reproduced. Several of these anonymous maps were given the name of Father Kunstmann to identify them. The one drawn between 1502 and 1503 is known as Kunstmann II. Unquestionably the cartographer took his information from Amerigo's voyage. The coasts of Brazil and Argentina extend to below 45° south. The illustrations of the map are as interesting as the coastline. The interior of Brazil shows a meticulously drawn scene of a spit being slowly turned by a kneeling Indian, and on the spit a naked white man being roasted over the flames. This drawing was to be repeated on subsequent maps.[1]

Amerigo set down certain considerations on the subject of cannibalism. It was the custom, he said, to eat enemies taken prisoners of war. After making use of the women captives for a time, they shot them and their children with arrows and ate them at great banquets celebrating past victories. Smoked human legs

1. The first known representation of the natives of the New World is an engraving with an inscription in German, the original of which is in the New York Public Library, and which is reproduced by Stevens in *American Bibliographer*, No. 1, January 1854, pp. 7-8. It is a cannibal scene, based on Amerigo's relation.

hung from the rafters of their houses like hams, and they fattened children for their larder. The Christians took pity on ten such tender victims–"destined to the sacrifice, not to say malefice"–and bought them.

The Indian men pierced their lips and cheeks and inserted into the openings stones of green and white alabaster, some of them half a handspan long and as thick as Catalan plums. This seemed a brutal custom to Amerigo, but he saw that the people were healthy and lived many years. They counted time by moons, marking each moon by a stone. "I met an old man who indicated to me by stones that he had lived 1,700 moons, which make 132 years." The conditions under which Amerigo gathered his information made for only relative accuracy and left to the imagination a margin that he does not try to hide. But undoubtedly the open-air life the savages led eliminated plagues such as he had known in Florence. What a difference between the tropical surroundings and life in the cities lately emerged from their medieval congestion! "A doctor would die of starvation here," Amerigo writes of his New World.

As in all Amerigo's writings, mention of gold is conspicuous by its absence. Moreover, when he does refer to it here, it is with certain subtle ironical touches. The King, he states, has sent them out to discover, not to seek immediate gain. Discovery, naturally, implied observing what riches there might be, but Amerigo was on his guard against optimistic calculations that might lead to false suppositions. Beyond doubt, he remarks, the land has wealth, though the natives seem in no hurry to display that which would interest the Europeans most. They themselves prize feathers more than gold or silver. The King of Portugal would profit greatly from the new colony. The natives "recount many wondrous things about the gold and other metals and drugs. I am of those who, like St. Thomas, are slow to believe."

The first things to impress the traveler were of the vegetable kingdom. Other maps based on Amerigo's accounts included, besides the Christian on the spit, trees and parrots. Amerigo speaks of logwood and *cassia fistula*. He discovered among the stones many crystals unfamiliar to him, and the same was true of spices and drugs. He stated, however, that he had no idea of their use.

One can imagine the excitement of the navigators as they proceeded down the coast, discovering capes, bays, river mouths, islands. They traveled with the saints' calendar in their hand, in a kind of mystical guessing game: what will St. John bring us tomorrow, or St. Lucia? The geographical surprise hidden behind each indentation of the coast was credited to the miracle-working power of a saint. The names were not given by the commander of the fleet, nor suggested by the pilots; they came from the calendar. On October 28 they saw a cape, and as it was the day of St. Augustine, this became Cape St. Augustine. He had given it to them; therefore it belonged to him. On October 16, St. Roque's Day, Cape St. Roque. On November 1, All Saints' Day, Bay of

All Saints. This seemed a special gift of heaven to Amerigo, son of All Saints' parish in Florence. And on December 13 another wonder! This was the day of St. Lucia, and the full name of the parish in Florence was Saint Lucia of All Saints. The river discovered that day became the St. Lucia River. January 6 was another date dear to Amerigo's heart, the day of the Three Kings. This was a favorite theme with the Florentine painters, the subject of that wonderful scene by Benozzo Gozzoli in the Medici palace. The day found them in sight of an inlet of the sea, which became Kings' Bay. So it went: On January 1, the River of January, Rio de Enero (Rio de Janeiro). On the 20th of the month, the island of St. Sebastián. On the 22nd, St. Vincent harbor.[2]

On February 15 an event of importance to the expedition, and even more to Amerigo's biography, took place. They had now been wandering over sea and land for ten months without seeing an end to their trip. They had sailed so far south that they were now below the Tropic of Capricorn. They had discovered no large city, no mines, nothing mentioned in the accounts of the Orient. They tied up the boats, went ashore, and seated themselves on the beach, an assembly of sailors, a town meeting, a council of wandering explorers, of comrades. They were not

2. F. A. Varnhagen: *Historia geral do Brasil*, says: "With the calendar in his hand, the leader of the expedition went along baptizing the different areas of the coast, leaving to posterity the knowledge of the date of his arrival at each one" (Vol. I, pp. 93-4).

acting as rebels; nobody was in revolt. They all knew that their expedition had not been dispatched to bring back gold, but to seek out the routes of the Atlantic. They had seen the world that Cabral had left virgin, and this had repaid their venture. Amerigo was not in the least disillusioned. To him this majestic world, in its simple floral grandeur, was the broadening of geography's horizons, the growth of man's knowledge. The meeting was opened; everyone had his say, the ignorant, those with more learning. The question they asked was "Shall we continue?"

Moreover, an unforeseen question had come up. The coast was now veering westward, and the new lands lay outside the area in which the King of Portugal was empowered to make conquests. For in May 1493, immediately following the first voyage of Columbus, the Catholic Monarchs, Ferdinand and Isabella, had secured from the Pope bulls establishing the division between Spain and Portugal of islands or mainland henceforth to be discovered. The line fixed by Alexander VI was one hundred leagues west of the Azores. Everything to the east of this meridian would be exclusively Portugal's, to the west of it, Spain's. The King of Portugal, John II, had objected to this boundary and had sought, through direct negotiations with the Spanish sovereigns, an arrangement more favorable to him. Ferdinand and Isabella had agreed to the change, which was formulated in the Treaty of Tordesillas in 1494. By the terms of the treaty, the demarcation line was moved 270 leagues farther west, and as a consequence of this the discoveries made along the coast of Brazil came under the dominion of Portugal. Accordingly, at the point where Amerigo and the crew members were holding their council, the coast was emerging from Portugal's jurisdiction to enter that which, under the revised treaty terms, was the province of Castile.

It has not been established who was in command of the fleet. It is presumed that it was Gonzalo Coelho, the Portuguese. By the terms of the Treaty of Tordesillas, "If the aforesaid ships of the King of Portugal should discover any islands or lands in the area ascribed to the King or Queen of Castile, of León, of Aragón, etc... all is to be and remain for the aforesaid King and Queen of Castile..." In other words, from that point on, unless the coast swerved eastward again, the discoveries they made would be for Castile. The Portuguese captain resigned his command. "As a result of our council," Amerigo relates, "it was agreed that we should continue that voyage if I so decided, and I was given full command of the fleet."

Thus for the first and only time Amerigo became the commander of a fleet. He had not been chosen for this by any king, nor had he seized power. He had suggested the route to be followed, his conclusions had proved correct, he had acted as cosmographer. The crew acknowledged him.

This date of February 15, 1502 should be regarded as a redletter day in America's calendar. It is noteworthy that no violent clash occurred in the first democratic assembly held on the continent, and that the majority of votes were for a man whose knowledge had come to him from the stars. What did Amerigo offer? He did not invite the men to follow him in the hope of riches. He offered them a mettle-trying adventure at a moment when they were weary and exhausted. He fired their minds with an exploration toward regions whose only lure was that they might hold a passage to the East. López de Gómara says in his history that "Amerigo Vespucci, Florentine, was sent out by the King of Portugal to the coasts of Cape St. Augustine in the year 1501 with three caravels to seek on those coasts a passage to the Moluccas."[3] His election conferred no power on Amerigo. He assumed a responsibility.

"I then ordered the fleet to be provisioned with a six-months' supply of water and wood, for that was the time the officers of the ships calculated that we could sail them." They were soon made ready, and set out for the Argentine coast.

No longer was the object to enter the land they were skirting. A few days later–ten degrees farther south–they descried a promontory that later appeared on maps with the name Pinachullo Detentio, or Pinaculo de Tentacão–that is, the "hill where a stop was made." There the city of Montevideo was later established. Then came the estuary of an immense river, the Plata, which they baptized the River Jordan. They were now 35° below the equator, as far

3. López de Gómara: *Historia general de las Indias*, p. 211, in the Biblioteca de Autores Españoles edition.

south as the ships of Vasco da Gama and Cabral had gone when rounding the Cape of Good Hope.

The tradition that Amerigo had discovered the Rio de la Plata asserted itself on the Italian maps and documents. Following the Florentine calendar, the date they give is 1501 instead of 1502. The discovery took place at the end of February or the beginning of March, before the change of year in Florence. On a mappemonde preserved in the library at Palermo one may read: "This is the river of the Plata, which is the river of Silver, discovered by Amerigo Vespucci, Florentine, in the year 1501." On a copy made after 1526 it says: "The Silver River, first entered by Amerigo Vespucci in the year 1501."

It was no small achievement to have reached the estuary of the Plata. Nevertheless, Amerigo sailed on. He logged five hundred leagues from the shore where the ships' council was held to the coast of Patagonia, arriving there during the first week in April. He planted no flag. All that he left was the name of a river, the Cananor. Shortly before the Cananor, he had given another stream the name of San Antonio. As the date did not coincide with the name in the saints' calendar, he must have called it after one of the crew members, or perhaps one of the Vespucci, his brother Antonio, or his uncles, Giorgio Antonio and Guido Antonio. It would have been around March 24 that he reached the San Antonio River, and this was the birthday of Guido Antonio, the Ambassador. Similar conjectures might be made for naming harbors San Vicente and San Sebastián. But why Cananor?

Cananor was a name whose associations were meaningful to Portuguese and Florentines alike. Cananor and Cochin were the two most important ports for the exportation of pepper and cinnamon on the Malabar coast. Pepper was indigenous to Malabar, and pepper was the spice most used in Florence. It was employed in both kitchen and pharmacy. It was a medium of exchange. Ghino Frescobaldi paid an annual rental of one pound of pepper for the lands he had in lease from the Humiliati friars in Ognissanti parish in Florence. Cabral's voyage was to convert the port of Cananor into a center of Portuguese activities, and Amerigo must have had advance information of this from his talks with Gaspar at Cape Verde. To be sure, the Cananor River emptied on a barren, arid shore. But to give it that name was in the nature of a bridge of hope projected toward the East.[4]

They sailed on. Their reading was 52° south latitude. This was the farthest any European navigator had sailed. On April 3

such a tempest arose that we had to close-haul all sails, and run bare-masted before the wind, which

4. The confusion that has arisen among the commentators of this voyage is due, in great part, to the mistaken interpretation of two very different points on the maps: Cananor and Cananea. The point has been definitively cleared up by Roberto Levillier in his monumental work: *América, la Bien Llamada*.

was libeccio; *the waves were mountainous, and the gale was such that all aboard were terrified. The nights were very long, and we had one, that of April 7, which lasted fifteen hours, because the sun was just emerging from Aries, and in this region it was winter, as Your Magnificence can imagine. In the midst of the storm on April 7 we sighted a new land, along which we sailed for twenty leagues; the coast was rough, and we saw no harbor or people, because of the cold, I think, which was so intense that none of the men could defend themselves from it or endure it. Finding ourselves in such peril with such a storm that we could hardly see from one boat to another because of the huge waves and the fog, we decided, after consulting the captain major, to signal the fleet to assemble and set its course for Portugal. And this was a wise decision, for if we had kept on that night we would all have been surely lost. Even after we had put about, the storm increased so that we were afraid we would be lost, and we made vows of pilgrimage and other ceremonies, as is the way of sailors in such moments.*

Amerigo had sailed along the coast of the New World to a point not far from the strait opening into the Pacific. The maps which were made after his voyage showed the coast as far south as 50^0 or 55^0. The Strait of Magellan lies within these limits. The storm prevented Amerigo's approach to it. The maps that go by the name of Kunstmann II (1502), Canerio (1502), Waldseemüller (1507), Ruysch (1508), Ptolemy (which Waldseemüller drew for his geography, 1513), and Waldseemüller (1516), all show the

Cananor River, the last place to which Amerigo gave
a name, whose mouth is at the forty-fifth parallel.
Roberto Levillier has made an exhaustive study of
the name of Cananor, based on the cartography of
the years 1502-90, for the purpose of putting to rest
all doubts with regard to the coastal extension covered by Amerigo on his voyage. The established fact
is that all the maps drawn up prior to the voyage of
the *Newen Zeitung* (1514), that of Díaz de Solís (1515-
16), and that of Magellan (1519-22) could have been
based only on information supplied by Amerigo.

The infrequent use of the name of *Jordan* to the
south would indicate that the voyage had given up
exploration by land and was confining itself to maritime exploration. Amerigo and his companions were
trying to get all they could out of their battered ships.
At the council on the coast of Brazil they had allot-
ted them a six months' life span. They now found
themselves extremely far south, and were thinking
of the return voyage when the tempest hit them.
They only glimpsed the outlines of the coast without venturing to try a landing. Whoever took one
step beyond Amerigo's findings would discover the
strait, as Magellan did thirteen years later. When his
men hesitated to proceed, he said to them: Amerigo
Vespucci came this far; it is our duty to go farther.
The historian Alberto Magnaghi, in spite of his doubts
as to the authenticity of Amerigo's letters, goes so
far as to accept that Amerigo may have sailed below
the Cananor River, as far as the harbor or Bay of San
Giuliano, close to the entrance to the strait. "It may

be that the name of San Giuliano, so familiar to a
Florentine, was given to it by Amerigo, and that
Magellan kept it."[5] This name first appears on the
map of Pigafetta of 1522. Everything would seem to
indicate, however, that it was not Amerigo, but
Magellan who gave it this name.

A contradiction in three of Vespucci's accounts
has puzzled many of his critics. In his first letter to
Lorenzo di Pier Francesco de' Medici he describes
the voyage as related here and as it appears on the
maps. But in a later letter, of which only fragments
are known, and which he sent to the gonfalonier of
Florence, he says that when they reached 32° south
latitude, instead of continuing west, following the
coast, they changed course and traveled east, which
would bring them to Africa. This led certain historians of the nineteenth century to the opinion that the
latter part of his relation had to do with the coasts of
Africa. Why did Amerigo change his course from
west to east in the last two letters?

Levillier has made a special study of the matter to
prove that such a change of course could not have
taken place. All the maps and contemporary accounts
disprove it. There is a general agreement on this
point. Then what could have happened? According
to Levillier: "We had already denied in 1948 that the
voyage was interrupted at 32° south latitude, but we
thought the figure might be a mistake, just as *si-*

---

5. A. Magnaghi: *Amerigo Vespucci*, p. 199. Magnaghi's hypothesis is
refuted by Levillier in *América, la Bien Llamada*, Vol. II, p. 86

rocco (southeast wind) instead of *libeccio* (southwest wind) might be a lapsus. After careful study of
the fragmentary letter that repeats the figure of 32°
and repeats *sirocco*, we have reached the conclusion that the sudden change from SSW to SSE was
not accidental, but a slyly inserted adulteration."[6]

Amerigo was writing from Lisbon. The political
factors, which were leading the Portuguese cartographers to deflect the coastline eastward to bring it
within Portuguese jurisdiction, while the Spaniards
were doing just the opposite to uphold the claims of
their sovereigns, were already in play. The sworn
testimony of the pilots was no longer ingenuous,
nor were their relations; they now served to extend
or curtail royal claims. Magnaghi arrived at conclusions similar to those of Levillier:

*May it have been that for reasons we do not know
Vespucci did not wish to reveal the nature of the coast
south of the twenty-fifth degree? Or may it have been
that the Portuguese government did not allow the
delineation of territory that might lie to the west of
the line of demarcation and consequently belong to
Spain? Facts to back up such a hypothesis are not
wanting. In the testimony of Ferdinand Columbus
on the subject of the Moluccas at the Council of
Badajoz in 1524 it was shown that the Portuguese
were past masters in the art of changing the routes
and the configuration of the land on maps allowed*

6. R. Levillier, article published in *La Nación* of Buenos Aires, May
1954, on the occasion of the fifth centenary of Vespucci.

outside the kingdom, and that from 1504 King Manuel forbade the reproduction on maps of the itinerary followed by the Portuguese fleets traveling to India beyond the Manicongo (Congo) River, and ordered that those which were to be used by the Portuguese in their navigations be deposited with one Jorge de Vasconcelos.[7]

Outrunning the storm, the ships moved northward toward the equator. The air and the sea were growing calm. The men still played with the idea of visiting the coast of Africa. "It was our intention to go and explore the coast of Ethiopia," the name then given to West Africa. On May 10, 1502 they reached Sierra Leone, and spent a fortnight ashore. It was months since they had had such a rest. From Sierra Leone they proceeded to the Azores, where they arrived toward the end of July. "And we stayed there another fortnight, taking some recreation." They reached Lisbon in September 1502 with only two ships: "We set fire to the other in Sierra Leone because it was no longer seaworthy." And "here I am," Amerigo wrote to Lorenzo, "waiting to see what the King is going to decide about me. May it please God that I comport myself in the manner best suited to His holy service and to the salvation of my soul."[8]

---

7. A. Magnaghi, op. cit., p. 189.

8. A. von Humboldt: *Géographie du Nouveau Continent,* Vol. V, p. 107, says: "The examination I have made of the letters of Amerigo Vespucci relative to his third voyage suffices to establish the quality of truth inherent in these documents."

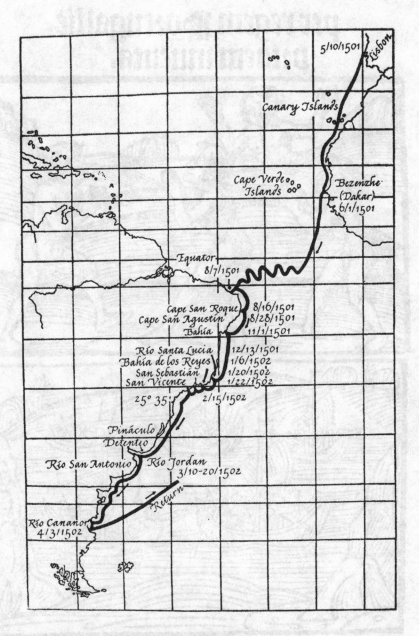

Route of Amerigo's third voyage, 1501-1502.

De ora antarctica

per regem Portugallie
pridem inuenta.

XVII

THE NEW WORLD
(1503)

Amerigo returned satisfied with his experience. The reality of what he had seen had far outstripped his imagination. His news traveled quickly, first to Seville, to the Cerezos, María, his wife, and Fernando, his brother-in-law. And at the same time to his nephew Giovanni, the son of Antonio, who had come from Florence to Seville to carve out a career with his uncle's aid. Giovanni Vespucci possessed great skill in the designing of maps, thanks to which he was to make a name for himself in Spain.

The Florentines in Seville were so proud of Amerigo's voyage that everyone was asking why King Manuel had not rewarded him with a governor's appointment. The fact was that Amerigo had not requested it or wanted it; it had not entered his mind. He was more in love with the stars than with the earth, and he did not see the possibility of hitching his wagon to a star.

A letter written by Piero Rondinelli from Seville to Florence gives us an idea of the state of mind of the Italian colony. "Amerigo Vespucci," he writes,

will be arriving here in a few days. He has undergone great hardships and has derived small profit. He deserves a better fate. The lands he has discov-

*ered have been leased by the King of Portugal to a
group of new Christians, who have pledged themselves to send out six ships every year and to explore
three hundred leagues farther each year, and to build
a fortress in the land discovered... They will pay in
logwood and slaves, and perhaps they will find other
useful things...*[1]

Rondinelli's remarks about the new Christians were
exact. Portugal utilized the Jews expelled from Spain.
At first it arranged for their admission into the country with an eye to developing the economic life of
the kingdom. Later the Church tried to get them to
accept Christianity: those who became converted
received special advantages from the King. Rondinelli
was well informed. Moreover, he had good connections. He came from a prominent Florentine family
that had become wealthy in the wool trade. He went
to Seville as did so many others who saw an opportunity to profit by the victory over the Moors and
the expulsion of the Jews.

The news of Amerigo reached Zaragoza, too, and
direct from Lisbon. Pietro Pasqualigo, the Venetian
Ambassador, was in Zaragoza, and he transmitted
the news to the Signoria of St. Mark's: "The caravels
that were sent out last year to make discoveries in
the land of the Parrots and Santa Cruz returned on
July 22. The captain states that he has discovered
more than 2,500 miles of new coast without having

---

1. *Raccolta Columbiana*, Part III, Vol. II, pp. 120, 121.

come to the end of it. The caravels returned with cargoes of logwood and cassia. They brought no other spices..."

The news was dispatched to Flanders by the noble and circumspect Baron Conrad van der Rosen, a native of the kingdoms of Germany, who happened to be in Lisbon. The Baron procured his information of Cabral's and Vespucci's voyages from a notarial statement drawn up by Valentin Fernandez de Moravia. "Two years later (after Cabral's departure)," wrote Fernández, "another armada of this same Most Christian King set out which, after following the shoreline for nearly 700 leagues, discovered peoples speaking the same language, baptized many of them, sailed to the latitude of the antarctic pole, 53° south, and having encountered severe cold, returned to their native land..." Then he adds: "This drawing–that is, of these men and a crocodile–are sent by the illustrious gentleman Jodo Draba in eternal remembrance of His Most Serene Majesty to the Chapel of Christ's Blood, founded in Bruges, city of Flanders."[2]

But all this information was as nothing compared with the accounts from the pen of Amerigo himself to Lorenzo di Pier Francesco de' Medici and his friends, complementary to his first letter from Cape Verde. These accounts brought to its culmination the geographical revolution that was in intellectual gestation. The conclusion Amerigo reached was the

2. A. Fontaura da Costa: *Cartas das Ilhas de Cabo Verde de Valentin Fernandes*, p. 91.

following: the mainland they had seen was not Asia. With this he put on record his complete disagreement with Columbus's contention. In the first letter–probably written in September or October 1502–he said: "We reached a new land which we discovered to be mainland... I reached the region of the antipodes, which according to my navigation is the fourth part of the world."

This was not enough. It was necessary to state matters in such a way that everyone could understand. Amerigo gave further thought to his report, and the result was the letter known as *Mundus Novus*, one of the most famous documents in all history. None of those who read it failed to grasp its importance. It must literally have been worn out by much reading, for not even a copy of it remains in the Medici archives. It was a short letter, but from its opening lines it establishes the scope of Amerigo's discovery: "In days past I wrote you of my return from those lands that we have sought and discovered with a fleet fitted out at the expense and at the orders of this Most Serene King of Portugal, and which I can licitly call the New World." And farther on: "We learned that that land is not an island, but a continent, because it extends along far-stretching shores that do not encompass it and it is populated by innumerable inhabitants."

Thus Amerigo brings a hemisphere out of the shadows of centuries and rectifies the opinions of the philosophers. Many had denied the existence of this fourth part of the world. Others stated that if such a continent existed, it was uninhabitable. "I have discovered the continent to be inhabited by many more peoples and animals than our Europe, or Asia, or even Africa, and have found the air more temperate and pleasant than in other regions known to us..." As for its situation: "A part of this continent lies in the torrid zone on the other side of the equator toward the antarctic pole, whereas its beginning lies 8° above that equinoctial line..."

It was then that the expression *New World* took on its full significance. Until that moment it might have been a common-place, careless manner of foretelling other things. When Bartholomeo Marchioni wrote to Florence in 1501 about Cabral's voyage, he said: "This King recently discovered a new world on this voyage, but it is dangerous to sail the vastness of those seas." Columbus had said to the Catholic sovereigns: "Your Majesties have another world here." His brother, Bartholomew Columbus, in 1503 drew a map bearing the inscription *Mondo Novo*. Peter Martyr used the terms *Nova Terrarum, Novo Orbis, Orbe Nove*, from 1493. But they employed these expressions in referring to islands or in speaking of matters having to do with Asia. It was a way of glorifying the discoveries. Columbus had said that this was Asia, and nobody could budge him from that position. For that reason he never made the impression that Amerigo's letter made. The latter presented the unknown quarter of the globe, the whole new hemisphere, and specifically differentiated it from Europe, Asia, and Africa. This meant a complete change in existing ideas. Nobody before had ever conjectured what Amerigo had seen. This was not *a* new world; it was *the* New World, to be written not in small letters, but in capitals. After he had thus baptized it, the term passed into general use as something never before thought of. Even today, when we wish to refer to this hemisphere in words conveying its uniqueness, we say the New World.

Stefan Zweig has said:

The actual event of this letter consists oddly enough not in the letter itself, but in its title–Mundus Novus– two words, four syllables, which revolutionize the conception of the cosmos as had nothing before... These few but conclusive words make of the Mundus Novus a memorable document. They are, in fact–some two hundred and seventy years before the official one–the first Declaration of Independence of America. Columbus, up to the hour of his death, blindly entangled in the delusion that by landing in Guanahani and Cuba he had set foot in India, has with this illusion actually decreased the size of the cosmos for his contemporaries. Only Vespucci, by destroying the hypothesis that this new country is India and insisting on its being a new continent, provides the new dimensions which have remained valid to this day.[3]

Mundus Novus was addressed to Lorenzo di Pier Francesco de' Medici, but it was passed on to his circle of close friends, to Giorgio Antonio Vespucci,

3. S. Zweig: *Amerigo, a comedy of errors in history*, pp. 31, 38 ff.

Zenobio Acciaiuoli, both pupils of Toscanelli (Ficino and Poliziano were dead by this time). The exciting news spread quickly, bringing the Florentines pleasant relief from the problems of the moment. Florence was undergoing a period of confusion and misfortune. The demagogic legacy of Savonarola's disciples still weighed heavily on the city. The year before, Guido Antonio Vespucci had died, disillusioned, after a stormy session in the Signoria, during which the populace drowned out his voice with catcalls and stamping. Thoughtful men saw no cure for the evils that had beset the city except in a new sort of government, and talked of naming a lifetime gonfalonier. Lorenzo di Pier Francesco de' Medici, the recipient of Amerigo's letter, had only a short time to live. But the letter lifted everyone's heart, There was animation in the palace of the Signoria, and it was decreed that the houses of the Vespucci in Ognissanti parish should be illuminated for three nights. This had been done only on rare occasions in the Republic's history.

The news had the effect of exalting the memory of Florence's illustrious sons. This was Toscanelli's third triumph, the other two being the voyage of Vasco da Gama and that of Columbus. Only Magellan's feat was needed to establish the sphere in its place in space. Archbishop Antonino came in for his share of glory, too, for he had defended the theory that the fourth part of the world was as yet undiscovered. It was like a miracle to see his portrait with that of Amerigo in Ghirlandaio's fresco. If Columbus, by sailing out of the Pillars of Hercules, had proved that the ocean was navigable from shore to shore, the Atlantic should rightfully have been called the Sea of Columbus. The new continent revealed by Amerigo might be known—But the idea had not yet occurred to anyone.

And this was not all. For years the city, its academies, its philosophers, everybody in Florence had been fired by the idea of discoveries—of dis-covering objects, ideas, statues, books covered over by time, space, prejudice, ignorance. Submerged philosophies re-surged. Greek and Roman marbles, which had disappeared for centuries, re-appeared. Plato, who had been veiled, was re-vealed. Everything seemed to be born again: it was the Re-naissance. And the route was dis-covered by which to reach the land of spices more quickly and safely, the new markets, the new skies, the terrestrial globe. This was not abject reverence for the past. It was a revolutionary impulse that mocked the immediate past with ironic, sarcastic jeers. It was the antithesis of the dialectic school.

But the original creations that emerged were also significant. The new paganism, the new Platonism, the new languages, went to prove that antiquity was only a point of departure, not a goal. There is an abyss between the *Republic* of Plato, the *Politics* of Aristotle, and *The Prince* of Machiavelli. Everything was informed by a *Vita Nuova*, and no better title could have been hit upon for Amerigo's letter than *Mundus Novus*. The business interests of the mer-

chants and the curiosity of the navigators both felt
the lure of wresting its secrets from a virgin geography. There was also a radical difference between
the geography Ptolemy had taught and the reality
described by Amerigo.

Moreover, Amerigo's announcement had already
been foretold. It was to become one more chapter in
the novel of the thousand and one discoveries the
world was living through. Now the veil had been
lifted from the Atlantic, too. The bold standard-bearers
of the most advanced schools of thought had not
erred. Toscanelli had been right. The illumination of
the houses of the Vespucci had something in common with those almost mystical ceremonies at which
fresh flowers were laid before the bust of Plato. The
prophecies of the oracle had come to pass.

Among those who had had a presentiment of the
new world was the poet Luigi Pulci, a friend of the
Vespucci, a singer of Simonetta's beauty. He had set
this forth clearly in his *Morgante*. As soon as the
Morgante was published, it was passed from one
Vespucci to another. These verses are typically
Florentine in that scientific themes form a part of
their poetic inspiration. Amerigo discovered a constellation and thought of Dante; he saw a landscape
and it brought to mind the paradise of Pollziano; he
reached the New World, and to hand were the verses
of Pulci, another fervent admirer of Toscanelli.

Pulci's poem was published in 1481, eleven years
before Columbus ventured to leave behind him the
"Non Plus Ultra" inscribed on the Pillars of Hercules.

Now the ships bound for the other hemisphere sailed safely by. Even though the sea looks flat, says Pulci, the earth is as round as a wheel. The manner in which it is suspended among the sublime stars, and the fact that there should be cities, castles, empires in the antipodes, which the setting sun bathes with its light on the other side of the planet are divine mysteries. Amerigo may have repeated Pulci's verses:

> *Know then that this opinion is untrue,*
> *For it is possible to sail on,*
> *Since the sea everywhere is flat*
> *Even though the earth be round of form.*
> *Men were bolder in those days*
> *And a blush may well redden the cheeks*
> *Of Hercules for having set that sign*
> *Since their ships did sail beyond.*
>
> *And descent to the other hemisphere may be,*
> *Since everything to the center is affixed*
> *just as the earth by mystery divine*
> *Suspended hangs amidst the heavenly stars.*
> *And there below are cities, castles, kingdoms,*
> *Which to those of old were all unknown.*
> *See how the sun quickens its march*
> *To where below I say it is awaited.*[4]

4. *Sappi che questa opinione è vana*
   perchè più oltre navicar si puote,
   però che l'acqua in ogni parte è piana,
   benchè la terra abbi forma di ruote;
   era più grossa allor la gente umana,

Amerigo not only put the most exciting news of his day into circulation, but also presented it attractively. The letters of the traders were raw historical material. Amerigo's had natural literary charm. In his letter on the New World certain details concerning the male sex organs and the artifices employed by the women to arouse men's desire have brought a blush to the cheek of many a scholar. But this was the Florentine manner, and it was in high favor. Lightheartedness or fervor was the order of the day in Amerigo's world. Queen Isabella left a library made up of a splendid collection of the lives of the saints, illuminated texts of the Gospels, the works of the Church Fathers—and Boccaccio's *Decameron*. Amerigo says of the peoples he visited in Brazil that "they lived according to nature, and can more rightfully be called epicureans than stoics." And he gives his reasons.

His letter circulated in manuscript copies until it fell into the hands of a famous humanist and architect of Verona, Fra Giovanni Giocondo. Fra Giovanni

tal che potrebbe arrossire le gote
Ercole ancor, d'aver posti que' segni
perchè più oltre passaranno, i legni.
E Puossi andar giù nell'altro emispherio,
però che al centro ogni cosa reprime;
siche la terra per divin misterio
sospesa stà fra le stelle sublime,
e laggiù son città, castella, e imperio;
ma nol cognobbon quelle gente prime.
Vedi che il sol di camminar s'affretta,
dove io dico che laggiù s'aspetta.

had been invited to Paris by Louis XII to direct the building of the Bridge of Notre-Dame. His stay in the French capital lasted for a number of years, possibly from 1499 to 1507. His fame grew; he had charge not only of the Bridge of Notre-Dame, but also of that of the Hotel de Dieu and the golden chamber of Parliament. He was famous as an epigraphist. As collaborator of Manuzio, he had undertaken the publication of a number of classical works: the *Letters* of Pliny the Younger, the *De Prodigiis* of Giulio Ossequente, and Cæsar's *Commentaries*. He built hydraulic works in Venice, and in Verona the most beautiful of Renaissance palaces.

Fra Giovanni translated Amerigo's letter into Latin,[5] in which language it was published. It was the most breathtaking piece of news an Italian living in Paris at the time could give out. In a short time three editions had appeared, It was printed in Paris, in Florence, and in Augsburg in the printing establishment of Johannes Omar Vindelice. These were followed by translations into the living European languages, German and Dutch being the first. With the Latin edition the manuscript copies that had circulated in Italian disappeared, and in 1507 Francanzio de Montalbodo made an Italian translation from the Latin text. This is

---

5. A. Magnaghi's lengthy reasoning, in *Amerigo Vespucci*, to prove that Fra Giovanni del Giocondo's literary qualities make it impossible to consider him the translator of Amerigo's letter, a translation he finds mediocre, is not sufficient to outweigh the statement of Vautrin Lud, editor of the *Cosmographiæ Introductio*.

the famous version that goes by the title of *Paesi
novamente retrovati et Novo Mondo da Alberico
Vesputio florentino intitulato*. The popularity of this
Italian version was so great that another Latin translation was made from it by Archangelo Madrignano
and published in Milan in 1508. The changes, vari-
ants, and alterations suffered by Amerigo's letter at
the hands of copyists, translators, printers,
re-translators, re-editors can be seen by comparing
the different versions. Little did Amerigo know that
he was releasing a paper dove that would visit every
country of Europe. It flew far and wide. Everyone
was acquainted with the letter. Its diffusion was in
keeping with the enthusiasm aroused in Amerigo by
his discovery. He had not been mistaken. The emer-
gence of the New World implied a revolution.

The little pamphlet, unpaginated–there was no
need to number four sheets of paper–was printed in
close-set Gothic characters. It displayed a woodcut
of the globe set in a circle of stars. Above the globe
stood the figures of two men: the European and the
man of the New World. The European above, the
New World man to the right of the sphere, the two
standing, firmly held to the surface of the planet by
the force of gravity.

Persuaded of the fact that in this brief treatise of
irrefutable facts he was contradicting the assevera-
tions of the most famous books that had preceded
it, the translator adjoined, on his own responsibility,
this moral: "Here this stands so those who assume
too much may know that it is not possible to know

everything… Here the temerity and pride of our audacious nature, which thinks it can know all, are refuted."

To the reader of travels Amerigo's letter was one
more chapter in the swift, dazzling succession of
surprises the world was offering. There was not time
enough to give each new episode its individual value.
Amerigo's voyage was one more relation that went
to swell the "collections." When the edition of Milan
was published in 1508, the editor, looking for an at-
tractive engraving for the cover, used the one with
which he had illustrated Mandeville's *Viaggio*, edited
in 1497. It is a most impressive design. Against a marine
background, the ships move through well-kempt
waves. The foreground displays the broad plain of a
walled kingdom traversed by a river. On one side of
the river, the Christian horsemen; on the other, a king
carried in a litter, before whom strange visitors are
kneeling. The scene is laid in Asia, and the king may
represent the Great Khan. There could be no better
example of the rapid linking of the new geographic
images. The use of this engraving from Mandeville's
history on Amerigo's letter is in the nature of a bridge
joining the era beginning with the news of the New
World to the discoveries of the centuries that preceded it, which were confined to the coasts of Asia.[6]

It is a waste of time to argue about the importance
of *Mundus Novus*: Europe's response was decisive.
But it is not without interest to point out certain

6. L. Olschki: *Storia letteraria delle Scoperte Geografiche*, p. 9.

changes of opinion. In 1926 Professor Alberto Magnaghi wrote: "Fra Giovanni del Giocondo was a man of exemplary life and habits. Would he have been a party, at his age in 1504, to describing so many and such lewd details concerning the customs of the savages merely for the sake of pandering to the low taste of readers of books of travel?"[7]

But Amerigo's descriptions are no more lascivious than those of Bishop Peter Martyr in his letters to the Pope. Nor did they outdo works being translated every day from the Greek, or the songs sung in the streets of Florence by Lorenzo de' Medici's companions, among whom Fra Giovanni would have been happy to count himself.

It is hard to say which of the errors contained in *Mundus Novus* the author should be blamed for and which the translators. Amerigo was aware of the fact that what he had seen was too important to be limited to letters to friends, written hastily and without too much thought, and he was preparing a small book, of which he often makes mention. He said that he was putting into it information he had collected about all the noteworthy episodes of his voyages. He was always excusing himself for overburdening his correspondents with his news. He went into lengthy apologies, particularly in his letter to Soderini. In his book he would be able to give things the space they deserved and talk of his

7. A. Magnagbi, Op. Cit., p. 27.

stars without embarrassment. "I have seen many other beautiful stars whose movements I have set down in careful detail in a certain little book of mine, which I wrote especially on this voyage."

The little book was lost. Amerigo had a foreboding that this was going to happen. He knew that royal wishes were orders, that orders were to be obeyed, and that kings–and queens, too–did as they pleased. On one occasion he wrote to Lorenzo: "I was on the point of sending you an extract from the book, but this Most Serene King has it; I will do it when he gives it back to me." And later on: "A certain little book that I especially wrote during this voyage this Most Serene King has at the moment, and I hope he will return it to me."

But he never returned it. Amerigo had dreamed of enlarging and revising it. The reputation he hoped would live after him was to have been based upon it. But this was not necessary. Two words had sufficed for his glory.

Giorgio Vasari, Paolo dal Pozzo Toscanelli, *from a detail of a mural in the Palazzo Vechio at Florence.*

XVIII

FLORENTINE INTERMEZZO
(1504)

The Florentine loves controversy, criticism, argument. So he is today, and so he was in Amerigo's time. After the illumination of the Vespucci houses and the first enthusiasm came the criticism of Amerigo's letter. There was no way of convincing the scoffers that the people of the New World went naked. Or that they were white. Or that there were thickly settled areas. Amerigo's theories on how to take the co-ordinates of longitude on the high seas did not carry conviction. Least of all did his statement that there were people who valued feathers more than gold.

Amerigo's friends rose to his defense. These friends were in all probability his brother Girolamo, his uncle Giorgio Antonio, and Zenobio Acciaiuoli. The three of them, friars, were living in the Convent of San Marco. They had received their investiture at the hands of Savonarola himself. They all spent a considerable part of their time in the fabulous library that had belonged to the Medici of the oligarchy, which, when the palace was sacked, had been transferred to the convent and put in charge of Giorgio Antonio. Girolamo had returned from Rhodes, gentled by the life of privations he had undergone there. Acciaiuoli was at the peak of his intellectual powers. From them Amerigo

"Los Guayanas", Illustration from the book Il Costume Antico e Moderno, *by Dr. Jules Ferrario, Milano, 1827.*

undoubtedly received a careful summary of the objections to his letter. The news reached him in Lisbon.

How mistaken one can be–he must have thought–when passing judgment on things one has never seen! And he immediately sent off an ironic, jesting letter, at times sarcastic, dotting the *i's* and crossing the *t's*. All that has been preserved of this letter is a fragment that was discovered and published in 1937 by Professor Roberto Ridolfi.[1] Until that time it had lain unknown in the archives of the family of Ginori Conti. It is not known to whom it was addressed. It has been conjectured that it might have been Lorenzo di Pier Francesco de' Medici, but the tone would seem to belie this supposition, and it may well be that Amerigo already had had news of Lorenzo's death. Everything would seem to indicate that it was intended rather for Zenobio Accialuoll or, perhaps, Giorgio Antonio Vespucci. In any case it is the document that best reveals Amerigo's polemical gifts, his style, more like speaking than writing, when he was irked.

"As I have already said," Amerigo writes, "the people of that land go naked. That is based on natural reasons, and because I saw too many of them to count... As the philosopher says, 'custom changes nature.'" Those who contradicted Amerigo based their

1. In the *Archivio Storico Italiano*, Vol. I, No. 1 (Florence, 1937). A Spanish translation was published by R. Levillier in *El Nuevo Mundo*. p. 154. Ridolfi is of the opinion that the letter was addressed to Lorenzo di Pier Francesco de' Medici, in which I think he is mistaken.

arguments on the fact that if the natives lived in the fifth, sixth, or seventh climate, following the geographers' classifications, they would be exposed to greater cold than the Europeans, who went warmly clothed. Amerigo answered: I have made three voyages... I have seen some 2,000 leagues of coastland and over 5,000 (of?) islands, a great many of them inhabited. I found the mainland to be full of innumerable people, and I never saw one of them clothed, or even with their private parts covered, much or little. Both men and women."

Amerigo's explanation of the reasons for the color of the natives is worth setting down in its entirety. It is his contribution to natural science:

As for the opinion I have expressed that the people of that region are white and not black, and especially those who inhabit the torrid zone, I have this to say, with all respect to the philosophers. It is not necessary that all the men dwelling in the torrid zone be black because of nature and scorched blood, as are the Ethiopians and the greater part of the people who inhabit the region of Ethiopia. As I said before, I have sailed through all the parallels from Morocco to the end of Ethiopia, and have reached a point 32° south of the Line. I have been in many parts of Africa and Ethiopia, at Cape Catim, Cape Anghila, Zanaga, Cape Verde, Rio Grande, Sierra Leone, lying 7° on the equator. I have seen and spoken with countless people there, and they are all black in color, more so in certain areas than in others. And even if such knowledge lies within the province of the philosophers, I shall not re-

frain from expressing my opinion, be it well or ill received. I hold that the main reason is the compression of the air and the nature of the land, because all the land of Ethiopia is very sparsely populated, and there is a lack of fresh water, little rainfall, and the soil is very sandy and scorched by the heat of the sun. There are vast sandy deserts and very few woods or forests, and the prevailing winds in that region are the levanter and the sirocco, both hot. Also nature has turned blackness into habit, and we see this in our own country: Negroes engender Negroes, and if a white man has offspring with a Negress, the child will be brown—that is to say, less black than the mother and less white than the father. Or inversely. Which indicates that nature and habit are more powerful factors than the compression of the air and the land. For this reason I deduce that as the land and air I have discovered in the same position as the aforesaid land of Africa and Ethiopia, or, to put it more clearly, between the same parallels, is much pleasanter and more temperate, and of better compression, for that reason the people are white, though verging on tawny, because, as I say, in that region the air is more temperate than in Ethiopia; and the land is much more agreeable and abounds in fresh water, and the dew falls there nearly every day. The winds are southerly and westerly, so that the heat there is not so great as in Ethiopia. For that reason the trees there are always green and covered with foliage. These are the facts. Anyone who does not believe them can go there and see for himself, as I did...

The extent of Amerigo's voyages was also put in doubt. How could he state that he had seen so many lands, both north and south of the equator, and even tell which meridian he had reached?

To corroborate briefly what I have related, and to justify myself against the criticisms of the malevolent, I say that I have known this by the eclipses and the conjunctions of the moon and the planets. I have lost much sleep nights to reach an accord with the scholars who have constructed the instruments and written on the movements and conjunction and appearance of the eclipses of the two luminaries and the erratic stars, such as King Alfonso the Wise in his Tables *and Regiomontanus in his* Almanac, *and Bianchino, and the almanac of Rabbi Zacuti, the Jew, which is for all time, all drawn up in different meridians: that of King Alfonso in Toledo, and that of Regiomontanus in Ferrara, and the other two in Salamanca. And it is a fact that I found myself so far to the west—not uninhabited but densely populated— that I was 150° from the meridian of Alexandria, which is eight hours from the equatorial hour. If anyone, through jealousy or malice, does not believe this, let him come to me with his objections, and I will explain it to him with authorities and witnesses. And let this suffice for the longitude. If it were not for the fact that I am very busy, I would send you the explanation of everything and of the many conjunctions I observed. But I do not want to enter into all this. These are writers' doubts, and they lie outside the ability of those who have propounded them. And let this suffice.*

Amerigo rested his conclusions on the authorities who constituted the basis of existing knowledge in the science of navigation. His first reference is to the Alphonsine Tables, which had been drawn up in 1252 during the reign of Alfonso the Wise, and which were undoubtedly based on observations made by the Moors in the time of the Caliph Omayyad. His next reference is to the *Almanac or Ephimerides* of Montereggio, or Regiomontanus (Johann Müller of Königsberg), which was published in Nuremberg in 1474 and was very famous at the time. Columbus is believed to have made use of it in his observation of an eclipse in Jamaica in 1504. Regiomontanus died in 1474, after having published the *Astronomica* of Manilius, probably at Toscanelli's suggestion. "Although Regiomontanus always referred to Toscanelli as master and supreme authority in matters of science," writes Uzielli, "he belonged more to the humanistic than to the experimental school, of which his learned Florentine friend was the head."[2] Giovanni Bianchini the astronomer was a friend of both Regiomontanus and Toscanelli. There was an exchange of letters between Bianchini and Regiomontanus on the subject of Toscanelli's tests with the sundial of the Cathedral of Florence to determine the angle of the equatorial plane to the ellipse. Along with Bianchini, Amerigo quotes Abraham Zacuto, the Jew, whose

2. G. Uzielli: *Paolo dal Pozzo Toscanelli*, p. 80.

almanac–with which Columbus, too, was familiar–
circulated along with that of Regiomontanus among
navigators, especially the Portuguese.

The question was raised whether Amerigo had
really passed the Tropic of Capricorn. *"Semplice
domanda"*–a foolish question. They had only to look
at his map to see that he had not only passed the
tropic at 23°, but had sailed as far as 50° south latitude. Certain things are not worth while explaining;
they are obvious, and can be left to the understanding of the judicious. The fact that the seasons in the
Southern Hemisphere are the opposite of those in
the north is a well-known fact. "The longest day we
had in that region was one 2nd of December, and
the longest night, the 2nd of June." Amerigo explained this variation on the basis of the position of
the sun, as any good teacher of the period might
have done. "And I could give you infinite other reasons. But let these, for the time being, suffice."

*They attack me because I said that those people
hold in low regard gold and the other riches esteemed and prized by us. They argue that I contra-
dict myself when I say we bought slaves. The
objection seems to me so unfounded that I regret
the loss of time and of ink and paper to answer them.
The person who raised the question should be called
a metimastician (one who half chews) rather than
a mathematician. I have said that life there is epicurean rather than stoic or academic, and I pointed
out that they do not hold property privately, nor do
divisions into kingdoms or provinces exist. In a*

word, everything is in common. If they gave, or sold, us slaves, as I said, it was not for pecuniary gain, for they were given almost gratis, in exchange for a wooden comb or a looking-glass not worth four farthings... And they would not have traded the looking-glass or the comb for all the gold in the world. We often tried to give them crosses of gold and rings set with stones, and they did not want them. We even asked them for the things they valued most, and they gave them to us without recompense. I can give you this example: when I went out to discover for the King of Castile on my second voyage, we came to a land where we bartered 119 marks of pearls, which were evaluated in Castile at 15,000 ducats, and I don't think they cost us 10. In exchange for a hawkbell an Indian gave me 157 pearls worth one thousand ducats. And don't think he thought he had made a bad trade; the minute I handed him the bell he put it in his mouth and sprinted for the woods. I never saw him again. He was probably afraid that I would rue the bargain.

It surprised Amerigo that his correspondent had not quickly answered the simple things that everyone should know. When he was asked for a description of the climates to answer the questions of his detractors, he said: "It amazes me that you should not have answered for me." Another question he was asked he termed "of little weight and less substance." He could permit himself this irony for he had a final argument that none could dispute: he had been in the regions he spoke of. The role of his commentators was limited to seeking the explanation of the facts; they could not deny them. Furthermore, "I cannot imagine who is the simpleton that asks these things about a letter written to a friend. As a matter of fact, you are filling me with vainglory by making me think that my letter is considered a great paper, when I dashed it off as one writes to an acquaintance."

Again in this letter Amerigo speaks of his plan to write a more extensive work. If God grants him three years of life, he says, with the help of a learned person he will write his book. And once the book is written, he can die peacefully, knowing that he has left papers proving the trials he underwent to discover the things of the New World.

The echoes of this futile debate died down amid the silence of the archives, and their only result was a few hours of amusement to Amerigo's friends. But the maps that came out of Lisbon—some of them the work of Italians—at once brought an awareness of the advances that had been made in coastal discovery. Everything would seem to indicate that the news of the New World aroused an echo everywhere. In that same year (1502), cartographers quickly began to include the outline of the southerly coast. First came an Italian planisphere that goes by the name of King-Hamy. It was bought by a traveler, Dr. King, in the nineteenth century, and later became the property of Dr. Hamy, the first to describe it. Some held it to be the work of an Italian, others of a Portuguese. In any case, it shows the coast extending below the

35th parallel, and includes a part of the discoveries to the south of the Jordan River, as far as Patagonia. Another map of the same year, published by Kunstmann–one that shows the scene of the Christian being roasted on a spit–extends to the Cananor River. This is the first map to carry the names of many of the places visited by Amerigo; it served as the basis of most of those which followed. Another planisphere of the same year is in the Oliveriana Library of Pesaro. It is the first, as Roberto Levillier, the Argentine, has pointed out, to convey the idea of the "continentality" of South America, the first to employ the term *Mundus Novus* given to it by Amerigo. It was also in 1502 that a Genoan, Nicolai de Canerio, made the map bearing his name, which also extends to the Cananor River.

Four maps that have come down to us (and there is no way of knowing how many that have disappeared) bear witness to the immediate repercussions of Amerigo's voyage. The Florentine disputations were idle chaff.

There may have been one more proof of Amerigo's voyage. Father Cazal states that at the mouth of the Cananea River, a piece of marble four handspans high, two wide, and one thick, bearing the arms of Portugal, was found planted on the mainland. Magnaghi says: "This marker could have been put there only by the Vespucci expedition of 1502."[3] The strange thing about it is that the marker should have been placed on the very spot at which the assembly of sailors that gave the command of the fleet to Amerigo was held, and where they believed Portugal's jurisdiction ended.

The name of Cananea, mentioned by Father Cazal, appears only on later maps. It was surely not conferred by the sailors who accompanied Amerigo. They were less concerned with naming the place than with the question of whether the lands to which the Crown held claim ended there. The problem that arose immediately in Portugal was that of concealing the boundary line, of altering the direction the coast followed, or at least of delaying the matter. The first three maps that were made showed all too clearly the westward swerve of the coast, which was the equivalent of saying that it moved toward the dominion of Castile. On the map of Caneiro the coast changes direction, swinging eastward, with the bulge toward Africa. This map set a fashion that had its reasons. King Manuel had set up in Lisbon the House of the Indies, one of whose functions was to safeguard reports. Jorge de Vasconcellos was the curator of the sailing charts. The death penalty was decreed for anyone divulging information classified as secret. It was the duty of the pilot major to "efface from the works of cartography new discoveries best kept secret, and he was granted by the Crown the exclusive right to supply approved maps, drawn according to official specifications."

This was the nature of the discussions in Lisbon. We have already seen what they were like in Florence. Interests varied greatly in the sixteenth century.

3. Ayres de Cazal: *Corografia Brasilica*, Vol. I, p. 228; A. Magnaghi, op. cit., p. 190.

XIX

FORERUNNER OF MAGELLAN
(1504)

The news of the discovery of a new continent on the western side of the Atlantic caused a profound change in Portuguese policy. A new possibility of colonization was suddenly revealed. Up to that moment the Portuguese, lacking the population to found colonies, had concentrated on opening new world trade routes. Amerigo's voyage, which had been conceived as a survey, had turned into the discovery of a mighty land mass that could not be held merely by setting up a marble marker. It called for settlers, forts, the planting of the flag, and enforcement of respect. Paper and parchment alone would not do the trick.

There was the example of Spain for all to see. She had already built cities on her islands and had thrown up the first lines of defense. Columbus had been as much concerned with the economic aspects of his conquests as with the geographic problems of the discoveries. On his first voyage he founded a city. On the second he put a major effort into the immediate exploitation of the colony. Amerigo did not share Columbus's ambitions, but he knew perfectly well the purpose for which territory was won. "It is not to be wondered at," he had written to Lorenzo, "that, moving as rapidly as

John Ogilby, Fernando de Magallanes, *from* America being the latest and most accurate description of the New World, *London, 1671.*

we did, we did not learn of all the possibilities of gain, for the natives attach no value to anything, either gold, or silver, or jewels... I have the hope that with this Most Serene King sending out explorations, not many years will elapse before they bring great profit and income to this Kingdom of Portugal...

The first to realize the promise the new lands held were the Jews, the new Christians the Florentine of Seville had referred to. Portugal was running over with freshly baptized Jews. When Spain had expelled them, King Juan of Portugal had offered them temporary asylum. In return for the payment of a tax, he agreed to receive them for as much as eight months. Then he would see what he could do to help them get to other countries, for which purpose he promised them ships. It was a golden opportunity for Portugal. Ninety thousand entered the country. The King took the tax money and then did not give them the ships. Many were made slaves. The children were sent to the island of Santo Tomas to live or to die. When in 1496 a marriage was arranged between King Manuel and the daughter of Ferdinand and Isabella, the first request Their Catholic Majesties made of him was to purge his kingdom of Jews. He agreed, and the decree of expulsion was issued in 1497. But carrying it out would have caused an economic collapse, and King Manuel had no desire to repeat Castile's experience. Instead he decreed compulsory baptism for all Jews and Jewesses between the ages of four and twenty-four. In one month the Christian community was enlarged by twenty thousand new members. The new Christians or *marranos* were not permitted to leave the country. Things went along in this manner until, in 1506, there was a slaughter of Jews in Lisbon in which two thousand of them were killed. The following year they were permitted to leave Portugal, and the majority went to Holland.

One of the leaders of the new Christians of Lisbon in 1502 was Fernando de Noronha. He represented an affluent group.[1] Noronha saw that the New World might be profitable as a business venture and that, above all, it held out the hope of living without fear. It was an enterprise of as much interest to the King as to the group for which Noronha was acting. An arrangement was worked out. Partly in furtherance of this plan, on May 10 of that year six ships set out from Lisbon, possibly under the command of Gonzalo Coelho. Amerigo sailed as captain of one of them.

Gonzalo Coelho and Fernando de Noronha were interested in colonizing; Amerigo in discovery. The discrepancy between their aims was deep. In his *Mundus Novus* letter Amerigo had written: "I am thinking of making still a fourth journey, and as I have decided to do it, they have promised us two ships, fully outfitted, so I may prepare to seek new regions to the south." It is possible that Amerigo was sup-

---

1. R. Levillier: *El Nuevo Mundo*, p. 48.

ported in this idea by the Italian merchants, and had the approval of the Crown, which maintained its traditional interest in discoveries. The expedition, therefore, represented two opposed interests.

Amerigo's imagination was still fired by the idea of finding a passage to the Indies, of reaching the island called Malaccha, the fame of whose riches had reached his ears. It was the emporium for all the ships from the Sea of Ganges and the Indian Ocean. He hoped to find the southern passage. In this he was Magellan's precursor.

The expedition dropped anchor along the coast of Sierra Leone, a customary halt. Amerigo asked himself why they were wasting time in Africa. The captain of the fleet impressed him as being vain and stubborn. "He wanted to explore Sierra Leone… without the slightest need for it. All that mattered to him was to show that he was the commander of the six ships, disregarding the wishes of all us other captains."

The voyage began badly. The weather during the exploration of the African coast could not have been worse. Finally they charted their course for the voyage's agreed objective. But in the middle of the Atlantic a surprise was in store for them. It was an island, "a true wonder of nature." Minute in size, not more than two leagues long and one league wide. They found it to be uninhabited, but it had an abundance of fresh water, many trees, marine and land birds so tame that they allowed thernselves to be taken, and many lizards and moles.

"The island was unlucky for the whole fleet, for I may tell Your Excellency," Amerigo wrote later to Soderini, "that as a result of the poor judgment and orders of our commanding captain, he lost his ship there." In fact, the fleet broke up. The captain had asked Amerigo to look for safe anchorage for the ships, and Amerigo relates that he found an excellent harbor and they waited there eight days for the commander. They finally sailed out to see what had happened and found that the flagship had disappeared. One of the other ships informed them that she had gone down.

All these incidents would seem to indicate that the differences between the commander and Amerigo had worsened, and that they deliberately decided to lose one another. Humboldt, who studied Amerigo's letter, checking it against other documents of the day, ascertained that the other ship had not gone down. Amerigo's letter takes a dramatic tone. He wrote that on the island "we were very displeased with the way things were going, and the men remaining on my ship were so fearful that I could not hearten them... We set out... They told us that the flagship had gone down... And the anguish this caused us Your Magnificence can well imagine, finding ourselves one thousand leagues from Lisbon, and on the high seas, and undermanned; nevertheless, we braved fortune, and pushed farther on." The King's orders were that even if a part of the fleet was lost, the remaining ships were to continue the voyage.

Amerigo kept on and reached Brazil. He dropped anchor in All Saints' Bay, which he already knew and where he felt at home. But it would have been rash and dangerous to continue with only two ships toward the island that he had heard was the trading-place of the treasures of the Orient. So he made only a brief exploration of the coast and began the construction of a fort. He says that he left twenty-four Christians in the new settlement, took aboard a cargo of logwood, and turned homeward. "We could not continue farther because we were short of men, and much of our gear was gone."

He left everything he could possibly spare with those who remained behind. Provisions for six months, twelve cannon, arms. He says that they explored the region to a distance of forty leagues inland. In his letter to the Florentines, written shortly after his return, he did not feel that it was necessary to give further details of what he had seen on this voyage—so trifling in results when compared with the three previous ones. Benvenuto, who was carrying the letter, he added, could fill in the gaps.

Amerigo was not happy over his experience. "This voyage was not carried out in keeping with the plan I had." We know what his plan was, but it is interesting to hear the version of the historian, López de Gómara: "Americo Vespucio, Florentine... tells how he went... to look for a strait in that coast through which to go to the Moluccas."

Up to that time the person Amerigo had kept informed of his voyages was Lorenzo di Pier Francesco de' Medici. Lorenzo was now dead. The person to whom to address his letters was the new master of Florence, Piero Soderini, who had been elected lifetime gonfalonier. Amerigo and he had been fellow students of Uncle Giorgio Antonio. Many years had gone by, but the ties of friendship formed in youth are not easily broken. Besides, the relationship between Giorgio Antonio and Soderini had continued, both of them being friends of Marsilio Ficino. Ficino consulted Giorgio Antonio on his translations from the Greek and sent Soderini copies of his letters, which have come to be the most important documents in studying the life of the philosopher. When Ficino was accused of spreading works of magic and demonology, Soderini was one of those who came to his defense. When Ficino made his will, Giorgio Antonio was one of his witnesses.

Moreover, in his public activities Soderini had had connections with Amerigo's other uncle, Guido Antonio Vespucci. On Guido Antonio's second embassy to the King of France, shortly after the death of Lorenzo the Magnificent in 1492, he was accompanied by Piero Capponi, who succeeded Piero Soderini and Gentile Becchi. The growing ambitions of Charles VIII and the disorder Savonarola's fanaticism was spreading in Florence made these delicate and difficult missions. On his return from France, Guido Antonio assumed an active role in Florentine political life, becoming the head of the party that finally sent Savonarola to the stake. In 1498 he was named gonfalonier. Soderini's election came later, in 1501.

Soderini was not so wise as Giorgio Antonio or so forceful as Guido Antonio. He stood for the golden mean in everything. He was a man with a spirit of compromise, representing that middle-of-the-road policy the Florentines were seeking like a bridge to lead them to a less impassioned, less controversial existence. The tone Amerigo uses in his letter would indicate that he knew Soderini's character well. Cerretani, a contemporary who wrote the history of those years, describes Soderini at the time he assumed office as lifetime gonfalonier: "He is rich and childless. There are not too many men in his family, and he is not overburdened with relatives. He is fifty years old, of medium height, sallow-skinned, with a broad forehead and large head, and thin, black hair; he is grave, eloquent, witty, not over-strong of will or mind nor too erudite; vain, closefisted, religious, devout, and without vices..."

But Soderini had an interest that was very important to Amerigo: his curiosity about voyages. The Florentines in Lisbon were well aware of this. Amerigo wrote in his letter: "The principal reason that has moved me to write to you was the request of the bearer of these presents, Benvenuto Benvenuti, one of our Florentines, and a devoted servant of Your Magnificence, as he has demonstrated, and a great friend of mine." The letter to Soderini is dated September 4, 1504, three months after Amerigo's return. He took this occasion to give a résumé of his four voyages. The previous letters had been fragmentary and familiar in tone.

But here for the first time he was addressing himself to the head of the Republic, and he gave an orderly summary of his experiences. "I recall," he says to the gonfalonier, "how in the days of our youth when I was your friend--now I am your servant--we went to learn the principles of grammar following the example and the teaching of that venerable monk, friar of San Marco, Guido Antonio Vespucci, whose counsels and precepts would it had been God's will that I should follow, for, as Petrarch says, I would have been a different man than I am. Nevertheless, I do not complain, for I have always taken pleasure in virtuous things, and even though this fabulous news of mine is not on the level of your virtue, I will say to you, as Pliny said to Mæcenas: 'There were once days when my jests found favor with you...'" Here, as Canovai points out, Amerigo made a mistake: Pliny did not make the remark to Mæcenas, but Catullus to Cornelius Nepos. But Amerigo was more concerned with giving his relation a well-turned introduction than with academic accuracy. So he wrote the first thing that came to his mind and went on: "Now that Your Magnificence is continually engaged in public affairs, in some hour of rest you take, in some moment of leisure, you may find pleasure in reading of amusing, pleasant matters. As one takes fennel after a succulent meal to help digestion, to relieve your mind of its many cares, you can ask them to read you this letter of mine. It will give you surcease from the relentless cares and unremitting engrossment with state affairs. And should I prove too prolix, I ask your indulgence, My Magnificent Sir..."

The letter to the gonfalonier spread as swiftly as the *Mundus Novus.* Readers were avid to continue the exciting relation of Amerigo's adventures. An Italian edition appeared in short order, probably printed in Florence, perhaps in 1505. From Italian it was translated into French and Latin. The Latin edition consisted of thirty-two pages. Stefan Zweig wrote: "Thus thirty-two pages... represent the entire literary output of Amerigo Vespucci–a tiny and not very solid piece of luggage for the journey into immortality. Never has any writing man become so famous on such meager production; coincidence after coincidence, error after error, had to accumulate to raise it so high above its time as to make even us cognizant of the name that floats skyward with the starry banner."[2]

A comedy of errors? Certainly not. The report Columbus made of his discoveries contained more errors. The explorations Amerigo had carried out in 1504 were more extensive than those of any other mariner; his information was more accurate. In none of his letters, neither those carelessly written, nor the one to the gonfalonier, did he introduce any change in his true status on the voyages. His discoveries in the field of astronomy, navigation, and

2. S. Zweig: *Amerigo, a comedy of errors in history,* p. 38.

science were as fortunate as in that of literature. But the final outcome is even more far-reaching than Zweig grasped: not one, but twenty-two flags wave in the free air under the single name of America.

Amerigo made no mistake in writing to Soderini, the proper person in Florence to inform of his fourth voyage. What he accomplished in 1504 was quickly repeated by another Italian traveler, Giovanni da Empoli, who also sailed under the flag of the King of Portugal. The cases of Amerigo and Empoli were very similar. Empoli first worked in Bruges in the service of the Florentine bankers, who decided to send him to Lisbon to join the voyages of exploration to the Orient. Empoli signed up with the expedition that sailed under the command of Alfonso de Albuquerque in April 1503, one month before Amerigo set out for Brazil. Like Amerigo, Empoli returned to Lisbon in 1504, but he left for Bruges to give the bankers an account of what he had seen. From there he went to Florence. What happened after that is related by his uncle Girolamo:

He carried letters for the Magnificent Piero Soderini... and he called on him to present them. Soderini received him most cordially. After they talked together at length, the gonfalonier told him he would appreciate it very much if he would come to see him again. He returned the next day and found the gonfalonier in his audience chamber with many other leading citizens. Giovanni thought he had had them come to hear the news of his voyages from his own lips. And after greeting the gonfalonier with due reverence and courtesy, the latter asked him about things having to do with those countries.[3]

Soderini ordered Empoli to write out the account of his travels. In this manner things were learned which were of immediate importance, and which have been helpful later for the purpose of history. Between the two–Empoli's report and Amerigo's letter–it is possible to reconstruct in original and pristine simplicity the natural course these matters followed.

Amerigo concluded his letter to Soderini with the final news of his fourth voyage: "After so many trials and hazards we entered this port (Lisbon) on June 18, 1504. Praise be to God! Here we were warmly received. They could hardly believe it. The whole city had given us up for lost, for the other vessels of the fleet were lost because of the vanity and madness of our captain, for thus God punishes pride... "As a matter of fact, as Humboldt points out, the ships had not been lost; but this has no bearing on our story, and besides Amerigo did not know it. Then Amerigo adds:

At the moment I find myself here in Lisbon, and I do not know what the King may want with me; I have a great need of rest. The bearer of this letter is Benvenuto de Domenico Benvenuti. He will inform you of my state, and of certain things, I have omitted so as not to be prolix. But he has seen and heard them. I have made

3. Giovanni da Empoli: *Archivio Storico Italiano*, Appendix III (1846).

*my letter as brief as I could, and have left many things
unsaid that might well be included, so as not to be
long-winded. Your Magnificence will forgive me, and
count me among your servants. I commend to you my
brother Antonio and all those of my house. I pray that
God may give you long life, elevate the state of our sublime Republic, and reward Your Magnificence, etc.*

Amerigo had fulfilled his obligations toward the
King of Portugal, and was now free. He gave the
King a report of his voyages, now lost, together with
many other of his papers. In Lisbon, Amerigo was
closer to the Florentine colony than to the Portuguese. The King made use of the Florentines with
calculated prudence. Like all the Italians, they were
valuable because of their business connections and
their money. But where maritime matters were concerned, Portugal was unwilling to share her secrets
and knowledge with other countries.

Amerigo felt neither cheated nor flattered. He had
seen what he wanted to see, voyaged as far as he
could. The only thing that distressed him, of which
he constantly complained, was that the King did not
return his papers. In his letter he did not allude to a
circumstance that irked his fellow Italians: the fact
that only Fernando de Noronha had profited by this
last voyage. The island that Amerigo had seen, "one
of nature's wonders," was granted to Noronha by
the King. It is now known as the island of Fernando
de Noronha. An injustice? Not at all. This island represented the money the King had received and the
obligations he had contracted with this new Chris-

tian. If anyone respected the rights of those who put up money for an enterprise, it was Amerigo.

Amerigo's mission in Portugal was over. His home and his friends were in Seville. María Cerezo was in Seville, as was his nephew Giovanni.

His last two voyages had left Amerigo with the conviction that there was a strait to the south through which it was possible to reach the spice islands. Magellan would turn his presentiment to reality.

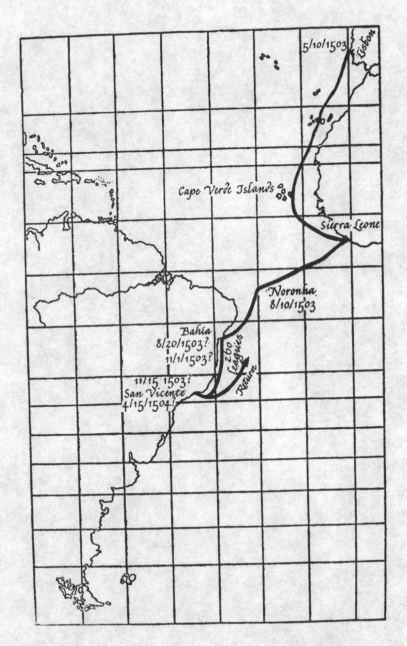

Route of Amerigo's fourth voyage, 1503-1504.

XX

Citizen of Castile
(1505)

History moved swiftly in those days. From 1501 to the beginning of 1505–the years Amerigo had spent in Portugal–great changes had taken place in Spain. The State had been steadily growing more powerful and more intolerant. Cisneros had been using toward the Moors a policy similar to that which had ejected the Jews from Spain. Disregarding the capitulations of Granada–which had left the former inhabitants a wide margin of liberty in the preservation of their language, their religion, their customs, their traditions–the Cardinal, as though taking a leaf from Savonarola's book, had built in Bibarrambla bonfires into which thousands of volumes on religion and statecraft were thrown. Treasures of Islamic art were lost forever; exquisite miniatures in gold, red, and blue, drawings, calligraphs, representing the painstaking labors of centuries, crackled in the flames like burning autumn leaves. In indignation the Moors of the Albaicín revolted and besieged Cisneros's palace. But nothing came of it. In the ensuing tumult the last sparks of Moorish liberties were stamped out.

As this policy of official intolerance, so contrary to Spanish medieval habits, gained headway, the perspective of a new world, where a different life was possible, grew more enticing. The dream of a new Spain, across the sea, was taking shape.

Death had come for Queen Isabella. She died in Medina del Campo, and her unembalmed corpse, with a Franciscan habit for a shroud, was borne on a black litter to Granada. "From the moment the cavalcade set out from Medina, one gloomy November day, it moved through a wild storm of wind and rain all the way to Granada. In many places the roads were impassable, the swollen streams having washed the bridges away, and little brooks had grown to the volume of the Tagus, while low-lying plains had been converted into lakes... Neither the sun nor the stars were visible during the three weeks of the journey. Raging torrents at times swept away horses and mules, and in some cases the riders were lost, too..."[1] People screamed with woe, women tore their hair, and the churches echoed with solemn chants. The procession, garbed in black at the outset of the journey, reached its destination caked with mud. In this manner the bones of the Queen arrived at the Monastery of San Francisco of the Alhambra, to rest in a setting of Moorish associations.

Nothing could have been more in keeping with this drama than the memories Columbus had brought with him from his last voyage. Amerigo found him

---

1. W. Starkie: *La España de Cisneros*, p. 2.88.

weary, aged, resentful, full of strange fancies. Columbus had reached Spain on the eve of the Queen's
death, Amerigo shortly afterward. With the death of
Isabella, Columbus had lost the woman who four times
had held out a helping hand to him. Ferdinand assumed the regency of Castile in the name of his melancholy daughter, Joanna the Mad, Isabella's heir.
Ferdinand felt himself closer to Amerigo than to Columbus.

Everybody in Seville was happy to have Amerigo
back. The most respected and experienced pilots
talked with him by the hour. The news he brought
back from Portugal helped Spain to establish an ambitious general policy of discovery. King Ferdinand
lost no time in summoning him to court, wanting to
make immediate use of his services. Ferdinand found
money for the voyage; he wrote to Alfonso Morales:
"Treasurer of Her Most Serene Majesty Doña Joanna,
my dear and beloved daughter: I order you that of
whatever maravedís you may hold you will at once
give and pay to Amerigo de Espuche, residing in the
city of Seville, twelve thousand maravedís, which I
am bestowing on him toward his expenses..."[2]

Columbus placed all his hopes on what Amerigo
could do for him at court, talking with him about
things he did not even venture to put on paper.
Columbus had always been like that, a man of mystery and whispers. He wrote to his son Diego:

2. Navarrete: *Viajes*, Vol. III, p. 294.

My very dear Son: Diego Méndez left here on Monday, the third of this month. After he had gone I talked with the bearer of this, Amerigo Vespuchy (who) is going there to the court where he has been summoned in connection with matters of navigation. It has always been his desire to give me pleasure; he is a man of good will; fortune has proved contrary to him as to others; he has not profited from his labors as justice would demand. He is acting on my behalf moved by a great desire to do something which shall be to my benefit if it lies within his power. From here I do not know what I can enjoin upon him that will be to my benefit, because I do not know what they want of him there. He is determined to do everything possible for me. See there what would be advantageous, and work toward that end, and he will do everything and talk and put it into effect; and let all this be done secretly so no one gets wind of it. I have told him everything I could in connection with this, and have informed him of the payment I have received and receive.[3]

Each having concluded four voyages, these two Italians, Christopher the Genoese and Amerigo the Florentine, found themselves in very different circumstances. Columbus's days were running out. In another year he would have departed this world. The King paid him slight heed. He had been given privileges, and his family had received opportuni-

3. Ibid., Vol. I, p. 498.

ties and distinctions, but he, as Admiral of the Ocean
Sea and Viceroy of the Islands, was finished. Columbus himself was thinking of nothing but law-
suits and claims. At times he talked with haughty
pride, at times with tragic abasement, mingling the
upbraidings of an Old Testament prophet with the
lamentations of Jeremiah. Whereas Amerigo had returned from each voyage with increased prestige and
had grown in estimation, Columbus, who always set
out loudly announcing mighty undertakings, had
come back each time more discredited, more miserable, more tortured by his complexes.

To be sure, he had returned in triumph from the
voyage of 1492. His prow had traced a pathway
through the Atlantic for all time. That first voyage
had marked the coronation and end of his prolonged
youth. From that moment on he was an old man.
On October 12 the earth had emerged from his hands
a sphere–a small sphere, it is true, but a sphere.
Those were the days when people flocked from the
hills to the roadside to see him pass with his Indians, his parrots, and his gold. The second time he
had returned a frightened man, dressed in penitent's
garb, seeking the seclusion of a convent, feeling himself the object of calumny and spite. The Queen had
had to hold out her wand to conjure away his fears
and bring him to court. The third time he had arrived in chains. He had been fettered like a common criminal in Hispaniola–his own island–by the
King's justice–his King! Columbus had wept tears of
shame, rage, humiliation, as though he had drained

the lees of his cup of sorrow. But the Queen was still alive, and she remembered that Columbus was Columbus. Her words of comfort and reparation must have echoed in Christopher's heart like the distant tinkle of the glory bells. The night before, the sound that had filled his ears had been the clank of the chains of shame around his ankles.

Then came the fourth voyage. His tragedy now passed belief. On the raging water of Panama, where his fevered imagination had seen visions of a Veragua paved with gold, he had been caught in a Caribbean hurricane, which had stripped away his sails, and then the shipworm had come, eating away his timbers. He reached Jamaica captaining a fleet of ships so unseaworthy that they could be used only to build shelters for the marooned shipmen. A cruel sun blazed down on this group of starving men. It was then that Columbus wrote one of the most heartrending letters the world has ever read, full of imprecations in the style of the Old Testament, shot through with phrases that reveal the grip his madness had taken on him. There is his soliloquy after he had heard the voice of Heaven: "Oh, foolish and slow to believe and serve thy God! What more did He do for Moses or for David, His servant? From the day of thy birth, His watchful care was for thee. Marvelously He made thy name to sound through the earth. He gave thee the Indies for thine own, to partition them as thou didst choose, and He gave thee power to do so…" He finally was saved from his disastrous wreck by the devotion and help of

Diego Méndez. When at last he reached Spain, it was to find the Queen dying. He felt himself surrounded on all sides by envy and treachery.

Exactly the opposite happened with Amerigo's four voyages. He had never set out with fanfare of any sort or as the leader of a noteworthy enterprise, but he had always found more than he had expected, and he had never met with disaffection on the part of those who received him on his return. He generated an atmosphere of confidence. He and Columbus moved on different planes. He had no great aspirations. He never sought the kings; it was the kings who sent for him. Now, when, at the end of his life, Columbus was trying to buy a funeral litter in which to be carried to court, or secure authorization to ride a mule, Amerigo traveled in genteel fashion to see King Ferdinand, who had sent him the money for the trip.

The antecedents of the commission Columbus had entrusted to Amerigo can be discerned through Columbus's letters to his son Diego. Columbus was persuaded that a certain Camacho and one Shipmaster Bernal were poisoning the court against him. "This Shipmaster Bernal," he wrote, "it is said began the treachery; he was arrested and accused in many cases, and for each of them he deserves to be quartered... For over a week Camacho has been afraid to leave the sanctuary of the church because of bearing false witness and the incontinence of his tongue... I am going to ask for a writ because I think it would be an act of mercy to punish him;

he is so dissolute of tongue that someone must punish him with the law..."

His letters reveal the object he was pursuing. "I have already told you," he wrote to Diego,

that what you are to ask of His Highness is that he fulfill what he wrote me with regard to the ownership and the rest that was promised to me... His Highness should realize that all he has given me is as one to a hundred compared with the increase of his power and revenue; and what has been done is as nothing to what remains to be done... The dispatch of a bishop to Hispaniola should be delayed until I can speak with His Highness... The ships from the Indies have not arrived from Lisbon. They brought a rich cargo of gold and none for me... I have never seen such a mockery, for I left 60,000 pesos smelted...[4]

Shortly after this, Columbus died. Amerigo had fruitful years ahead of him. On his arrival at court, he talked with the King, and they reached an understanding. Amerigo made a decision that gave a new course to his life. He became a citizen of the Kingdoms of Castile and León. Until that time he had been a member of the Florentine colony, and his commissions for the monarchs had been carried out on that basis. As a citizen of Spain, Amerigo would be one of Ferdinand's distinguished subjects. The King conferred naturalization upon him in these terms, in the name of his daughter:

4. Ibid., p. 497.

Doña Joanna, by the grace of God, etc... To honor and favor you, Amerigo Vezpuche, in consideration of your fidelity and certain good services you have rendered me, and as I hope you will continue to do in the future, by these presents I make you a native of these my Kingdoms of Castile and León, and that you may have and hold any royal and municipal public offices that may be given and entrusted to you, and that you may enjoy all honors, benefits, and rewards, privileges and liberties, exemptions, pre-eminences, prerogatives, and immunities...[5]

The King arranged for a meeting with Amerigo and Vicente Yáñez Pinzón. The three gave thought to a new colonial policy that should have two objectives: to work out the strengthening and defense of the settlements in the Caribbean, and to pursue the discovery of the southern passage to the lands of spice. The documents begin to refer to Amerigo and Vicente Yáñez as "captains." Ferdinand instructed them to fit out ships with all possible speed. It is evident that the three conferees shared a common understanding. The King's conception of a strong national policy, Yáñez's idea of colonizing, and Amerigo's desire to complete his explorations combined to form a single realistic, far-reaching plan. It was a joint, hard-headed enterprise whose purpose was to further and protect Spain's power.

5. Ibid., Vol. III, p. 294.

Vicente Yáñez Pinzón had accompanied Columbus on his initial voyage, as captain of the *Niña*. Later on he had become the champion of that sector of opinion which challenged the Admiral's privileges and demanded freedom of discovery. In large measure it was as a result of Yáñez's efforts that in 1495 the sovereigns had authorized anyone so desiring to engage in discoveries. Later he had made a voyage to the islands, and in 1499 he had set out to explore the coast of Brazil, following the route of Amerigo's second voyage.

Under the new plan, Yáñez's area of activity was to be the colonization of the Antilles. He was named warden, and instructed to build a fort at his own expense in San Juan, Puerto Rico. He would act in the capacity of captain and chief magistrate. He would settle the island, in return for which the King would give him life tenure of it, with the right to will it to his heirs. Amerigo was to set about preparing the expedition to seek the westward passage.

Amerigo and Vicente Yáñez went to Palos de Moguer to assemble and outfit their ships. The King was to be a full partner. He was to pay half the expenses, and receive half of the profits. A Genoese, Francisco de Riverol, advanced money to the King for the immediate expenses. Amerigo and Yáñez Pinzón were in constant touch with the royal secretary, Gaspar de Gricio. The general idea of this understanding had been worked out by the three participants, the King and his two captains. Pedro Miranda was the messenger who went back and forth from the court to Palos and from Palos to the court, carrying letters and consulting with Amerigo and Yáñez about the fleet.

Everything was going along briskly when suddenly a political shift left the two navigators practically high and dry. Joanna the Mad and Philip the Handsome suddenly entered the Spanish political scene. King Ferdinand had been ruling in his daughter's name. Now Philip, supported by German soldiery, entered Castile determined to rule. Ferdinand, only recently widowed, had just married Germaine de Foix, the niece of the King of France, and this had not set well with the people. He had no choice but to step aside in favor of Philip. There followed a great scurrying on the part of the courtiers as they turned their backs on Ferdinand and rushed to curry favor with Philip.

Where did this leave the plans Ferdinand, Amerigo, and Yáñez had worked out? The two captains in Palos asked each other whether Gricio would continue as secretary of the new King or whether he would be replaced, as seemed likely. What would be the reaction of the new officials to the planned expeditions? Would Amerigo and Yáñez Pinzón enjoy the favor of the new sovereign? This would have to be discovered firsthand, and the person who seemed best fitted for such an exploration was Amerigo. He was better versed in diplomacy and politics. The Trade Board for the Indies in Seville, under whose supervision the ship-outfitters always had to operate, gave Amerigo letters for Philip's Lord

Chamberlain, M. de Vila, and for the secretary, Gricio. In addition, it gave him five reports to be delivered. These had to do with the dispatch of the fleet, with a watchtower King Ferdinand had ordered built on the Pearl Coast, with the caravels journeying to Hispaniola, and with the fortress under construction there. Amerigo was to inform Gricio on all these matters and give him a memorandum setting all this forth. It might be that the secretary would find the outlay too great, inasmuch as the expenditures were already more than the King had estimated. In this connection Amerigo was to explain that the price of bread had risen and that the budget had been calculated on the basis of the salary of two hundred men for four months instead of six. If all this could have been discussed personally with King Ferdinand, there would have been no problem. But now it was necessary to set it all down in black and white. "An authorization is required," said the memorandum for Gricio, "stating whether in the future expenses of the aforesaid fleet, and other undertakings, King Ferdinand is to pay half and receive half of the profits that may ensue, and just how this is to be done to avoid confusion and so that everything may be orderly and clear…"

The truth of the matter was that the captains, as well as the Trade Board, were caught between two fires, between two kings, and were fearful of the possibilities this change of government might hold. Nothing reveals this more clearly than the postscript to Amerigo's letter of instructions:

*If Gricio is at court, and still serves in matters hav-
ing to do with the Indies, give him the letter, show
him the reports; he will see that the King receives you
and gives you favorable attention. We have been informed that the King has entrusted the affairs of the
Indies to M. de Vila, his Lord Chamberlain. If that is
the case, go to him directly. What we especially want
cleared up is the agreement between Our Lord the
King (Philip the Handsome) and King Ferdinand,
so we shall know our obligations to each.*[6]

Amerigo's mission was completely successful.
Philip the Handsome quickly grasped what it would
mean for his reign if a passage to the Spice Islands
was discovered which would rival that found by the
Portuguese, thanks to Vasco da Gama. Without for-
getting the other commissions entrusted to him,
Amerigo stressed the search for the passage. The
thing to do was to move swiftly and secretly to prevent the Portuguese from discovering these plans
through their spies and then putting obstacles in the
way of the voyage. It was decided to push the construction of the ships in Biscay. Philip and Amerigo
were probably agreed that it would be better to make
preparations far from the prying circles of busybod-
ies, from whom no secret could be withheld, in
Seville and Cádiz, cities of easy access to the Portuguese. Moreover, the experience of the Basques in
Atlantic navigation could be turned to good advan-

6. Navarrete: *Colección diplomática*, Document CLX, p. 352.

Pages 410-411: *Giovanni Stradano*, Allegory of Amerigo and América,
the latter in a hammock, Florence, late sixteenth century.

tage. Before a year had elapsed after Amerigo's conference with the King word was received from Biscay that the ships were ready and on their way to Cádiz. "It is my wish," the King wrote to the officials of the Trade Board, "that the aforesaid fleet set out as quickly as is possible because of the disadvantages that would ensue from its delay."[7] These disadvantages were that the Portuguese had already got wind of what was going on and were doing everything in their power to hamper the expedition. The King prodded the officials, asking them if the supply of sea biscuit had been laid in, and instructing them to talk with Vicente Yáñez and Amerigo to see if they could leave before the winter set in.

This was in August 1505. Several weeks later, on September 25, Philip the Handsome died. He had been displaying his strength and agility in a game of handball with a group of Basques; overheated, he drank a pitcher of ice water. The fever that followed ended his days and his rule. Doña Joanna completely lost what little she had left of her wandering wits. King Ferdinand was in Genoa at the time. He quickly returned, and resumed the reins of government. Precious time had been lost.

The Portuguese openly formulated their objections to the expedition. Ferdinand had too many problems already to expose himself to more. But he was a Machiavellian character. He knew how to bide his

---

7. Navarrete: *Viajes*, Vol. III, Document V, p. 296.

time. With much publicity, he ordered the fleet disbanded. The ships were assigned to the Hispaniola service. The larger one, called the *Magdalena*, was assigned to Diego Rodríguez de Grajeda. After he had sailed her to Hispaniola, he bought her with his own money. The smaller one, which Amerigo was to have commanded in the voyage to discover the passage, meant nothing to him now that the voyage had been called off. It was taken over by Juan de Subano. Amerigo took charge of outfitting it, as though his activities henceforth were to be merely routine jobs.[8]

But this was not the case. Amerigo was fifty and full of vigor and plans. The search for the passage had been postponed, but there was much to do in the colonization of the Antilles and in the building of the fortress on the Pearl Coast, matters he had discussed at length with Vicente Yáñez. These were all parts of the same plan, and it had been demonstrated that Amerigo, the newly naturalized citizen of Spain, could get along with any king. So he busied himself transferring wheat, flour, and wine from the Trade Board to the ships, buying drills and augurs for a small caravel being dispatched to Hispaniola, and sea biscuit by the hundredweight. The record of his activities is on the books of the Trade Board. He had the rank of captain and was on the Crown payroll.

8. Ibid., Vol. III, p. 328.

In December 1506 a ubiquitous Venetian, Girolamo Vianello, who had served with the armies of
Spain, who had traveled widely and spoke Arabic,
who had carried letters from the King of Spain to
the Senate of Venice, who had sent the Venetians
the news of the death of Philip the Handsome, wrote
to the Signoria of Venice: "Two ships have arrived
here from India, dispatched by My Lord the King,
which went out to discover under the command of
Zuan the Biscayan and Amerigo the Florentine."[9]

Of this voyage, only this single mention exists.
"Zuan the Biscayan" is undoubtedly Juan de la Cosa.
On previous voyages carried out, like this one, as a
mission for the King of Castile, Amerigo had communicated the news to Florence, for he was still a
Florentine citizen. Now he had sworn allegiance to
another flag. The voyage may have been made simply for the purpose of corroboration. Possibly it
reached the coasts Columbus had seen, the only
section Amerigo did not know. In any case, if the
voyage was actually made, it was to the Pearl Coast
and other parts of the mainland; it lasted three
months, and he then returned to Spain. On this occasion there were clashes with the Indians, their villages were fired, and gold and pearls were acquired
through barter. In his letter Vianello says: "They found
many houses from which numerous Indians came
forth to greet and honor them, who told them that

9. *Raccolta Columbiana*, Part III, Vol. I, pp. 185-7.

one of them had already announced to them how certain ships would come out of the east, which belonged to a great king who was unknown to them, who would hold them all as slaves, and that these people were immortal and would arrive dressed in strange garb. They said that when our ships appeared, their King said to them: Behold the ships foretold to you ten years ago. This King appeared in a breast-plate of solid gold fastened to his chest, with a chain of gold and a mask of gold, and four bells fastened to his ankles..." From the description of these jewels, they would seem to be of the type of workmanship characteristic of certain regions of what is today Colombia and of Central America, and suggest the possibility that the voyage was along those coasts.

Vianello's letter remained unknown until the time of Humboldt, who was informed of its discovery by Leopold Ranke. Ranke had come upon it in Sanuto's Diary in the Marciana Library of Venice. It was first published by Baron Varnhagen in 1869. It immediately suggested the possibility that Amerigo had made a fifth voyage. This assumption was inadmissible to Humboldt, as to Varnhagen and many others who followed their opinion, down to Alberto Magnaghi. To be sure, Vianello was a responsible person. There is exact information about him, not only as a traveler, but also as a cartographer. The letter he wrote, with its wealth of details, left Burgos in December 1506 and arrived in Venice in January 1507, as is borne out by the Venetian records. On the other hand, however, Humboldt, basing his opinion on

Martín Fernández de Navarrete, found it impossible
to accept the possibility that Amerigo was away from
Spain at the supposed time of the voyage.

Martín Fernández de Navarrete, an outstanding historian, member of the Academy and editor of a major part of the documents having to do with the
voyages of discovery, enjoyed, and still enjoys a reputation admitting of no dispute. His utterances were,
for the most part, accepted without reservation, even
by persons as cautious as Humboldt. In his *Exact
Information Concerning Amerigo Vespucci,* Navarrete had written: "On September 15, 1506, the officials of the Trade Board wrote to Secretary Gricio
that they were sending Amerigo Vespucci to report
to King Philip I on the state of the fleet King
Ferdinand had ordered outfitted, which could not
sail before February 1507."[10] Navarrete changed the
two dates. Amerigo did not visit the court in 1506,
but in 1505. It slipped the distinguished scholar's
mind that in September of 1506 Philip the Handsome had been dead for a year. He forgot that in the
collection of documents he himself had published
the document to which he refers is dated 1505. And
Humboldt, without using the necessary caution,
under the spell of Navarrete's authority, repeated:
"In September of 1506 the directors of the Trade
Board in Seville instructed Amerigo Vespucci to go
to the court, which was probably at Villafranca, to

10.   Navarrete: *Viajes,* Vol. III, p. 327.

report... He was entrusted with the delicate mission of securing the approval of the two sovereigns, who were not on good terms, the Archduke King and his father in-law, Ferdinand the Catholic. For his negotiations he was advised to seek the mediation of M. de Vila or the Secretary of State, Gricio, whichever seemed best."[11] Later Varnhagen and Vignaud followed the same erroneous path as Humboldt.[12]

It is perplexing how such a patently mistaken piece of information as this adduced by Navarrete could have served as the basis for denying one of Amerigo's voyages. But the incident is an instance of the difficulties in the way of drawing up an accurate biography of the Florentine. In the last analysis, this is the importance of the fifth voyage.

To return to "Zuan the Biscayan"–that is, Juan de la Cosa, the author of the first map of the New World that we know–he was an old friend of Amerigo's. Undoubtedly he utilized the information brought back by Amerigo on his first voyage to draw up his map on which Cuba appears as an island. The two of them accompanied the expedition of Hojeda, Amerigo's second voyage to the Caribbean. They had been associated in the designing of maps, in court intrigues, in the study of Portugal's activities. De la Cosa was more active in this than Amerigo. He was sent as a

11. A. von Humboldt: *Géographie du Nouveau Continent*, Vol. V, p. 159.
12. A. Varnhagen: *Amerigo Vespucci*, p. 117; H. Vignaud: Améric Vespuce, p. 170.

spy to the court of Don Manuel. He was discovered there and put in prison. The King of Castile had to use his influence to secure his release. The history of such incidents is to be found in the books of the Trade Board, as is the manner in which the Crown paid its agents: "To Juan de la Cosa on the 22nd day of the month of August 1503, ten gold ducats to go to Portugal and find out or learn secretly about the voyage the Portuguese made to the Indies with four vessels on which they brought back Indians as slaves, and logwood, and made another voyage to the same land."[13] The success of Juan de la Cosa's espionage is attested by the following entry: "To Niculoso Espindola in the name of Juan de la Cosa 2,620 maravedís for two mariner's charts which he gave to Our Majesty the Queen and to cover his expenses of travel to Portugal and the court in the matter of the news concerning the logwood and Indians that the Portuguese had brought…"[14]

In all this plotting and spying the gallant Biscayan pilot was closely associated with the Italians, with Amerigo and with Nicolas Spinola, one of the Genoese merchants who gave assistance to Columbus and took an important part in the growing trade between Spain and Hispaniola.

13. E. de Gandia: *Antecedentes diplomáticos de las expediciones de Juan Díaz de Solís, Sebastián Caboto y don Pedro de Mendoza,* p. 22.
14. Ibid., p. 24.

On November 26, 1507 the King summoned Amerigo and Juan de la Cosa to the court. In 1508 the two made the same trip again, carrying the gold that had arrived from the Indies. Both received an equal sum of maravedís for their traveling expenses.

Amerigo and De la Cosa did not appear at court alone. They were accompanied from Seville by Vicente Yáñez Pinzón and Juan Díaz de Solís. These four aces of the sea deserve study as the most notable foursome of their day in the great adventure of the discovery. Yáñez Pinzón was an Andalusian, De la Cosa a Basque, Díaz de Solís a Portuguese, and Amerigo a Florentine. They came, messengers from the four cardinal points, to show the King of Castile the allurements of the mariner's rose. The four did not make the trip to Burgos in silence, one may be sure. Each of them had a wondrous tale to relate. Amerigo's we already know; that of Juan de la Cosa can be guessed at from what we have seen of his espionage activities; the other two were no less fascinating.

As the four traversed the Castilian plain, it was like a peripatetic school of master mariners. Their travels and encounters recall those of Don Quixote and his squire, and they must have delighted in that teeming world of fantasy and hard common sense from which Cervantes drew the substance of those immortal dialogues between a mad hidalgo and a poor peasant. The maritime history of Spain could not be written without the names of these four wanderers, each of whom left his name linked to maps, seas, legends, the new continent.

We have said little of Díaz de Solís. "The probabilities are," writes José Toribio Medina,

that his family had its origin in Asturias de Oviedo; from there they went to Portugal, where they settled, and where he was probably born. After having made several voyages to India as a sailor, he left the service of that nation, irked at not receiving his wages, and signed up, no doubt as a pilot, with French corsairs; in company with them he seized a Portuguese caravel returning to Europe from La Mina, and after receiving share of the booty, he appears in Spain in the latter months of 1505.[15]

The King seated himself at the round table of adventure with the four mariners. Ferdinand, who had just returned from Naples, was eager to rekindle the fires of discovery, which had died down in his absence. The idea of seeking the passage to the spice islands came up once more in these conversations. De la Cosa kept harping on the Pearl Coast. Perhaps the King, perhaps all of them, spoke of the need of organizing a better control of the expeditions, of the preparation of mariners, of the drawing up and safeguarding of the maps, and of setting up in Seville a central organization headed by a pilot major. These things were already being done in Lisbon. This was what Amerigo had seen in operation, and this was perhaps the best idea he could contribute to the systematic organization of

15.   J. T. Medina: *Juan Díaz de Solís,* p. xxiii.

the Spanish voyages. From the web these four mariners were weaving out of these pieces of heterogeneous information, the King saw emerging the image of a living map of future realms. The standard of Castile would float over remote seas, outrivaling the exploits of the Portuguese.

Díaz de Solís and Yáñez Pinzón set out to find the passage. They failed because they were not in agreement. They returned in 1509. Juan de la Cosa left for the Pearl Coast. In a landing near Cartagena, on the Caribbean coast, he died from Indian arrow wounds.

The King kept Amerigo in Seville. He had decided to put all his navigational enterprises under the Florentine's supervision: he would be the Pilot Major.

XXI

PILOT MAJOR, AND DEATH
(1508-1512)

When the four sea captains set out from Seville in February 1508 for the court, they took with them a mule carrying six thousand ducats in gold from the New World. On the record books of the Trade Board their names appear as follows: "Juan de la Cosa and Amerigo and Vicente Yáñez and Juan Díaz de Solís." As already pointed out, Amerigo was known by his first name by reason of the musical quality of the word, and because for the Trade Board people, as for the rest of Seville and for his friends, he was like one of the family. We know the results of this visit to the court. Yáñez and Díaz de Solís left to search for the passage, and returned at outs; De la Cosa had a rendezvous with death in the Caribbean, and Amerigo came to be Pilot Major of Spain. His appointment was made with almost undue haste. It was an instance in which the King acted without hesitation. The four captains had arrived at court at the end of February, and on March 22 the Florentine's appointment was signed.[1]

1. A. de Herrera: *Decadas*, I, Book VII. For the details of the functions of pilot major, the text of the appointment, and notes on Vespucci's successors in the post, see J. Pulido Rubio: *El Piloto Mayor de la Casa de Contratación de Sevilla.*

Amerigo Vespucci looking at the Polar Star *(detail).*
Stradanus/Gallé, 1590.

Castile had a rudimentary, almost nonexistent naval tradition. The Basques and the Catalans were the sailors. The Portuguese too were excellent seamen. All of them were trained in the practical school of commerce, of fighting pirates, of nautical charts, of sailors' tales. Castile's participation in matters pertaining to the sea had been limited to the port of Seville. When the gold mines of Guinea were discovered and Castile's suzerainty over the Canary Islands was established, Italians and people from other places offered their services to the Castilians, partly to assist them in their undertakings, partly for their own profit. These chance contacts with Africa and the disputes with the Portuguese over sea rights were as nothing compared with the great training school of Portugal. Columbus transformed all this. Castile's real wealth had been its plains, producing wheat, olives, chick-peas, onions, hidalgos, bold soldiers. With Columbus, Castile took ship. Spain completed its unity on the sea. Men from all its provinces came together on the caravels. And the King had to open a new front in the government of his realm.

The idea was so completely new that when, on March 22, 1508, the King said: "Amerigo is to be Pilot Major of Spain," he gave a new orientation to his government; he entered upon a path the laws of the land had not envisaged. There were precedents for barter, land grants, right of conquest, settlement, but none for the post of pilot major. Its antecedents were to be found in Portugal. Amerigo had seen it functioning there. Several months had to elapse until on

August 6, the duties of the new superintendent of the sea were defined. It was then that Ferdinand devised a plan which, by reason of its logic and the manner in which it concerted the interests of trade, Crown, and science, agreed completely with Amerigo's ideas. His experiences in Florence and on his voyages, his acquaintance with the Portuguese school, his close contact with the Italian colonies of Seville and Lisbon, his dissatisfaction with existing mariners' maps, his understanding of the objectives of Spain, all now found an outlet. Ferdinand could not have chosen a better counselor for his new administrative needs. One or two generations earlier the Vespucci had drawn up for Florence the codes governing sea routes and the rights and obligation of its merchants in Bruges. It now devolved on Amerigo to do the same for Spain, but on a more ambitious scale. And he also had a teaching mission: he was to be the head of the university of mariners.

The investigator wishing to learn the names of the ministers Ferdinand availed himself of to lay the bases of a policy that came to be the natural corollary of the Trade Board would discover that they were "Juan de la Cosa and Amerigo and Vicente Yáñez and Juan Díaz de Solís."

The first part of the royal decree of August 6 reads as though it had been lifted from Amerigo's letters. Experience and the information received, it says, go to show that because of lack of experience on the part of the pilots and lack of the knowledge needed to sail the ships traveling to the islands and the mainland, many mistakes have ensued, the crews have undergone great perils, and the property of the King and merchants has suffered serious risk. The cause, in large part, has been the inability to use the quadrant and astrolabe to discover latitudes and work out the ships' positions at sea. As the Crown plans to make further voyages and extend its discoveries, "it is needful that there be persons who are more expert and better trained, and who know the necessary things... so those who travel under their command may go more safely." The King ordered all pilots and those who in the future might wish to act as pilots to be trained in the use of the quadrant and the astrolabe, so that, "joining practice with theory," they might make use of them on their voyages

...and without this knowledge they may not sail on the aforesaid ships as pilots, nor receive a salary for pilotage, nor may merchants engage them as pilots, nor shipmasters take them aboard unless they have first been examined by you, Amerigo Despuchi, our Pilot Major, and receive from you a certificate of examination and testimony that each of them knows the aforementioned; with which certificate we order them to be considered and accepted as trained pilots wherever they show it, for it is our pleasure that you be the examiner of the aforesaid pilots.

The appointment carried with it the understanding that Amerigo was to open a school of navigators. The King decided that it should be in Amerigo's own home in Seville. He was to teach anyone so desiring who would pay him the fee agreed upon. At first there would be no approved pilots, but as the business of the voyages could not be halted because of the serious consequences this would entail, Amerigo was empowered to select the most skilled from among the pilots and mariners who had already seen service and make them ready for one or two voyages. On their return he would examine them and complete their instruction.

As important as the training of the pilots was the problem of navigators' charts. Amerigo had long had this in mind, and he alluded to it in his letter to Soderini, of which he must have given a copy to King Ferdinand, as he told the Duke of Lorraine. Thee King now gave the following order: "There are many general charts drawn up by different shipmasters depicting and indicating the lands and islands in the Indies of Our possession... which vary greatly one from another." To establish consensus and unity, the King decided that there should be one general chart showing each point of land, each island, each river mouth, each bay, in its proper location. "We order our officials of the Seville Trade Board for the Indies to bring together the most skillful of all our pilots who may be ashore at the time, and in the presence of you, the aforesaid Amerigo Despuchi, our Pilot Major, to settle upon and draw up a master map of all the lands and islands of the Indies discovered to this moment belonging to our kingdoms and realms, and on the basis of their opinions and discussions and on the decision taken by you, our aforesaid Pilot Major, a master chart be drawn up, to be known as the royal chart, by which all pilots are to govern and guide themselves."

Ferdinand used his imperial authority. The title of pilot major became a law without appeal. No pilot might use any chart other than that drawn up by Amerigo "under penalty of fifty doubloons' fine to go to the Trade Board for the Indies in the city of Seville." Any and all pilots henceforth voyaging to the Indies, discovered or to be discovered, on finding anything not appearing on the master chart, were to go to Amerigo's house to report their findings. In this way the chart grew in accuracy and was kept up to date for the use of other navigators.

Any pilot setting out on the ocean sea without his quadrant and astrolabe and the knowledge of how to use them was to be declared unfit for his employment for the time of the Crown's pleasure and to pay a fine of ten thousand maravedís. Amerigo was empowered to carry out all these provisions.

Amerigo received a copy of the decree, and its contents were publicly announced.

We order Prince Charles, our very dear and well-beloved son, and princes, dukes, prelates, counts, marquises, gentlemen, masters of orders of our tribunals and chancelleries, and the other priors, commanders, subcommanders, governors of castles and fortresses, country seats, and council members, mayors, magistrates, officers of the law, knights, squires, officials, and good men of all the cities, towns, and villages of our kingdoms and realms; and all ship captains, pilots, master mariners, and mates, and any other person whom the contents of this concerns or may concern, to have and hold you as Our Pilot Major.

The voice of the King descended from the uplands of Castile to the ports of Andalusia and over the plains of the sea. Everything was stated in careful detail, according to medieval practice. Salamanca remained the university for law and the humanities, for theologians and rhetoricians; Amerigo's house in Seville became the university for the ocean sea and the New World. But the New World was called "the Indies." This name was of no concern to Amerigo; he respected the one that had been employed by Columbus.

In order that no one might claim ignorance of the law, it was ordered that people be called together by the town crier, to the sound of drum, and the letter be publicly read in the customary places in the city of Seville, of Cádiz, and all other cities, towns, and hamlets of all the kingdoms and realms. In those days people knowing how to read were akin to actors. Their voices, as they boomed in the market places and squares, recalled the theater. In sonorous tones they pronounced the name of the new master of the school of the sea as pleased them best: Espuche, Despuche, Espuchi, or Bespuchio.

It is strange that so marked a distinction as the post of pilot major should not have aroused anyone's resentment. Amerigo had no enemies. He was always the same affable, agreeable, unpretentious person. He was a member of a noble house of Florence; but with María Cerezo and the seamen he was one of the populace of Seville. Without seeking authority or power, he now held a position such as Columbus had never occupied. Columbus was the Admiral of the Ocean Sea, a title that was mostly façade, and which the stern hand of Bobadilla in San Domingo did not respect. The unhappy Genoese, during the time of his admiralship, had oscillated between dreams of grandeur and the humiliations of reality. Amerigo, bearing a more modest title–pilot major–was the superintendent of the seas. A living map was entrusted to him, and he watched it grow and augment. It was not the circumscribed America that we know, where everything is in its set place, but a mobile New World, which revealed itself by surprise, as when the mist rolls away from the landscape at dawn. If ever Amerigo dreamed of being something, he could have conceived of nothing better.

The good impression caused by his appointment in Spain must have spread to the New World. The first pilots crossing toward the end of 1508 carried the news. Nicolás de Obando, Governor of Hispaniola, had just informed the King that several ships homeward bound from the island had landed at French ports for lack of dependable skill in navigation. The King answered him that this would never happen again. "It has been provided," he wrote, "that no pilot will sail without having been examined by my pilot major, who will give him a certificate of competence, and a master map will be drawn up from all the various maps, and all must know the use of the quadrant, and to this end I have ordered Amerigo Vespucci to instruct them in its use in Seville."

Amerigo's family of seafaring friends was growing as was the Spanish family of navigators. One by one they came to Amerigo's home, where they stayed weeks or months receiving his instruction and leaving to spread his fame beyond the sea. They found the sea which Amerigo mapped for them safer, less fraught with accident, and they respected him. Nobody had an unkind word to say about him.

Moreover, Amerigo was now being the Italian uncle to Giovanni, the son of Antonio. Giovanni looked after his papers, listened to his teachings. It was he who received the greatest benefit not only from Amerigo's knowledge, but also from that of those who visited him. He, in turn, was becoming a teacher of pilots and a cartographer.

Amerigo had imagination. He did not permit his appointment to become a routine post. On one occasion the Venetian Ambassador, Francesco Comer, talked with him and learned that the new ships being built in Biscay were to be plated with lead at Amerigo's orders. It was a good idea to encase them in metal to protect them against the perils of the stormy Caribbean.[2]

Nor did he ever lose his sense of comradeship. He helped Diego Nicuesa secure the money he needed to travel to the New World, going security for him. On March 13, 1509 Nicuesa pledged himself to honor the obligations assumed by Amerigo and the others who had helped him.

2. *Raccolta Columbiana*, Part III, Vol. I, p. 94.

Amerigo's duties as Pilot Major were heavy. He could not spare the time to look after his own affairs. He appointed Andrés de San Martín his attorney to act for him before the Queen or the Archbishop of Seville, and before mayors, judges, or notaries in the event of trial, or without trial, and to collect whatever was due him, in maravedís or doubloons, "or in wheat bread, barley, oil, or fowl." Some of the mariners may have paid for their instruction with chickens, as is often the case with village doctors. In the wording of the powers of attorney of those days, Andrés de San Martín could give or take oath for Amerigo, and swear "by his soul." And Amerigo was bound by all his present and future possessions.[3]

The Archbishop, Francisco Ximénez de Cisneros, whose influence had been so decisive during the reign of Queen Isabella, enjoyed equal prestige with King Ferdinand, and in 1507 Pope Julius II, at Ferdinand's request, made him a cardinal. From then on, history knows him as Cardinal Cisneros and as the Grand Inquisitor, to which dignity he was raised by the King, and rightly so. He was stern, unyielding, and most zealous in matters concerning dogma. And as his post in the government was of the highest importance, of necessity he had to concern himself with matters having to do with the Indies. He sought out Amerigo: he was interested in finding a

3. The complete text of this power is published in *Colección de documentos inéditos para la Historia de América*, Vol. X, Appendix II, pp. 451 ff.

way to guarantee the royal prerogatives, to work out a fiscal policy for the colonies. Would a monopoly be the best solution, or should the traders be given a free hand? Should an agency be set up to look after such matters? Might it be well to follow the systems of the Portuguese?

In reply to the Cardinal's question, Amerigo wrote him a letter that is the document of a statesman. It is dated December 8, 1508, in Seville. It begins by analyzing the mercantile policy followed by the King of Portugal in order to point out the differences between Portugal and Spain. No concrete plan had yet been worked out with regard to Brazil. It was not until Amerigo's second voyage for King Manuel that a plan for colonizing there was conceived. But there was still no Portuguese settlement such as those the Spaniards had founded in the Antilles as early as the days of Columbus. All the King of Portugal did was to send merchandise to his factors to be sold to the Moors of Africa. This was a market with which they were familiar, and the goods were paid for in ivory, gold, or spices. But in the New World the Spaniards had to supply their colonists with a variety of implements they needed to set themselves up, and to send them articles suitable for barter. The settlers needed building materials for houses, for setting up agricultural enterprises, for the construction of cities. If certain of these articles—particularly livestock—Amerigo wrote the Cardinal, could be secured more advantageously in the Canaries or in Portuguese islands than in Spain, a system could be worked out allowing a margin of freedom to buy them there and then levy a tax on them when they were brought into the colonies. Or this trade could be left in the hands of merchants, who would divide their profits with the Crown. The indispensable step was to set up control bodies to see that under the protection of such liberties fraud and contraband did not spring up.

The understanding of the situation and the problems revealed by Amerigo in his plan show him to have been a man of vision far in advance of the foremost ministers of the Crown.[4]

Antonio de Herrera writes in his history that in 1511 "word was received that the Portuguese, desirous of sailing the ocean which belonged to the Crown of Castile, importuned Amerigo Vespucci for maps."[5] Amerigo's post was one of the greatest sensitivity in those days. He had everything in his hands. But at the same time he offered the greatest guarantees to the Crown because, his own loyalty being above all doubt, he had firsthand knowledge of what the Portuguese were after. Amerigo was fully aware of the aims, the plans, the ambitions of Lisbon. And no one knew better than he the methods by which Spain could best defend herself. His role was that of wise counselor, one who recommended shrewdness and astuteness rather than force.

Spain had become a kingdom built upon subterranean currents of espionage. And, as so many times

4. *Cartas de Indias*, December 9, 1508.
5. Herrera; *Décadas*, I, Book V11, chapter xii.

before, Ferdinand turned to his old friends, to those of Amerigo's group, to defend himself.

In October 1510 it was discovered that the Portuguese Alonso Alvares had been holding secret talks with various pilots, trying to get what information he could out of them for Portugal. Swift measures were taken in Seville. Alvares was arrested and tortured into confession. It was learned that with the help of the pilot Juan Ruiz de Mafra he had been trying to induce Spanish pilots with experience of the voyages to Urabi, Veragua, Paria, and the Pearl Coast to enter the service of King Manuel. The officials of the Trade Board, undoubtedly with Amerigo's approval, commissioned Vicente Yáñez Pinzón to win the confidence of Ruiz de Mafra and put him in the custody of Bishop Fonseca. Yáñez carried out his mission unerringly, and Mafra came into the power of the Bishop. Portugal made protests, to which Ferdinand replied politely but firmly that Castile had no intention of giving up her secrets or allowing her pilots to be stolen from her.[6]

As is apparent, Seville was not solid land, but a sea of plots, bribes, and double-dealing through which Amerigo had to steer his course. For his defense he had the training he had received on his trip to Paris with his Ambassador uncle, Guido Antonio. The maze of plots through which he had to thread his way was the same he had had to circumvent

6. E. de Gandía: *Antecedentes diplomáticos de las expediciones de Juan Díaz de Solís, Sebastián Caboto y don Pedro de Mendoza*, p. 117.

when he was working for Lorenzo de' Medici, the Popolano. He came through each test with the heightened admiration of the Crown and its officials. From the day he was made a citizen of Castile and named Pilot Major, he never again wrote to Florence. His conduct was that of a loyal Castilian subject, with one slight difference: he asked nothing. He was happy in his post.

Death came to Amerigo on February 22, 1512. María Cerezo and Giovanni, his nephew, were at his side. He left no child in Spain, nor governance of any sort in legacy, nor remuneration for any discovery. He received no title of nobility from the King, no coat of arms. He had never been ambitious for such things. There is no record of any request for such honors. If flowers were laid on his grave, perhaps the wasps of his Florentine coat of arms came to sip their nectar, the golden wasps of Peretola under the azure sky of Seville.

Two days after his death the canon of the Cathedral, Manuel Catafio, called at the Trade Board of the Indies to collect Amerigo's final wages. He was acting in the capacity of executor, and claimed this money in the name of María Cerezo. He received 10,937 $^{1/2}$ maravedís.[7]

Amerigo's real legacy was his school, his university for pilots. The most expert navigators of Spain studied there, and it prepared the new generations of seamen. His diary, his papers, his maps were left

7 Navarrete: *Viajes*, Vol. III, p. 308.

to his nephew. The King appointed one of Amerigo's friends as his successor, the Portuguese Juan Díaz de Solís. But Díaz de Solís was not made the sole custodian of the royal map, the master map of Spain; he shared this responsibility with Giovanni Vespucci. Moreover, Giovanni was authorized to keep the map, revise it, make copies of it, and sell them to the navigators. Aside from Giovanni only one other person was authorized to make such copies: the Spaniard Andrés de San Martín, Amerigo's old attorney. Giovanni became known as one of the most noted map-makers, and his testimony, based on Amerigo's diaries, carried great weight in the discussions that took place between the pilots of Spain and Portugal over the respective claims of the two crowns.

After Amerigo's death the Crown did not forget that he had been a loyal servant. It treated his widow and nephew with consideration. Giovanni was made pilot and cartographer. María Cerezo was assigned a part of the salary of the new Pilot Major, Díaz de Solís. Of his annual salary of 50,000 maravedís, 10,000 were set aside for María. On the death of Díaz de Solís, his place was taken by Sebastián Cabot, and the same deduction from his salary was made for Amerigo's widow. The fact that the Pilots Major agreed to this withholding from their salaries is proof of their generous tribute to the memory of the man who had founded the school of pilots. It is likewise possible that they utilized the papers of Amerigo in the possession of María Cerezo and Giovanni Vespucci. The Crown was fortunate in having had for nearly half a century the services in this post of a Florentine, a Portuguese, and a Venetian. The first Spaniard to receive the appointment was Alonso Cháves, in 1552. Amerigo had been appointed in 1508.

The respect the name of Vespucci enjoyed in Castile did not escape the notice of Pope Leo X, the son of Lorenzo the Magnificent, whose first steps up the ecclesiastical ladder had been guided by Guido Antonio Vespucci. Shortly after coming to the throne of St. Peter, Leo X saw in the proposed marriage between the son of King Ferdinand and the daughter of the King of France a threat to his international policy. To scotch the plan he sent as his personal ambassador Giovanni Vespucci, the son of Guido Antonio.[8] The mission was completely successful. The Vespucci were old hands at games of this sort.

8. Uzielli: *Notes to the Life of Vespucci by Bandini*, p. 80.

An old engraving depicting a geographer taking measures of the globe with a compass.

XXII

THE NAME AMERICA
(1507)

Why, when, where, and how did the New World get the name of America? Who coined it?

Deep in the heart of Lorraine, where the slopes of the Vosges form quiet folds covered with pines, stood the ancient monastery of Saint-Dié, a haven of peace in the sixteenth century. In the seventh century St. Deodatus de Ververs–or Deodaturn or Theodatus or St. Deodati–had withdrawn to these forests to found the monastery. Three centuries went by, and a chapter of canons was established. Another century elapsed, and everything was wiped out by fire. Another century, another fire. In the sixteenth century Saint-Dié was little more than it had been in the preceding centuries–a church, a cloister, a few houses, and a wall. But now they were of stone. In the choir loft the canons sang the offices. This done, they strolled gravely through the cloisters, talking of rhetoric, engravers, and geography amid the peace of their mountains. The canons of Saint-Dié constituted a kind of miniature academy. They finally called themselves a Gymnasium, after the fashion across the Rhine–the Gymnase Vosgien. Their isolation and enthusiasm made them feel themselves somewhat the center of the world, or at least of their small world. Their thirst

Mantelpiece object from Switzerland or Austria with the name of America, seventeenth century. Cooper-Hewitt Museum of Design.

for news was insatiable; their fondest hope, to pass their information on to the world.

Saint-Dié was under the patronage of the Duke of Lorraine, René I. Theoretically, he was a king. His grandfather, René II, who in his youth was a king, ended his days as the Count of Provence. He did not win fame as a soldier, but he was esteemed as a poet and painter. The troubadours found him a generous Mæcenas. René II, his grandson, maintained the tradition of his grandfather in some degree. He was a Latinist, he was interested in geography, and he encouraged the literary enthusiasm of the canons of Saint-Dié. His secretary and chaplain, Vautrin Lud, became a canon of Saint-Dié. In 1507 Vautrin Lud was all-powerful in the monastery; he headed the chapter, he carried on the municipal administration and dealt out justice, he was supervisor of the mines, he built the chapel of Ortimont, he sang in the choir, he established pious foundations, he led the processions. As Saint-Dié was minuscule in size, these duties were not too onerous. But in addition Vautrin was a good man, who prayed for everyone, and he had the gift of kindly wit. "An excellent man... an irreproachable teacher," the poet Ringmann said of him, and he spoke with sincerity and knowledge.[1]

Vautrin, who was in the neighborhood of sixty, had surrounded himself with young men of great enthusiasm. His nephew, Nicholas Lud, persuaded him to

---

1. G. Save: *Vautrin Lud et le Gymnase Vosgien (Bulletin de la Société Philomatique Vosgienne, No. 35, Saint-Dié).*

set up a print shop in Saint-Dié, and offered his own house for this purpose.[2] It was a tiny press, but in their minds it was the press from which great works would issue. Each of those who worked in it was a scholar or poet of sorts. All of them were canons or on the way to becoming canons. One of the proof-readers was the poet Matthias Ringmann, twenty-two, the son of peasants who had lived in the mountains, but whom curiosity had led to Heidelberg, to Paris, from Paris to Italy, from Italy to Strasbourg, listening to the teaching of grammarians and humanists. He translated the *Commentaries* of Julius Cæsar into German. As illustrator and cartographer, and also as proof-reader, Lud had brought in a priest, some thirty years of age, who later became a canon. He may have studied with Albrecht Dürer, and his name was Martín Waldseemüller. He was born in Radolfszell on the banks of Lake Constance, and studied at the University of Fribourg. He was an intimate friend of the poet Ringmann. He used a Greek nickname: Ilacomilus. From Cologne or Fribourg or Basel a group of typographers and engravers had come to Saint-Dié. They had been trained in the Rhine schools, perhaps directly or indirectly by Dürer.

Another important member of the group was Jean Basin, vicar of the church and notary of the college of canons, who was born in Sandaucourt. Basin de San-

---

2. See *Bulletin de la Société Philomatique Vosgienne*, No. 36 (1911). The father of Nicholas Lud, Jean, was the author of a book, entitled *Dialogue de Johannes Lud* (1500), extolling René II.

daucourt, as he is generally known, was the author of a treatise containing general considerations on the art of speech, which distinguishes man from beasts, and on the manner of speaking with elegance, which distinguishes cultivated men from rustics.

In 1911 a marble plaque was placed on the house of Nicholas Lud, where Vautrin's press was set up, with an inscription reading: "Here, in the reign of René II, on April 25, 1507, the *Cosmographiæ Introductio* was printed in which the name of AMERICA was given to the New World. It was printed and published by the members of the Gymnase Vosgien, Vautrin Lud, Nicholas Lud, Jean Basin, Matthias Ringmann, and Martín Waldseemüller."

What was the *Cosmographiæ, Introductio?* Where did the canons get the idea of giving the New World the name *America?* Who suggested it?[3]

For some time Vautrin Lud had been interested in matters of geograpby. At the beginning of 1507 he had published in Strasbourg, at the Grüninger press, a small book entitled *Speculi Orbis Declaratio*–that is, *Explanation of the Mirror of the World.* In it, on a figure invented by him, the earth is represented in polar projection upon a moving disk, which, revolving about it, marks the hours. When Vautrin set up his press in Saint-Dié, he wrote to Bishop Hazards: "You will soon see, God willing, the most important

3. It was Alexander von Humboldt who, while writing his *Géographie du Nouveau Continent* in Paris, discovered the *Cosmographiæ Introductio* and initiated the study of the Gymnase of Saint-Dié.

publications from our plates, among which Ptolemy's *Geography* will please you."

Ptolemy's *Geography,* as has been seen, was the great book of those days, but the voyage of Columbus, the letters of Amerigo, the Portuguese explorations, the steady expansion of the limits within which the European world had had its being, had made this classic work of ancient geography the object of continual study and revisions. Vautrin Lud and his friends found that the current editions were not correct. A better job could be done, and this was the objective of the press set up in Saint-Dié "Human felicity," runs the dedication of Lud's brief book to René II, "does not consist in riches, nor in the savor of banquets, nor in the luxury of clothing or furnishings, nor in the exercise of power, nor in transitory or perishable things of this sort. It consists principally in the study of the secret workings of nature, in the investigation of its different elements, in the observation of all she offers as perfectly good in heaven, on earth, and in the rest of her works."

The *Speculi Orbis Declaratio* carried, as was the custom, a poem on the title page. It had been written by Matthias Ringmann. It was inspired by Amerigo's letter on the New World. It said, among other things:

A land exists unknown on your maps, Ptolemy,
Situated between the Tropic of Cancer and rainy
Aquarius,
Surrounded by the vast sea. In this land
Ablaze with light dwell many naked peoples.

A king, in whom Portugal takes just pride, discovered it,

Sending a fleet across the stormy sea. What more shall I say?

The lands and customs of these peoples, here, in this book, you will learn.

Ringmann had written the poem the year before, when he came by a copy of the *New World* letter, which he translated into German. Ringmann, whose youthful fervor knew no bounds, had the greatest enthusiasm for things Italian. His professor of rhetoric in Paris had been the poet Plubio Fausto Adrelino. He lived in Paris during the years when Giocondo, the translator of Amerigo's letter, was there directing the construction of the Notre-Dame Bridge. Later he went to Italy and made the acquaintance of Pico della Mirandola in Florence. He may very well have known Giorgio Antonio Vespucci: Mirandola's circle was that of Giorgio Antonio. A painting of Roselli's, in the Church of San Ambrogio in Florence, contains portraits of Pico, Ficino, and Poliziano. When Ringmann published Amerigo's letter, it was preceded by the poem reproduced in Lud's work.

Ringmann used as his pseudonym Philesius Vogesigena–that is, Philesius of the Vosges. Philesius was a name given to Apollo. It is apparent that the poet had a romantic cast of mind. Consumption carried him off in 1511, while he was still little more than a youth. At the suggestion of Canon Lud he wrote a very curious work, *La Grammatica figurata,* in which all definitions are conveyed by drawings. The whimsical art of the engravers of the Rhine had free rein in it. The noun was a priest, the proper name a chalice, the masculine gender a boy, the feminine a girl, and the bench on which the pupils sat was the neuter. The idea of this unusual grammar occurred to Lud as a rest cure for the romantic poet. "Bearing in mind the fact that not all our time," he told Bishop Hazards, "can be devoted to serious matters, but that we must have a little amusement, I believe the spirit should relax in intervals of repose. When in days past I saw Philesius, whom I have as proofreader in my print shop, surrounded by Greek folios and engaged, according to the precept of Horace, in tormenting them day and night, I told him that he should lay aside serious things for a little and try to amuse himself, and I suggested as a way of doing so... the idea of setting forth in designs of his fancy... the general principles of grammar."

At the end of the grammar, there is a passage as follows: "There is in the Vosges a spot known throughout the world which has for its name your own name, O Saint-Dié! There Gualterus Lud and Philesius have printed these just principles in admirable characters." And then: "Bishop Saint Dié: in the city that shines with your name, where the peaks of the Vosges rise, this work was printed; and in that same city, God willing, many other documents will soon be printed."

It can be seen that Ringmann and Lud had the most fabulous idea of this village of a few stone buildings, which they pompously called a city, and which, in their feverish optimism, they believed would shake the world. The curious thing is that they were not mistaken.

All of them were busily engaged in carrying out the plan of printing Ptolemy's work. Waldseemüller had written to the scholar Jean Amerbach of Basel, requesting a copy of the geography "for my patrons, Vautrin and Nicholas Lud." At this moment there came to René II's hands, and from his to those of the Saint-Dié group, Amerigo's letter to Soderini containing the account of his four voyages and a map of the regions Amerigo had visited or those which had been discovered by Spaniards and Portuguese. With this letter and the *Mundus Novus*, already known to Ringmann, geography underwent a complete change. The world as seen by Ptolemy was increased twofold. Never had such a revolutionary document fallen into hands so well fitted to make use of it. The canon and poet Jean Basin de Sandaucourt set about translating into Latin the text of Amerigo's letter, which had come to Saint-Dié in a French version. Ringmann and his companions set to work writing an "introduction to cosmography," Waldseemüller to drawing the new map of the world. These writings and this map would be the announcement of the new geography.

The excitement that gripped the little press of Saint-Dié is understandable. Columbus's letter of 1493 had not caused such an impression. Columbus had opened the possibility of another route to Asia, but Bartholomeu Dias and Vasco da Gama had found still another that seemed to lead more directly to the lands already known to the Italian and Portuguese traders. Islands such as those the Genoese admiral described were being told of by other navigators. Columbus's descriptions of the mainland, however rich in treasure he imagined it, were as nothing compared with the lavish courts Marco Polo told of in his *Book*. On the contrary, they evoked lands of fabled monsters: men with dog's tails, islands inhabited only by women, men without heads, with mouths and eyes in their stomachs. For all Columbus's enthusiasm, he still gravitated in the orbit of medieval geography. Now, after a lapse of four and one half centuries, realizing the true significance of his discovery, all this may strike us as absurd. But in his day the reports of his voyage never aroused the same excitement as Amerigo's news of the discovery of a new continent. This radically changed the concepts of the world in which men lived. Amerigo's report subsequently gave body to Columbus's discovery. This explains the rejoicing not only in Saint-Dié, but in the whole of Europe.

Historians have made a great problem of how Amerigo's letter to Soderini and his maps came into René II's hands. The letter as published in Saint-Dié appears with a special dedication from Amerigo to René. But Amerigo did not know René, nor was the letter addressed to René, but to Soderini. And there was also the question of the maps.

By 1507 the letter to Soderini was already known in many places. It had been written in 1504 and at least manuscript copies had circulated widely. The first Italian edition, of 1505 or 1506, was printed in Florence. Sandaucourt, the translator of Saint-Dié, stated that he made the translation from a French version. The letter was signed in Lisbon, and Amerigo said that he had sent it previously to King Ferdinand the Catholic. There may also have been a Spanish text.

Even though in the form in which the letter was published in Saint-Dié it appears addressed to René, there is no doubt that the letter is the one written to Soderini. Amerigo speaks in it of the days in which the two of them studied with his uncle Guido Antonio; he commends to him his brother Antonio, who was in Florence; he tells him the giants of Curaçao were the size of Francesco degli Albizzi, and so on. It was natural that King Ferdinand or René of Lorraine, when they heard about Amerigo's voyages, should have tried to obtain copies of the letter and that agents of theirs should have written to him asking for them. Many documents and relations circulated in this manner. All Amerigo did was to copy the letter, adding at the beginning a fitting dedication, which would give its recipient the impression that it had been written just for him, in keeping with a polite convention. That which René received begins:

To the illustrious Renato, King of Jerusalem and of Sicily, Duke of Lorraine and of Bar, Amerigo Vespucci, in humble reverence and due commendation. It may be, illustrious King, that Your Majesty will wonder at my temerity, seeing that I do not hesitate to write this prolix letter, in spite of knowing how engaged you continually are in arduous enterprises and urgent affairs of state. For this reason you might hold me to be not only presumptuous, but idle as well, employing my time in sending you matters little appropriate to your state, and written especially for Ferdinand, King of Castile, in a style not pleasing but completely barbarous, as an ignorant man alien to all culture. But my confidence in the virtues of Your Majesty, and the veracity of the things I am about to relate, which have not been written by ancients or moderns, way perhaps be my excuse.

In continuation Amerigo simply copies the letter to Soderini, from the place beginning: "Having been moved to write you this principally by the bearer of this, Benvenuto, the humble servant of Your Magnificence, and friend of mine..."

Moreover, it was indispensable, on publishing the letter in Saint-Dié, to do René the honor of putting his name at the head of the letter. It has been thought that this was the invention of the canon translator, but there is no reason why it could not have happened as set forth above.

Aside from the printed text, the *Cosmographiæ Introductio* was to carry Waldseemüller's maps, a planisphere, and a solid globe–that is to say, segments that could be cut out and pasted to a globe. This was the idea Amerigo had had when he did the same thing for Lorenzo the Popolano and sent him "a flat figure and a mappemonde of spherical shape, designed by my own hands."

It is possible that some agent of René's in Lisbon had got hold of both letter and maps in Lisbon. But it might have come to him through some of his friends in Florence or friends of Count Eberhard and Reuchlin, who had been trained by Giorgio Antonio Vespucci and closely associated with Zenobio Acciaiuoli. This can be deduced from a letter of Zenobio Acciaiuoli to Luigi Guicciardini, written in Lucca in May 1509. In this letter Zenobio asks Guicciardini to lend him once more, as he had done before, the planisphere and the globe, as a German astronomer had written to him in this connection. Zenobio says that the astronomer is "Johannes Teutonicus," and to put his mind at rest about the maps, he can have them copied by "Petrus Candidus," a monk of the Camaldolite Order. He tells Guicciardini that the map in question is the one showing the discoveries of which "the Portuguese and Spaniards boast," a phrase which, according to Magnaghi, "gives grounds for inferring that Acciaiuoli was of the opinion that at least one Italian had had a share in the discoveries."[4]

It will not seem at all farfetched to anyone who has followed this account attentively that Zenobio, the friend of Giorgio Antonio and Amerigo, related to the Medici, in touch with the Germans who had studied with Giorgio Antonio, should have been the person who made Amerigo's papers available beyond the Alps to someone who was following these events with curiosity. Waldseemüller's map, which

4. Zenobio Acciaiuoli's letter was published by Magnaghi: *Amerigo Vespucci*, p. 220.

was lost for centuries, turned up in Wolfegg Castle in Württemberg, and Reuchlin, Giorgio Antonio Vespucci's friend, was from Württemberg. This assumption would solve a problem that has been a source of perplexity for a long time. Nor is it out of the way that Guicciardini should have become the custodian of the maps that Amerigo sent to Lorenzo the Popolano. The Guicciardini were in the employ of the Medici, and were connected with the Vespucci. Nanna, Guido Antonio Vespucci's sister, was married to Luigi Guicciardini.

Poets easily become high-flown. The canon who translated Amerigo's letter felt it incumbent on him to precede it with a poem. It begins like this:

> *Whoever you may be, here you can find a sampler.*
> *Our pages, for your pleasure, may be as a ship,*
> *They contain shores and peoples newly found.*
> *Their aim, to arouse interest by their novelty.*
> *This purpose would have been better served by Maro,*
> *Putting such an event into choice words,*
> *He, who sailed the seas, and sang the Trojan hero,*
> *Would now have sung your sails, O Vespucci.*

The poem concludes with two lines well suited to a publisher who knows how to advertise:

> *As fame, eloquent witness, says that new things please,*
> *Here you have, reader; new things whose aim is to please.*

Basin de Sandaucourt's poem is followed by that of Ringmann, written for his German translation of the *Mundus Novus*. But he made a slight change. In the two previously published versions of the poem he had not mentioned Amerigo by name. Now he says:

Sed quid plura, situ, gentis moreq. reperte,
Americi parua mole libellus habet.

That is to say: "In this little book of Amerigo's you will see the regions discovered and the customs of their peoples." Amerigo's name was floating on the canons' lyrical tide.

The *Cosmographiæ Introductio* consists of a prologue, an epilogue, and nine brief chapters. These are followed by Amerigo's letter to Soderini, in a Latin version with the dedication to King René. Everything would seem to indicate that the text represents a joint effort. The first eight chapters have to do with mathematical matters. The ninth deals with the earth. Jules Marcou is of the opinion that the first five were written by Lud, possibly with the help of Waldseemüller. The style changes in the sixth; the theme broadens, there is reference to the New World. A new name appears in the margin, AMERIGE. By reason of its elegance Marcou attributes this to Basin de Sandaucourt. Chapter viii, on the winds, full of poems and quotations, "reveals the style and jesting character of Ringmann." Chapter ix, says Marcou, "much longer and more important, consisting of eight more pages dealing with the sphere, indicates by its style, first that the famous phrase so often quoted (in which the name *America* appears for the first time) is by the same hand that put into Latin the *Four Voyages,* for it has the same flowing poetic style. Then the description of the Old World in five pages of verse, in a kind of devil-may-care poetry, is completely reminiscent of Ringmann's manner as revealed in the mock elegiac composition on the reverse of the title page of the *Four Voyages...*"

Be that as it may, in this ninth chapter nine lines appear which have become world-famous. Translated from the Latin, they read:

But now that these parts of the world have been widely
examined and another fourth part has been discovered by Americu Vesputiu
(as will be seen in the following), I see no reason why we should not call it
America, that is to say, land of Americus,
for Americus its discoverer, man of sagacious wit, just as Europe and Asia received
in days gone by their names from women.

In the margin of this passage was written "AMERICA," and in another place: "It is fitting that this fourth part of the world, inasmuch as Americus discovered it, be called Amerige, or let us say, land of Americi, that is: AMERICA."

Whoever was the author of this passage of the cosmography, whether Sandaucourt or Ringmann, the

name must have been the object of debate among the
canons. In addition to the two poets, the Luds and
Waldseemüller no doubt participated in it. The poets,
who were eloquent, must have done most of the talking. What happened the night they hit upon the invention, the day they argued the point, was, on a small
scale, a foreshadowing of what took place in the world
later. Engravers and typographers in the print shop
may also have had their say. It was a wonderful name.
It fell more pleasantly on the ear than those of the
other continents. There could be no possible doubt.

Amerigo, in Seville, unaware of all that was going
on in that remote corner of the Vosges, never dreamed
that his first name possessed such a seductive quality. Even in Spain, although Columbus was never
called Christopher, but Columbus, Amerigo was always known as Amerigo not Vespucci. On Giovanni
Vespucci's map, which contains a reference to his
uncle on the coast of Venezuela, the name is not Val
de Vespucci, but Val d'Amerigo. The one who discovered the charm of the name and drew from it its
full sonority was one of those men who love to play
with words—that is, a poet. The name of America
was invented one inspired evening in the same way
that immortal verses are born.

Marcou believes that the invention was Sandaucourt's.
Charles Heinrich holds that it was Ringmann's. Sandaucourt represented Latin elegance; Ringmann, youth.
Among those of Saint-Dié it was Ringmann who discovered Amerigo's first letter, who was its translator
into German. Heinrich points out that in the two po-

ems published in *the Introduction to Cosmography*, Sandaucourt speaks of "Vespucci" and Ringmann of "Amerigo." Ringmann had proposed that the name of Alsatia be changed to Helvetia; he liked to play with geographical names. In an essay on the Muses, quoted by Heinrich, he says: "Why are names of feminine gender given to all the virtues, to the traits of intelligence, and to the sciences? What is the origin of this custom? Why is this use common not only to pagan writers, but to the Church authors? This comes from the belief that knowledge is destined to be fertile in good works. And just as maidens love the game of hearts, so the sciences are in the heart of the encyclopedias. Three parts of the Old World received the names of women."

The baptism was finally agreed upon, and Waldseemüller drew his map. On it he lettered the word that was to become immortal: AMERICA. Years later, when Ringmann was dead, Waldseemüller removed the name from his later maps. Sandaucourt was still alive. But the cartographer was not dominated by the uncontrollable fervor of Ringmann.

Waldseemüller's planisphere is a beautiful work of cartography and design. Possibly he did not do all the work. Perhaps some of the other draftsmen who worked with Lud had a hand in the ornamental border that serves as a frame. As some of these men were of the school of Dürer, it has sometimes been thought that the two portraits in the border were his. The matter has no foundation or importance. But the two portraits, one of Ptolemy, the other of Amerigo, are excellent. The first is shown wearing an Oriental headdress and holding a quadrant in his hand. The inscription reads: "*Claudii Ptholemei Allexandrini Cosmographi.*" Amerigo wears the dress of an Italian nobleman, with his hair hanging loose and his beard curled; he has a compass in his hands. The inscription says simply: "*Americi Vespuci.*" Beside these medallions appear the two hemispheres, reduced to scale, that of the New World to the right, beside Amerigo, and that of the Old to the left, alongside the portrait of Ptolemy. The winds blowing blasts from their puffed checks, clouds, and allegorical figures complete the design.

The planisphere is painstaking and profuse in the names that crowd the continent of Europe and the Mediterranean; fabulous in those of Asia; somewhat bare, delicate, virginal in the continent that was now baptized with the name of Vespucci. America is America, not another of the many Indies to be seen alongside Asia. For in Asia Waldseemüller lists India Gangen, India Extra Gangem, India Meridionalis, India, Indo China. America is now something different: it is the fourth part of the world.

The men of Saint-Dié were not working merely to satisfy their own thirst for knowledge. They wanted their works to be known throughout the world. Philesius–that is, Ringmann–wrote a poem dedicating the work to the Emperor "Augustus Cæsar Maximilian." "We should dedicate this map to you," he said, "Majesty whose name is venerated throughout the vast world, because you are the most powerful of kings, and your fame soars from the east, where the sun raises its golden head, to beyond the Pillars of Hercules, scorched by the glowing rays of midday, and even to the frozen surface of the ocean lying beneath the Great Bear..." Incidentally, on the diminutive mappemondes in the border of the large mappemonde the polar sea is shown in the shape of a frozen nipple, like the stem end of the pear Columbus referred to.

On the next page Ilacomilus–that is, Waldseemüller–sets down his dedication. He, too, addresses himself to "Divine Cæsar Augustus Maximilian." After considering the pleasure the invincible monarch will derive from feasting his eyes on this image of distant lands inhabited by other peoples–a delight known to all the world since the days of Plato, Apollonius of Tyana, and Homer–he says: "Studying to the best of my ability, and with the help of many people, the books of Ptolemy in a Greek copy, and adding the four relations of the voyages of Amerigo Vespucci, I have prepared for the use of persons instructed in such matters a map of the whole world, with an introduction, and for this I have made a solid sphere and a map to be projected upon it."

A year later the Duke of Lorraine died. His successor had little interest in the affairs of the Gymnasium. Nicholas Lud, who had been appointed secretary of the Duke in 1508, left Saint-Dié. Ringmann died in 1511 at the age of twenty-nine. Vautrin Lud, bereft of the circle that had glowed like a bright, short-lived candle, turned the press over to Jean Schot. It was he who brought out the *Geography* of Ptolemy. Ringmann had died, and the name *America*, as said before, was omitted by Waldseemüller this time. But in 1522, after Waldseemüller 's death, the geography was reprinted in Strasbourg by Johann Reichart, and the name *America* reappeared. From then on, it was impossible to leave it out of the atlases.

Waldseemüller had been a cartographer and geographer devoted to his art and science, but his title was merely that of proofreader. This, however, did not stand in the way of his addressing himself to the ranking figure of world politics, the Emperor. There was a nobility, if the term may be so employed, of craftsmanship. Neither he nor Ringmann nor their fellow members of the Gymnasium were unaware of Columbus's discoveries, but they reduced them on the sphere to what he really found: the Antilles. All those islands, said the map, had been discovered by Christopher Columbus by order of the King of Castile. It was obvious that Columbus had no knowledge of all the coast from Venezuela, along Brazil, and to Patagonia, which Vespucci had sailed. This was the part of the New World to which the name of America was given. It was not extended to what is today North America until 1538.

The little book of Saint-Dié made its way swiftly about the world. For reasons having to do with the business side of the printing establishment, two editions had to be brought out in Saint-Dié on the same day. One carries the dedications to the Emperor signed by Philesius and Ilacomilus; in the other the tributes were by Lud. It may have been that each of them wished to have his own copy, with his own name, and even pay his own homage to the Emperor, with an eye to the royal patronage everyone sought.

With this Latin edition of the four voyages available, nobody gave further thought to the Italian version. Now the name of Amerigo and America were engraved on the mind of Europe. Amerigo's letter had found a means of circulation throughout Europe which he never dreamed of, or even knew. The text of the Saint-Dié edition was reproduced and translated everywhere. Copies of the original edition are among the rarest and most valuable book-collectors' items. The fate of Waldseemüller's first maps is fantastic. The mappemonde disappeared from sight until 1900, when it was accidentally discovered by Professor Joseph Fischer in a book at Wolfegg Castle. The segments to be joined to the sphere had been discovered in more or less the same chance manner in 1871.[5]

During the Second World War, when the Nazi troops made the lightning advance of their first campaign in France, Saint Dié came under their power. The blow was so sudden that there was no opportunity for resistance. The people chewed the cud of their bitterness in silence, years of stunned silence. And then

5. Marcou: *Nouvelles Recherches sur le nom d'Amérique* (1888); D'Alvezac-Macaya: *Les Voyages de Améric Vespuce* (1858); H. Charles: *The Romance of the Name America* (1926); various contributors to different numbers of the *Bulletin de la Société Philomatique* have published interesting studies on the subject.

finally came the withdrawal. The military governor of
Saint-Dié, with all the efficiency of a good Nazi, one
morning ordered the inhabitants to withdraw from
the center to a sector of the city, as was often done in
routine operations. At a given moment, when all were
watching from behind the roped-off area, the city was
blown up. It had been mined. The first building converted to rubble was that which stood on the spot
where Nicholas Lud had set up his press, and where
the circle of poets gave America its name. There on
April 25, 1507 the inked rollers moved over the type,
and the lever of the press descended to stamp the
name of the New World for the first time. A stone
plaque records the event. The local chief of the Nazi
militia hated the name. It was the symbol of the freedom that was rolling back the tide of Nazism. He
lighted the fuse and destroyed the house. This was
not the first time Saint-Dié in its valley of pines had
suffered ordeal by fire. But the flames burned themselves out, a freer air blew through the ruined streets,
once more the sky was blue. The name of America
stands.

Waldseemüller's map, showing an imaginary portrait of Amerigo, 1507.

XXIII

THE CONTROVERSY

For centuries a controversy has raged around Amerigo
Vespucci. He has been presented as a sly thief who
cunningly robbed Columbus of his rightful glory. This
defamation of Amerigo is almost coextensive with the
history of America; scholars have repeated it; the text-
books of twenty nations have carried it.

Father Las Casas started this second black legend.
In his pen he had a magnificent tool for the fabrication of such legends, abetted by a verbal intemper-
ance in which he has had few equals. He wrote:
"And it is well to give thought here to the injustice
and offense that that Amerigo Vespucci seems to
have done the Admiral, or those who first printed
his four voyages, attributing to himself, or alluding
only to him, the discovery of this mainland."[1]

As a matter of fact, Las Casas had no knowledge
of how the edition of the four voyages came to be
published in Saint-Dié. But when he got started on
an argument he lost his self-control. What had at
first been a vague, tentative suggestion later became
an article of faith. "It amazes me," he subsequently

1. Las Casas: *Historia de las Indias*, ed. Aguilar, Madrid, Vol. I,
   p. 547.

Coriolano Leudo, Fray Bartolomé de Las Casas.

wrote, "that Don Ferdinand Columbus, the son of
the Admiral himself, and a person of goodly wit and
prudence, and who had in his possession those very
relations of Amerigo, as I know for a fact, did not
realize this theft and usurpation Amerigo Vespucci
had commited against his father."

Las Casas, who in many aspects had not emerged
from the Middle Ages, felt much closer to Columbus
than to Amerigo. Columbus had received his training in the thought of the Renaissance, and had utilized the theories of Toscanelli and the humanists,
but his experiences in Castile had turned him into a
renegade from the Renaissance. The opposition he
encountered among the friars of Salamanca, the intolerance that was mounting under Cardinal Cisneros,
and, perhaps, his Jewish ancestry taught him that it
was better to hold fast to the texts of the Church
Fathers, to take a prophetic, miraculous line, than to
range himself on the side of science. He went so far
as to state, in a famous phrase, that the mappemondes
had been of no use to him, but that he had been the
instrument Divine Providence had used to fulfill its
prophecies. The stubbornness with which he insisted
on this in his later days gave him a completely medieval stamp. And in this he and Las Casas stood
shoulder to shoulder.

To be sure, there are gleams of modern thought in
Las Casas. Volumes have been written to show that
his ardent crusade on behalf of justice put him well in
advance of his day in the field of human rights. But
one has only to read his treatise on magic to realize

how medieval his learning was. It is an encyclopedia of witchcraft. The Devil becomes a being so real that he can carry men through the air over mountains and valleys. Opposed to the Devil is the power of the miracle. If the Friar's books were not so voluminous, if his sermons did not lose themselves in a tedious labyrinth of endless erudite meanders, they would be a delightful source of shivery entertainment. The part of his writing that has remained alive is his diatribes against the conquistadors and Amerigo, the themes of the two black legends.

In contrast with Columbus, Amerigo represented, in Father Las Casas's eyes, the living culture of the Renaissance. Amerigo was the one who put all his faith in maps. His subtle, ironic, balanced, rational spirit stood in sharp contrast with the violent chiaroscuro in which Las Casas and Columbus moved.

All this explains the strong likes and dislikes that conditioned the thinking of a man of Father Las Casas's impassioned temperament. But there was still another factor. Las Casas's concepts, like those of all his contemporaries, were imperial. He looked upon the Indian as a childlike being deserving paternal solicitude, but he saw the New World as nothing but a colony. And Amerigo had set afoot a concept that was a forerunner of the idea of independence. These are the hidden seeds that take root in the subconscious. The term *New World* diminished the force of empire. *America* was a word that meant rebellion against the vocabulary the Crown was minting. It ran counter to imperial objectives. It never occurred to anyone that the new continent should be called Colonia, or Colombia, or Columbia. Las Casas never suggested such a thing. Spain wanted to keep the denomination *Indies*, which Columbus had given to his discovery. In line with this the Laws of the Indies were promulgated, the Indian Code was drawn up; the natives were called Indians, there was a profusion of histories of the Indies, an Indian policy was worked out, and so on. It was not a question of defending Columbus's glory, but of treating the New World as an appanage of Asia.

The gifted Crown historian Antonio de Herrera (1559-1625) followed in Las Casas's footsteps. In one passage of his *Décadas* he alludes to a suit instituted by the heirs of Columbus over the discoveries on the mainland. In the testimony of the witnesses, which he compares, there is no mention of any discovery by Amerigo. This was to be expected. Amerigo had been second in command on voyages that were not his, but King Ferdinand's. But, says Herrera: "By (the omission of his name) Amerigo Vespucci's slyness in appropriating to himself another's glory becomes more patent." And in another passage: "With great cunning Amerigo Vespucci transposes things that happened on one voyage to another to conceal the fact that the admiral, Don Christopher Columbus, discovered the mainland... The invention of Amerigo is clearly proved."[2]

2. A. Herrera: *Décadas*, Vol. I, Book IV, Chapter xi.

As the tendency grew to dramatize Columbus's life, Spain was made to seem more and more culpable. A series of unfortunate incidents, caused as much by the Admiral's maladroitness as by the overzealousness of officials like Bishop Fonseca and Francisco de Bobadilla, made Columbus suffer hell in this life. Already a reproachful finger was being pointed at Spain for not having spared the Genoese so much bitterness. This interpretation was coloring not only history, but drama, poetry, ballads, legend. And to men like Las Casas and Herrera the simple, obvious answer was to find a scapegoat, invent a villain to bear all the guilt. For this Amerigo was made to order. From that moment the river of adjectives insulting the thief of Columbus's glory began to swell and rage. Nobody had new facts to adduce; they simply repeated Las Casas's pronouncements, the shaky foundation of which are evidenced by the passages quoted from his own work.

Between 1825 and 1837 Martín Fernández de Navarrete published one of the most famous collections of documents relating to the discovery of America. It has been a source-book for scholars ever since. Fernández de Navarrete (1765-1844) was a distinguished researcher. Washington Irving, William Prescott, and Alexander von Humboldt were lavish with praise of him.

Columbus's sufferings, his poverty, the fetters with which he was bound in Santo Domingo, all of which were played up in the biographies that circulated in all lands and all languages, naturally weighed more heavily on Navarrete than on Las Casas or Herrera, and he was more eager to put the blame on Amerigo than to get at the facts. His "accurate" notes for Amerigo's biography afford abundant proof of this. But even more revealing is his correspondence at the time he was preparing his work. A letter to another notable scholar, Manuel González, is a case in point:

I am assembling materials for Volume III, which I plan to send to press in April. I would particularly ask you to bear in mind information concerning Amerigo Vespucci... If you can find information about him from 1496 to 1505, particularly, it would be very useful to follow his movements and know whether he really accompanied Alonso Hojeda on his two voyages, because he certainly did not go as captain or by order of the King, as he gives to understand and pretends in his Latin relations, which he gave out everywhere to usurp Columbus's glory of discovering the continent to which, through his slyness, he managed to give his own name. To prove this truth clearly I need the support of such documents and information as you may come by, for these are in the historical fields the proofs and demonstration of geometricians' theorems.[3]

The irresponsible way Navarrete states as a fact that Amerigo had said in his letters that he had sailed

---

3. This letter is in the National Library of Madrid, MS. 12,977, quoted by Manuel Serrano y Sanz.

as commander of the fleet (a thing he never said); that he wrote his relations in Latin (which he never did); and that he was the inventor of the name *America* (which he was not), for the ends Navarrete attributes to him (which never existed) is the result of a passion not confined to the intimate field of Navarrete's private correspondence, but carried into his books to the extent of altering documents. To show, for example, that Amerigo had not made the voyage of exploration of the coast of Mexico, Navarrete wrote that from December 1495, when Gianetto Berardi died, to 1498 Vespucci could not have set foot outside Spain because he was in charge of outfitting the fleets. He based his assertion on an entry in the Ledger of Fleet Expenses, he said, compiled by the scholar Juan Bautista Muñoz.[4] But Muñoz's book said nothing of the sort.

So unequivocal was Navarrete's statement that Humboldt fell into the snare. "The falsity of the sailing date–May 10-20, 1497–given by Amerigo," he writes, "becomes evident. Preparations for the voyage of Columbus to Haiti and Parias... kept Vespucci busy in Seville and in Sanlúcar from April-May 1497 until the departure of Columbus on May 30, 1498."[5]

Navarrete's fabrication, shored up by Humboldt's doubt, gave an Italian investigator, Alberto Magnaghi, his grounds for saying before a Congress of

4. Navarrete. *Viajes*, Vol. III, p. 322.
5. A. von Humboldt: *Géographie du Nouveau Continent*, Vol. IV, p. 267.

Americanists meeting in Rome in 1926: "Among the most powerful arguments of a chronological nature against this first voyage of Vespucci is the evidence to the contrary pointed out by Humboldt."[6]

Once the belief that Amerigo had robbed Columbus of the glory of the discovery, and that his first voyage was a lie was accepted, it was easy to doubt everything. "Is it conceivable," Navarrete asked himself, "that a monarch as cautious and circumspect as Ferdinand would have entrusted the command of a Spanish expedition of such importance to an adventurer who was not yet even a naturalized Spaniard?"[7] Navarrete harped once more on the command of the expedition–something Amerigo had never claimed–and overlooked the fact that Columbus, Cabot, and Díaz de Solís were as much foreigners as Amerigo in 1497. But his statement established a pattern, and in 1926 Magnaghi said: "Even if we were to grant that Amerigo's voyage had been tacitly permitted, the matter is not clear, for from June 14, 1496 until May 30, 1498 Columbus was in Spain at the peak of his glory and prestige, and his credit was ace-high not only at court, but also with businessmen... If the ships hired in 1495 (those which Amerigo outfitted) were not to be used in Columbus's third voyage, at any rate they were intended for it, as supporting and auxiliary vessels."[8]

6. A. Magnaghi: *Americo Vespucci*, p. 124.
7. Navarrete: *Viajes*, Vol. III, p. 336.
8. A. Magnaghi, op. cit., p. 121, 126.

The situation invented by Magnaghi shows Columbus at the height of his triumph when, as a matter of fact, his reputation was being subjected to careful scrutiny. His prestige on his return from the second voyage was low. Ferdinand, his son, says that he suffered jeers and mockery at court because of the adverse reports about him sent back from Hispaniola. The ships of 1495 were being readied for the very purpose of doing away with Columbus's privileges. As a result of the highly unfavorable reports he was receiving, the King was becoming aware of the need to investigate his activities and those of his brother Bartholomew in the governing of Hispaniola.

Nevertheless, Navarrete's asseveration, repeated by Humboldt, according to which Amerigo was occupied in Spain in 1497 and could not have been on a voyage, went unchallenged. Not until the scholar Henry Harrisse examined all the documentation on which Navarrete based his statement was the point cleared up. This is his conclusion:

...we must declare that there is no entry in the archives of the Trade Council for the Indies which refers directly or indirectly to these activities of Vespucci on any date subsequent to January 12, 1496. Nor is any such record in the 127 volumes containing the extracts and notes compiled by Muñoz in 1779 when he was commissioned by Charles III to write the History of America. As for the fleet mentioned by Navarrete, which consisted of twelve ships engaged by Berardi in 1495, it was dispatched from San Lúcar before the end of that year. All that Vespucci did in

*connection with the expedition was to supervise its
outfitting from April to November of 1495. He entered in Berardi's account the expenditures made in
his name, which were reimbursed by the royal treasurer on January 12, 1496. Following this date,
Vespucci's name disappears completely from the
Spanish documents, and does not reappear until February 5, 1505. There is not a shred of evidence, therefore, that Vespucci was in Seville or in Spain from
1496 until after 1498, and no proof, therefore, that
he could not have been at sea from May 1497 until
October 1499, as he states in the relation of his first
voyages of discovery."* [9]*

If Spanish historians of the school of Las Casas,
Herrera, and Navarrete altered basic facts in the fore-
going manner to render Amerigo's voyages impossible or to put in doubt the truth of his relations, it is
not to be wondered at that others outside Spain
should have followed in their footsteps. As eminent
a scholar as William Robertson in his *History of
America* called Amerigo "a lucky imposter," and
Ralph Waldo Emerson said: "*Strange...* that broad
America must wear the name of a thief. Amerigo
Vespucci, the pickle-dealer at Seville... whose highest naval rank was boatswain's mate in an expedition that never sailed, managed in this lying world
to supplant Columbus and baptize half of the earth
with his own dishonest name."[10]

9. H. Harrisse: *Americus Vespuccius,* p. 13.
10. R. W. Emerson: *English Traits,* p. 148.

The historians of Brazil and Portugal kept the ball rolling. If Vespucci could be discounted as the first to sight Brazil and sail half its coast in 1499, then this glory would be the trophy of Pedro Alvares de Cabral, who reached it in 1500. And if Amerigo was a liar, then the voyage of 1501 in Portuguese vessels could be discounted, too. The attack on Vespucci was led off by Father Manuel Ayres de Cazal in his *Corografia Brazilica* (1817). "It seems incredible," he wrote, "that King Manuel should seek a navigator outside his kingdom to sail with a fleet of his bound for a country where his own ships had already come and gone, steered by pilots of his own realms." Amerigo, adds Ayres de Cazal, "bequeathed to posterity three relations in two letters and a summary, which fundamentally are nothing but sheer inventions designed to glorify his own name and to make himself recognized by his compatriots as the discoverer of the Western Hemisphere."

After him came Viscount Santarem, a friend and correspondent of Navarrete, who worked along the same lines and toward the same end. The Viscount burrowed for references to Vespucci in the state papers of King Manuel, and, not finding them, he wrote to Navarrete telling him that this circumstance made him doubt Amerigo's claims. But the prize goes to Duarte Leite, who in *Descobridores do Brasil* (Porto, 1931), says: "This fatuous personage is nothing but a lying novelist, a navigator of the caliber of hosts of others, a cosmographer who repeated the ideas of others, a false discoverer who appropriated the glory of others. Despite this, he managed to impress generations of learned men who spent their days trying to interpret fantasies and make sense of his nonsense."

This mountain of adjectives heaped on Amerigo's memory had as its result that nobody believed his letters. He was not only a thief, but also a liar. Few documents in history have undergone so searching an analysis as Amerigo's letters. It was a fertile field for the scholar's amusement. The original manuscript texts had disappeared. They left the hands of Lorenzo di Pier Francesco de' Medici and Piero Soderini and began to circulate in copy or translation, in editions their author never heard about, and over which he never had control. Slight or important changes, altered words, have made them a scholar's jigsaw puzzle for more than a century. It should be mentioned in passing that the fate of Amerigo's documents was not unique. The diary of Columbus underwent the same treatment at the bands of Las Casas, who altered it to suit himself. Most of the relations of the conquistadors do not stand up under careful analysis. But as they either aroused little animus or were heroes who became the object of worship after meeting an untimely end, the documents they left have been accepted at face value, even with a generous margin of good will. The inherent charm of Amerigo's writings, their immediate fame throughout the world, did him harm. Erudite studies have been written on the Spanish words he employed, on his literary shortcomings, on coincidence of expression with Marco Polo or Michele de

Cuneo. Errors that well may have been those of a secretary, a copyist, or the translator who put the relations into Latin, or of another translator who turned them back into Italian, or an editor who wished to flatter a Mæcenas have all been laid at Amerigo's door.

To avoid problems, the Italian scholar Alberto Magnaghi, the last to establish a school, who has contributed penetrating observations and important studies on Amerigo, proposed at the Congress of Americanists in Rome in 1923 that the two most famous letters of Amerigo—the *Mundus Novus* and that to Soderini—be discounted and only those which are preserved in copy in the archives of Florence be accepted as authentic. That is to say, throw out the two most important letters, those which became famous in the sight and presence of Amerigo's family. With this Magnaghi would eliminate from Amerigo's history two voyages—one the most important of all. As the idea was presented with great trappings of lexicographical research, his book, though basically a work of sophistry, produced an effect.

What disturbed Magnaghi was the idea that Amerigo was guilty of improper literary conduct, and he took the stand that neither would he have written letters containing such outspoken sexual observations, nor would any distinguished humanist have been a party to their translation. His profound distaste is evident from the following lines, taken from the article he wrote to deny the authenticity of the last letter found in Italian archives, which remained unpublished until 1937: "If the letter were authentic it would upset everything once more, and would plunge us into that endless, tedious, fruitless, exhausting discussion that has gone on for four centuries... For that reason I, at least, cannot share the satisfaction the discoverer of the letter evinces."

On the other hand, the school of affirmative criticism which has attempted to explain Amerigo's history as a natural process has labored under the difficulties of trying to combat a legend cultivated with malice aforethought since the sixteenth century. The first of these was the Florentine abbot Angelo María Bandini. In 1745 he wrote *Vita e lettere di Amerigo Vespucci gentiluomo fiorentino* and published for the first time Amerigo's letter to Lorenzo di Pier Francesco de' Medici, dated in the year 1500 in Seville. It had been forgotten for two hundred and forty-five years. A second edition of Bandini's book was brought out fifty-three years later by Gustavo Uzielli, with copious notes.

Uzielli was a painstaking, dedicated investigator devoted to the cult of Toscanelli. His study of the great cosmographer is a model in its field. Carried away by his enthusiasm, he took the position that the New World should not have been called America or Colombia, but some variant of Toscanelli. The suggestion came late, and the name hardly lends itself to the purpose.

In 1879 Francesco Bartolozzi discovered and published the letter on the third voyage, dated in 1502 in Lisbon. It had been buried in the archives of Florence for three hundred and seventy-seven years. Baron Alexander von Humboldt was the first to make a scientific study of the voyages of Amerigo, in the second volume of his *Examen critique de l'histoire de la Géographie du Nouveau Continent aux XV et XVI siècles*. His book and that of Bandini set a new trend in the history of Amerigo. It was followed by many studies, including those of Armand-Pascal d'Avezac (1858), Francisco Adolpho de Varnhagen (1858-1872), Henry Harrisse (1892), and John Fiske (1892). Uzielli in 1892 compiled a bibliographical list of 280 titles, and this was incomplete.

Amerigo's polemic letter in defense of those he had written to Lorenzo the Popolano was published by Roberto Ridolfi in 1937–that is to say, four hundred and thirty-five years after it was written–and Amerigo's early correspondence was brought out by Ida Masetti-Bencini and Mary Howard Smith in 1902, some four centuries after it was written. This consists of seventy-one letters, which have never been collected in book form, and which appeared in a journal of history. Amerigo's composition book has not yet been published.

As scholars have concentrated their efforts on a study of the letters of Amerigo pertaining to his voyages, his life has come in for little attention. Up to the present there has been no biography of him as a person. There are a number of good biographies of Columbus and of nearly all the most important participants in the discovery and conquest, but we have only the raw materials for a life of the Florentine under whose name we live. A reading of George Northup's critical edition of Amerigo's letters (1916), Henri Vignaud's *Améric Vespuce* (1917), and, above all, the study of American cartography in Roberto Levillier's *América la bien llamada* (1948) give one the feeling that Amerigo is at last being discovered. After four centuries of wrangling about whether it was a good thing or a bad thing for the New World to bear his name, the simple reality of his life is beginning to come to light. And we find ourselves in the presence of a man who became famous without aspiring to be a hero and who without pursuing glory received it in full measure.

When Amerigo was born, five hundred years ago, Florence sang its babes to rest with enchanted lullabies. Many things about the Renaissance were in the nature of miracles. The government showed equal interest in politics and painters. Everything was an art. The year that Amerigo and Poliziano were born, refugees from Constantinople arrived in Florence bringing the gift of Plato. The Republic could give thought to the alliance with Venice and Milan as well as to the paintings Benozzo Gozzoli and Fra Angelico were working on; and a man like Lorenzo Ghiberti, who after many years' work had just finished the cathedral doors known as the Gates of Paradise, laid aside his burins to take up the pen and write a treatise on painting. Bookbinders gathered in the workshop to discuss Aristotle or Dante. At night the philosophers wandered into the streets

to sing love songs. On a smaller scale, the banks
were like those of today, with Florentine capital cir-
culating throughout two continents in letters of exchange, and the ships of the Republic sailing all the
seas. There were wars, but at the Battle of Anghiari,
which has become famous, the only casualty left on
the field was a single soldier who smothered in his
armor, as Machiavelli points out. Yet to commemo-
rate the battle Pedro Soderini, the gonfalonier, sent
for Leonardo da Vinci to paint the picture designed
for the hall of the palace.

In such an atmosphere the New World first came
into being in the imagination. Globes and plani-
spheres were designed before the ships set out on
the Atlantic. Geography showed its gratitude by
making these dreams come true. Spain opened the
transatlantic routes. Her ships, which history had
hardly taken account of until the day before, became the most famous. They were little wooden
castles out of which sallied heroes such as the world
had never before known: Balboa, Cortés, Pizarro,
Jiménez de Quesada, Hernando de Soto, Ponce de
León, Orellana, Valdivia. In fifty years the world
sphere had emerged from between their hands.

Amerigo followed the process of these events with
wide eyes, alert mind, a light heart, and a youthful
soul. He was the most interested spectator and the
most timely chronicler of this appearance of the New
World. He saw it all: the broad gulf of Mexico, ver-
dant Florida, the Pearl Coast, Venezuela reflected in
the waters, Brazil with its cinnamon trees and its

popinjays, the headland of Montevideo, Argentina, whose plains were then empty, and desolate Patagonia. But nothing so captured his imagination as the new stars, the skies of the south. Nobody equaled him in the freshness and enthusiasm with which he announced the news of the unknown quarter of the world that he was the first to see. He was a citizen of Florence and a citizen of León and Castile. With María Cerezo he was a Sevillian; and he was a transient, favored resident of Lisbon. His words threw a beam of light upon the assembly of poets and scholars of Saint-Dié. A representative man of the fifteenth century, a navigator formed by his own inquiring mind. Miracles were wrought in Florence, or in Seville, or in the Caribbean. The Mediterranean carried its fire as far as its restless waves spread. The Old World overflowed its bed, poured through the Pillars of Hercules, and found a larger world.

Illustration for the Sanctae peregrinationes *by Bernhard von Breydenbach , Mainz,1486.*

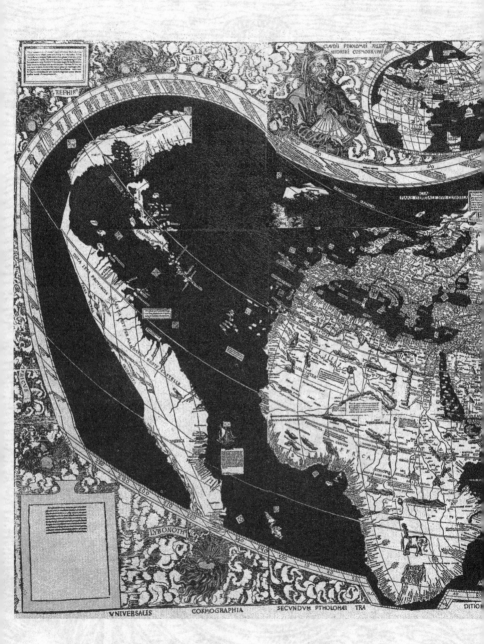

Waldseemüller's map, *1507*.

BIBLIOGRAPHY

ADAMS, EDWARD DEAN: *America and Americans, The Name and Its Significance*. New York: Privately printed; 1926.

ARCAYA, PEDRO M.: *¿Quién descubrió a Venezuela?* Mexico: Estudios de Historia de América, Instituto Panamericano de Geografía e Historia; 1948.

AVEZAC-MACAYA, ARMAND D': *Les Voyages de Améric Vespuce*. Paris: L. Martinet, 1858.

BANDINI, ANGELO MARÍA: *Vita di Amerigo Vespucci. Con le apostille inedite dell'autore. Illustrata e commentata da Gustavo Uzielli*. Firenze; 1898.

BARFUCCI, ENRICO: *Lorenzo de' Medici e la società artistica del suo tempo*. Firenze: Gonnelli; 1945.

BARGELLINI, PIERO: *Il Sogno nostalgico di Sandro Botticelli*. Firenze: Arnaud; 1946.

—: *Il Ghirlandaio del Bel Mondo Fiorentino*. Firenze: Arnaud; 1945.

BARTOLOZZI, FRANCESCO: *Apologia delle Ricerche Istorico-Critiche circa alle Scoperte d'Amerigo Vespucci*. Firenze: Cambiagi; 1789.

BERWICK Y DE ALBA, DUQUESA DE: *Autógrafos de Cristóbal Colón y Papeles de América*. Madrid; 1892.

BIBLIOTECA NACIONAL DE COLOMBIA: *Edición Facsimilar de las Cartas de Vespucci*. Bogotá: Publicadas bajo la dirección de E. Uribe White, 1942.

BROCKHAUS, ENRICO: *Ricerche sopra Alcuni Capolavori d'Arte Italiana*. Milan; 1902.

Bulletin de la Société Philomatique Vosgienne. Saint-Dié; 1900-1911.

BURLAMACCHI, FRA PACIFICO: *La Vita del Beato Ieronimo Savonarola. Publicata secondo il codice Ginoriano*. Firenze: Olschki; 1937.

CANESTRINI, GIUSEPPE: *"Intorno alle Relazione Commerciale de' Fiorentini co' Portoghesi avanti e dopo la Scoperta del Capo di Buona Speranza." Archivio Storico Italiano*, Ser. I, App. III; 1846.

CANOVAI, STANISLAO: *Viaggi d'Amerigo Vespucci. Con la vita, l'elogio e la dissertazione giustificativa*. Firenze: Pagani; 1817.

CAPPELLETTI, LICURGO: *Storia della Città e Stato di Piombino dalle Origine fino all'Anno 1814.* Livorno: Giusti; 1897.

CAPPONZ, GINO: *Storia della Repubblica di Firenze.* Firenze: Barbere; 1930.

CARACI, GIUSEPPE: *"Nuova Luce sull'Opera e la Figura di Amerigo Vespucci."* Rivista Geografica Italiana, XXXII; 1925.

—: *Amerigo Vespucci e un Moderno Critico Argentino.* São Paulo: Revista Historica Brasilera, No. 12; 1952.

CAROCCI, CESARE: *La Giostra di Lorenzo de' Medici messa in Rima da Luigi Pulci.* Bologna: Zanichelli; 1899.

CAROCCI, C.: *Amerigo Vespucci ed Alcuni Suoi Ricordi a Firenze e nei Dintorni.* Firenze: *Arte e Storia,* No. 19; August 1892.

CATALANO, MICHELE: *Vita di Ludovico Ariosto. Ricostruita su nuovi documenti. Geneve: Olschki; 1930.*

CAZAL, MANUEL AYRES DE: *Corografia Brazilica.* Rio de Janeiro; 1817.

CESARETTI, A.: *Storia del Principato di Piombino.* Firenze; 1788.

CIASCA, RAFFAELE: *L'Arte dei Medici e Speziali nella Storia e nel Commercio Fiorentino.* Firenze: Olschki; 1927.

Colección de Documentos Inéditos para la Historia de Hispano América. Madrid: Publicaciones del Instituto Hispano Cubano de Historia de América; 1930.

COLOMBO, FERNANDO: *Le Historie della Vita e dei Fatti di Cristoforo Colombo. A Cura di Rinaldo Caddeo.* Milano: Alpes; 1930.

CORTESÃO, ARMANDO Z.: *Cartografia y Cartografos Portugueses.* Lisboa; 1935,

COSTA, A. FONTAURA DE: *Cartas das Ilhas de Cabo Verde de Valentim Fernandes.* Lisboa; 1939.

DE ROOVER, RAYMOND ADRIEN: *The Medici Bank. Its Organization, Management, Operations and Decline.* New York: New York University Press; 1948.

DELLA TORRE, ARNALDO: *Storia dell'Academia Platonica di Firenze.* Firenze: Carnesecchi e Figli; 1902.

DENUCÉ, JEAN: *Magellan. La Question des Moluques.* Bruxelles: Mémoires de l'Academie Royale de Belgique, Classe de Lettres et des Sciences Morales, II series, Vol. IV; 1908-11.

DESJARDINS, ABEL: *Negotiations diplomatiques de la France avec la Toscane. Documents recueillis par Giuseppe Canestrini et publiés par A. D.* Paris: Imprimerie Impériale; 1859.

FERNÁNDEZ DE NAVARRETE, MARTÍN: *Colección de los Viajes y Descubrimientos que Hicieron por Mar los Españoles desde Fines del Siglo XV, con varios documentos inéditos*

concernientes a la historia de la marina castellana y de los
establecimientos españoles en Indias. (The first two volumes
have special titles: Vol. I: Relaciones, Cartas y Otros
Documentos Concernientes a los Cuatro Viajes que Hizo D.
Cristóbal Colón, etc.; Vol. II: Documentos Diplomáticos.)
Madrid: Imprenta Real; 1825-37.

FERNÁNDEZ DE OVIEDO Y VALDÉS, GONZALO: Historia General y Natural de
las Indias. Madrid: Edición de J. A. de los Ríos; 1851-5

FISKE, JOHN: The Discovery of America. Boston: Houghton, Mifflin; 1892.

FORCE, MANNING FERGUSON: Some Observations on the Letters of Amerigo
Vespucci. Read before the Congrès International des
Americanistes at Brussels, 1879. Cincinnati: Clarke; 1885.

FRACANZANO DA MONTALBODDO: Paesi Nouamente Retrovati & Novo
Mondo da Alberico Vesputio Intitulato (1508). Reproduced in
facsimile from the McCormick-Hoe copy. Princeton: Princeton
University Press; 1916.

GAFFAREL, PAUL-LOUIS-JACQUES: De l'origine du mot Amérique. Dijon:
Imprimerie Darantière; 1889.

GALLEANI NAPIONE, GIOVANNI FRANCESCO: Esame Critico del Primo Viaggio
di Amerigo Vespucci. Firenze: Molini, Landi & Co., 1811.

GALLOIS, LUCIEN-LOUIS-JOSEPH: Améric Vespuce et les Géographes de
Saint-Dié. Firenze: Ricci; 1899.

—: Waldseemüller, Chanoine de Saint-Dié. Société de Géographie de
l'Est; 1900.

GAMBA, CARLO: Botticelli. Paris: Nouvelle Revue Française.

GANDI, GIULIO: Le Corporazioni dell'Antica Firenze. Firenze:
Confederazione Nazionale Fascista dei Commercianti; 1928.

GANDÍA, ENRIQUE DE: Antecedentes Diplomáticos de las Expediciones de
Juan Díaz de Solís, Sebastián Caboto y Don Pedro de Mendoza.
Buenos Aires: Librería del Colegio; 1935

GASPAROLO, FRANCESCO: Pietro Vespucci, Podestà di Alessandria.
Alessandria: Jacquemod; 1892.

GAY, SYDNEY HOWARD: Amerigo Vespucci. (Narrative and Critical History
of America).

GHERARDI, ALESSANDRO: Nuovi Documenti e Studi intorno a Girolamo
Savonarola. Firenze: Sansoni; 1887.

GILLIODTS-VAN SEVEREN, L.: Cartulaire de l'Ancienne Estaple de Bruges.
Bruges: De Plancke; 1905.

—: Inventaire des archives de la ville de Bruges. Bruges: Gailliard; 1876.

GIORGETTI, ALCESTE: Nouveaux Documents Sur Améric Vespuce et sa
famille. Firenze: Revista Toscanelli; January 1893.

GÓMEZ IMAZ, JOSÉ,: *Monografía de una Carta Hidrográfica del Mallorquín Gabriel de Valesca. Madrid: Revista General de Marina*, XXXI; 1892.

GORI, PIETRO: *Le Feste Fiorentine attraverso i Secoli.* Firenze: Bempórad; 1926.

GORIS, J. A.: *Étude Sur les colonies merchants meridionales à Anvers de 1488 à 1567.* Louvain: Librairie Universitaire; 1925.

GRUNZWEIG, ARMAND: *Les Fonds du Consulat de la Mer aux Archives de l'Etat à Florence. Rome: Bulletin de l'Institut Historique de Rome*, Fascicule X; 1930.

HACK, WILLIAM: *Description of a Mapemonde by Juan Vespucci and of a Buccaneer's Atlas in the Possession of Bernard Quaritch.* London: Quaritch; 1914.

HARRISSE, HENRY: *Americus Vespuccius. A Critical and Documentary Review of Two Recent English Books.* London: Stevens; 1895.

—: *Bibliotheca Americana Vetustissima.* New York; 1886.

—: *The Discovery of North America.* London; 1892.

HEINRICH, CHARLES: *The Romance of the Name America.* New York: Privately published; 1926.

HERRERA Y TORDESILLAS, ANTONIO DE: *Historia General de los Hechos de los Castellanos en las Islas i Tierra Firme del Mar Océano.* Madrid; 1601-15.

HEYD, G.: *Storia del Commercio del Levante nel Medio Evo.* Torino: Biblioteca dell'Economista, S. V., Vol. X, Utet; 1913.

HORNE, HERBERT P.: *Alessandro Filipepi, Commonly Called Sandro Botticelli.* London: Bell; 1908.

HUDD, ALFRED EDMUND: *The Naming of America.* Bristol; 1931

HUGUES, LUIGI: *Di Alcuni Recenti Giudizi intorno ad Amerigo Vespucci.* Turin; 1891.

—: *Sopra un Quinto Viaggio di Amerigo Vespucci.* Rome: International Geographic Congress; 1884.

—: *Amerigo Vespucci. Notizie Sommaire.* Raccolta Colombiana.

HULUBEI, A.: *Étude Sur le Jouste de Julien et sur les Bucoliques Dediées a Laurent de Médicis. Paris: Humanisme et Renaissance*, II and III; 1936.

HUMBOLDT, ALEXANDER VON: *Examen critique de l'histoire de la géographie du Nouveau Continent et des Progrès de l'astronomie nautique aux quinzième et seizième siècles.* Paris 1836-9.

JOHNSON, VIRGINIA WALES: *America's Godfather.* Boston: Estes & Lauriat; 1894.

LANDUCCI, LUCA: *Diario Fiorentino del 1450 al 1516. Firenze; 1883.*

LANGTON-DOUGLAS, R.: *"The Contemporary Portraits of Amerigo Vespucci."* London: *Burlington Magazine for Connoisseurs*; February 1944.

LAPINI, AGOSTINO: *Diario Fiorentino.* Firenze: Sansoni; 1900.

LAS CASAS, BARTOLOMÉ DE: *Historia de las Indias. Editada por Gonzalo de Reparaz.* Madrid; 1927.

LASTRI, MARCO ANTONIO: *L'Elogio di Amerigo Vespucci Composto dal Proposto M. L.* Firenze; 1787

LEITE, DUARTE: *A Exploracao do Litoral do Brasil na Cartografia da Primeira Decada do Seculo XVI. (Historia da Colonizacao Portuguese do Brazil.)*

—: *Descobridores do Brasil.* Oporto; 1931.

LESTER, CHARLES EDWARDS: *The Life and Voyages of Americus Vespucius.* New York: Baker & Scribner; 1846.

LEVILLIER, ROBERTO: *América la Bien Llamada. Buenos Aires: Kraft; 1948.*

—: *"El Descubrimiento del Rio de la Plata y la Patagonia por Vespucio en 1502."* Buenos Aires: Argentina Austral, No. 256; November 1952.

—: *El Nuevo Mundo. Buenos Aires: Editorial Nova; 1951.*

—: *La Opinión de Duarte Leite sobre el viaje descubridor de la Argentina.* Buenos Aires: *Revista de Estudios*; 1952.

—: *A Proposito de Vespucio. Replica a Giuseppe Caraci.* Sao Paulo: *Revista Historica*; 1953.

LITTA: *Famiglie Celebri d'Italia.* Genealogical tables.

LOGOLUSO, PIETRO: *Sur le Origine del Nome America.* Trani: Laghezza; 1903.

LÓPEZ DEGÓMARA, FRANCISCO: *Historia General de las Indias.* Medina del Campo; 1553

LUCAS, HERBERT, S.J.: *Fra Girolamo Savonarola.* London: Sands; 1899.

LUNGO, ISIDORO DEL: *La Donna Fiorentina del Buon Tempo Antico. Firenze: Bemporad;* 1926.

—: *Gli Amori del Magnifico Lorenzo.* Bologna: Zanichelli; 1923

LUOTTO, PAOLO: *Il Vero Savonarola.* Firenze: Le Monier; 1900.

LUPI, CLEMENTE: *Nuovi Documenti intorno a Fra Girolamo Savonarola. Firenze: Archivio Storico Italiano,* Third series, III; 1866.

MAGNAGHI, ALBERTO: *Americo Vespucci. Studio Critico.* New Edition. Rome: Treves; 1926.

—: *Amici Portoghesi di Vespuci. Critica a Duarte Leite. Rome: Rivista Geográfica Italiana,* XLIII; May-August 1936.

—: *Il Planisfero del 1523 della Biblioteca del Rè in Torino. Firenze;* 1929.

—: *Una Supposta Lettera Inedita di Amerigo Vespucci sopra il Suo Terzo Viaggio. Critica a R. Ridolfi. Rome: Bollettino della R. Società Geografica Italiana,* LXXIV; 1937.

MARCONDES DE SOUZA, THOMAZ OSCAR: *Americo Vespucci e Suas Viagens.* Sao Paulo: Universidade de São Paulo; 1949.

MARCOU, JULES: *Nouvelles Recherches sur l'origine du nom d'Amérique.* Paris': Société de Géographie; 1888.

MARKHAM, C. R.: *The Letters of Americo Vespucci and Other Documents Illustrative of His Career.* London: Hakluyt Society; 1894.

MARZI, DEMETRIO: *Notizia intorno ad un Mappamondo e a un Globo Posseduto del 1509 de Luigi Guicchiardini. Firenze: Atti del 3 Congresso Geografico Italiano;* 1899.

MASETTI-BENCINI, IDA, & SMITH, MARY HOWARD: *La Vita di Amerigo Vespucci a Firenze da Lettere inedite a Lui Dirette.* Firenze: Francheschini; 1903.

MEDINA, JOSÉ TORIBIO: *Juan Díaz de Solís.* Santiago: Editorial del Autor; 1897.

MESNIL, JACQUES: *Botticelli.* Paris: Albin Michel; 1938.

MOLINARI, DIEGO LUIS: *El Nacimiento del Nuevo Mundo.* Buenos Aires: Kapelusz; 1945.

MORENO, NICOLÁS BESIO: *"El Meridiano de Tordesillas y el Descubrimiento del Río de la Plata por Vespucio."* Buenos Aires: *Ciencia e Investigación,* Vol. VIII, No. 9; 1952.

MÜLLER, J.: *"Documenti sulle Relazioni delle Città Toscane coll' Oriente."* Firenze: *Documenti degli Archivi Toscani, pp. 279-81; 1879.*

Narrative and Critical History of America, edited by Justin Winsor. New York: Houghton, Mifflin; 1889.

NERI, ACHILLE: *La Simonetta.* Torino: *Giornale Storico della Letteratura Italiana,* Year III, Vol. V; 1885.

NORTHUP, GEORGE TYLER: *Vespucci Reprints, Texts and Studies.* Princeton; 1916.

NUNN, GEORGE EMRA: *The Columbus and Magellan Concepts of South American Geography.* Glenside; 1952.

—. *The Geographical Conceptions of Columbus.* New York: American Geographical Society; 1924.

—: *The Mappamundi of Juan de la Cosa.* Jenkintown; 1924.

OBER, FREDERICK ALBION: *Amerigo Vespucci.* New York: Harper & Bros.; 1907.

OBERTI, EUGENIO: *Amerigo Vespucci alla Scoperta del Continente Sudamericano.* Torino: Paravia; 1932.

O'GORMAN, EDMUNDO: *La Idea del Descubrimiento de América. Historia de Esa Interpretación y Crítica de sus Fundamentos.* Mexico: Centro de Estudios Filosóficos; 1951.

OLSCHKI, LEONARDO: *Storia Letteraria delle Scoperte Geografiche.* Firenze: Olschki; 1937.

PASSERINI, LUIGI: *Storia degli Stabilimenti di Beneficenza della Città di Firenze, Firenze; 1853.*

PENNESSI, GIUSEPPE: *Pietro Martire d'Anghiera e le sue relazione sulle scoperte oceaniche.* Raccolta Colombiana.

PENROSE, BOIES: *Travel and Discovery in the Renaissance.* Cambridge: Harvard University Press; 1952.

PEREIRA FERRAZ, ANTONIO LEONCIO: *Américo Vespucci e o nome da América.* Rio de Janeiro: Imp. Nacional; 1941.

PÉREZ EMBID, FLORENTINO: *Los Descubrimientos en el Atlántico y la Rivalidad Castellano-Portuguesa hasta el Tratado de Tordesillas.* Sevilla: Publicaciones de la Escuela de Estudios Hispano-Americanos de Sevilla; 1948.

PESCE, AMBROGIO: *Il Matrimonio di Battista Fregoso con Iacopo Appiani. Archivio Storico Italiano,* Year LXXI, Vol. II; 1913.

PETER MARTYR (PIETRO MARTIRE D'ANGHIERA): *De Orbe Novo, Décadas del Nuevo Mundo.* Buenos Aires; 1944.

PICOTTI: G. B.: *La Giovinezza di Leone X.* Milano: Hoepli; 1927.

PIERACCINI, GAETANO: *La Stirpe de' Medici di Cafaggiolo.* FirenzeVallecchi; 1948.

PISANI, MARÍA: *Un Avventuriero del Quattrocento. La Vita e le Opere di Benedetto Dei.* Genève: Perrela; 1923.

POHL, FREDERICK JULIUS: *Amerigo Vespucci, Pilot Major.* New York: Columbia University Press; 1944.

POLIZIANO, ANGELO: *Opera.* Lugduni; 1539.

—: *Prose Volgari Inedite. Raccolte e ilustrate da Isidoro del Lungo.* Firenze: Barbera; 1867.

PULIDO RUBIO, J.: *El Piloto Mayor de la Casa de Contratación de Sevilla.* Sevilla: Zarzuela; 1923.

Raccolta di Documenti e Studi Pubblicati dalla R. Commissione Colombiana pel Quarto Centenario della Scoperta dell' America. Rome; 1892-4.

RAZZOLI, ROBERTO, O. M.: *La Chiesa d'Ognissanti in Firenze. Firenze:* Ariani; 1898.

REUMONT, ALFREDO: *Tavole Cronologiche e Sincrone della Storia Fiorentina.* Firenze: Vieusseux; 1841

RICHARDSON, MRS. ABBY: *The Christening of America.* New York, 1888.

RIDOLFI, ROBERTO: *"Una Lettera Inedita di Amerigo Vespucci." Archivio Storico Italiano*, Vol. 1; 1937

ROSCOE, GUGLIELMO: *Vita e Pontificato di Leone X. Tradotta e corredata, etc., dal Conte Cavaliere Luigi Bossi.* Milano. Sonzogno; 1816.

ROSSI, TRIBALDO DE': *Ricordanze. Delizie degli eruditi Toscani,* Vol. XXXIII.

RUIZ-GUIÑAZÚ, ENRIQUE: *Proas de España en el Mar Magallanico.* Buenos Aires: Ediciones Peuser; 1945.

SANTAREM, MANUEL FRANCISCO DE BARROS, VISCONDE DE: *Recherches historiques, critiques et bibliographiques sur Améric Vespuce et ses voyages.* Paris: Bertrand; 1842.

STARKIE, WALTER: *La España de Cisneros.* Translation by Alberto Mestas. Buenos Aires: Juventud; 1945.

STEIN, J. W., S.J.: *"Esame Critico intorno alla Scoperta di Vespucci circa la Determinazione della Longitudine in Mare Mediante le Distanze Lunari."* Rome: *Memorie della Societa Astronomica Italiana,* Vol. XXI, No. 4; 1950.

THACHER, JOHN BOYD: *The Continent of America. Its Discovery and Its Baptism.* New York: W. E. Benjamin; 1896.

TIBÓN, GUTIERRE: *América. Setenta Siglos de la Historia de un Nombre.* Mexico: Pirámide; 1945.

TOSI, CARLO ODOARDO: *La Famiglia Mini alla quale Appartenne la Madre di Amerigo Vespucci.* Cortona: Ravagli; 1898.

TOUSSAINT, MANUEL: *Carta de Amerigo Vespucio. Edición facsimilar con introducción de M. T.* Mexico: Imprenta Universitaria; 1941.

UZIELLI, GUSTAVO: *La Vita e i tempi di Paolo dal Pozzo Toscanelli. Raccolta Colombiana, Part V, Vol. I.*

—: Studies published in the review *Toscanelli.* Florence; 1893. Also notes to Bandini's *Vita di Amerigo Vespucci.*

—: *Toscanelli, Colombo e Vespucci.* Milano: Bellini; 1902.

VARNHAGEN, FRANCISCO ADOLPHO DE: *Amerigo Vespucci. Son caractère, ses écrits.* Lima, Mercurio; 1865.

—: *Historia geral do Brasil.* São Paulo: Melhoramentos; 1927.

—: *Nouvelles Recherches sur les derniers voyages du navigateur florentin.* Vienne: Gerold; 1870.

VASARI, GIORGIO: *I Ragionamenti e le Lettere.* Firenze: Sansoni; 1882.

—: *Le Vite degli Artisti.* Firenze: Salani; 1913.

VESPUCCI, AMERIGO: *Carta de Amerigo Vespucci al Cardenal Arzobispo de Toledo.* Madrid: Cartas de Indias, 1877.

—: For editions of Amerigo's letters, *see* works of Bandini, Bartolozzi, Magnaghi, Fernández de Navarrete, Northup, Montaboldo,

Levillier, National Library of Colombia, and Varnhagen listed in this
bibliography.

VIETIA LINAGE, JOSEPH DE: *Norte de la Contratación de las Indias
Occidentales*. 1672.

VIGNAUD, JEAN-HENRY: *Améric Vespuce*. Paris: Leroux; 1917.

VILLARI, PASQUALE: *La Storia di Girolamo Savonarola*. Firenze: Le
Monier; *1930*.

—: and CASANOVA: *Scelta di Prediche e Scritti di Fra Girolamo
Savonarola*. Firenze: Sansoni; 1898.

YASHIRO, YUKIO: *Sandro Botticelli*. London: Medici Society; 1929.

ZWEIG, STEFAN: *Amerigo, a Comedy of Errors in History*. New York:
Viking Press; 1942.

INDEX